Vitality and Dynamism

VITALITY AND DYNAMISM

*Interstitial Dialogues of Language, Politics, and Religion
in Morocco's Literary Tradition*

Edited by

Kirstin Ruth Bratt
Youness M. Elbousty
Devin J. Stewart

Leiden University Press

Cover design: Geert de Koning

Cover illustration: mrfiza / Shutterstock

Lay-out: TAT Zetwerk, Utrecht

ISBN   978 90 8728 213 4

e-ISBN   978 94 0060 185 7 (ePDF)

e-ISBN   978 94 0060 186 4 (ePub)

NUR   635

This book is distributed in North America by the University of Chicago Press (www.press.uchicago.edu).

Contents

****

Preface

The work, within your hands, is the first result of a plethora of conversations with many colleagues from different institutions. Those conversations began during two major conferences, the first at the University of Ibn Zorh in Agadir, Morocco and the second at the Moulay Ismail University in Errachidia, Morocco. The topics discussed at both of these conferences centered around the study of Moroccan Literature, viewed from a variety of differing angles and perspectives. Throughout these conversations, one major topic emerged, namely, the need to have works about Moroccan Literature published in English. Thus, we, the editors, took it upon ourselves to produce this current work and thus start the conversation in our field.

Each of the featured authors discusses themes that are germane to the issues Moroccan novelists write about in their narratives, such as immigration, social justice, equality, political governance, lack of transparency, magic, homeland, colonization, marginality, identity, and so forth.

We hope that this work will serve as a resource for both experts in the field and for students of Moroccan Literature, while simultaneously nurturing the sense of wonder and joy in learning!

Finally, we would like to thank the staff at Leiden University Press for their utmost professionalism. They have worked with us closely, making every obstacle as an opportunity.

Youness M. Elbousty
Berlin, 05/19/14

The Vitality of Tradition

Kirstin Ruth Bratt

Post-colonial theory recognizes that European and American scholars have traditionally defined the themes that are of interest in literary criticism; in Moroccan studies, these themes have tended toward questions of migration, identity, secularism, and religious fanaticism – typically questions regarding Morocco in its relationships with colonizing nations. For these edited books, we intend to re-define the themes of interest in Moroccan studies, looking toward more local themes and movements and relationships of sub-cultures and languages within Morocco. Questions in this volume regard concepts of the self, conflicting discourses, intersections of self-identity and community, and Moroccan reclamation of identity in the post-colonial sphere.

In 1999, historians Miller and Bourquia predicted, in their book on Moroccan history, that we would soon witness a surge in Moroccan studies, writing, "Collaborative efforts between scholars from the Maghrib and beyond are destined to increase as transnational research becomes the scholarly norm and joint efforts become more common."[1] Thus far, unfortunately, their prediction has failed to become reality, at least in the field of Moroccan literature. While poets and authors in Morocco have flourished in recent years, literary theorists have yet to stay abreast of the burgeoning body of literature being produced in this period of Moroccan literary achievements.

Recent decades have brought a period of stability and development to Morocco, and the reign of the current king has been an especially fertile time for literary accomplishments. This book examines the literature of Morocco produced during the reigns of Hassan II (1961–1999) and Mohammed VI (1999-present), and examines many of the socio-political forces at work during the two reigns. The works of literature produced during the reign of Hassan II were produced primarily in exile or, if written in Morocco, written under tight censorship controls. Since the beginning of the current king's reign, authors have enjoyed relative freedom, although many still write in exile or from established homes in the West.

With the ascent of the current King of Morocco in 1999, a series of democratic reforms were set in motion, many of which affected the climate for literary production. The king developed a global reputation of tolerance, resulting in a growing field of Moroccan literature. Somewhat free of the fear of censorship, exile, and imprisonment, authors now write freely, and on a wider range of topics than they would have prior to 1999. This is not to say that writers enjoy complete freedom, as questioning the authority of the king or of Islam remain a punishable offense.

Tahar Ben Jelloun, in an interview, explains that the writers of his generation assumed that they would be the last to write in French. They expected, with the arabization movement begun in the 1980s, that authors would begin to publish exclusively in Arabic more and more. While this is increasingly true to some extent – many works are currently produced in Arabic – it is also true that French continues to be a viable language for Moroccan authors. Furthermore, as Daniela Merolla very fully describes, there is a flourishing body of work in Amazigh that is being produced throughout Morocco. Her comprehensive survey of this literature should be of great interest for scholars working in all areas of Moroccan literature. It is also true that translations of Moroccan works from Amazigh, Arabic, French, and English are proliferating in various world languages.

These volumes will include various essays that celebrate Moroccan literature produced in recent decades but, more than that, they aim for a critical investigation of the work produced and the themes introduced by these authors. The goal is to extend the discussion of Moroccan literature for scholars working primarily in English.

Identity in the Moroccan Context

Anti-colonial literature is not necessarily "combat literature", as Fanon and Déjeux have both suggested in their own writings.[2] While it is often combative, there is also anti-colonial literature that emphasizes the human and the humane rather than the oppositional and contentious; it cannot be fair to label all anti-colonial literature as combative, even if one were to expand the definition of "combat" to include peaceful struggles against oppression or dehumanization. Oppositional forms of literature are certainly present in the Moroccan landscape of literature, but to consider Moroccan literature as always fighting from under a rubric of combat or tyranny is to label it away from many of its moderate and moderating themes and again to define it in terms of its relationship to colonizing nations.

Because of their relatively short history of colonization, their relatively peaceful transition to post-colonial sovereignty, and their friendly relations with other nations, many Moroccans consider themselves and their nation to be peaceful and tolerant. Literature of Morocco often presents itself as moderating – often critical of fanatics, intentionally dislocated persons, and political activists. Moroccan writing is often introspective, deeply spiritual, place-bound, and identity-based.

This volume provides in-depth discussions of several prominent Moroccan authors, including Abdelkebir Khatibi, whose work is described as a balance of sociology and artistry by Sam Cherribi and Matthew Pesce; and Mohammed Choukri, whose relation to the Beat Generation and its clash with traditional Moroccan values is the subject of Anouar El Younssi's chapter.

Moroccan homes have an international reputation for tolerance and peace, a reputation that is sometimes upheld in Moroccan literature and sometimes challenged. The literature produced in Morocco is sometimes a moderating force and sometimes a reflection of a population in transition or conflict. For example, as Mohamed Elkouche argues in this volume in "Cultural Encounter in Moroccan Postcolonial Literature of English Expression," some Moroccan literature emphasizes peaceful encounters of one "other" with another. The theme of colonial encounter, the direct contact or meeting between peoples of different cultures and civilizations, and especially between the West and its cultural Others, is an important and recurrent subject addressed in numerous Moroccan texts written in English. Sometimes, the encounters involve conflict or tension between the two different cultures, as in the case of Abdellatif Akbib's *Tangier's Eyes on America* and Mohamed Mrabet's stories, "A Woman from New York" and "What Happened in Granada?". Sometimes, these encounters tend to be familial, as in the case of Anouar Majid's *Si Yussef* and Driss Temsamani's *Rewind*. Elkouche sheds light on how different Moroccan authors generally reflect such cross-cultural relations and how they conceive of the question of Otherness.

Ilham Boutob focuses on Moroccan migration literature of the early twenty-first century CE, examining the issues that drive Moroccans to seek migration and the unforeseen factors that cause problems for migrants. More importantly, Boutob examines the often unexamined motivators that undergird migrant dreams and also, perhaps, nightmares. Recently, the king of Morocco spoke about Morocco as a nation that loses people to migration, that gains people from migration, and that hosts people in transit, and migration continues to be a common theme in Moroccan literature.

Morocco has a long history of multi-culturalism and multi-lingualism, reflected in its social history and in its literary history, as well. Authors in Morocco write in various languages, and translations of Moroccan literature into European languages and into Arabic are common. The work of translators is particularly important in Morocco, both in typical social interactions and in literature. The translator is essential in Moroccan daily life and in Moroccan arts. Yet the faithfulness of, and personal motives behind, various translations of Moroccan works has been called into question. Reactions from Moroccan writers to visiting writers such as Paul Bowles can provide illustration. Maghnougi explains how Moroccans responded to the interpretation of Morocco by Paul Bowles, suggesting that many believed Bowles brought his own depravity to light rather than uncovering depravity in Moroccan contexts, as he claimed to have done.

Several of our authors suggest that the relationship between the West and the rest of the world has been imagined as a relationship of Self (the West) to Other (the rest of the world), ordered and bordered geographically by the whims of Europeans and creating a Center-Periphery paradigm. These invented boundaries of humanity serve to separate geographical sites, but more, they serve to enclose the Empire and exoticize other cultures. Boundaries are often spatial, but more often they are related to relationships and colonialization. Changes within the Periphery, especially those that are due in part to European influence, create adjustments in borders, whether real or imagined, and those in the periphery often find themselves in a defensive posture, fighting misconceptions and accusations from the center. Of course, one of the most overwhelming aspects of colonialism has been the imposition of European languages.

Moroccan and Foreign Contexts

Throughout the volume, we will see an emphasis on place that demonstrates deeply passionate emotions connected to specific locations within the Moroccan landscape – some of these deep passions are more positive than others, but no matter – what matters is the verve with which many Moroccans feel a deep resonance and affinity with home.

Ian Campbell's article discusses the mapping of Fez in its intrinsically Moroccan and its colonized iterations. Innovations in mapping, Campbell writes, have led us to a new understanding of how geography contributes to social and linguistic turns; the Western gaze even comes to change the way that the city is mapped and understood. Campbell introduces us to two novels, Sefrioui's *Box of Wonders* and A. Ben Jalloun's *In my Childhood*: in each novel we learn how the main character interacts with and is influenced by the labyrinthine city of Fez. Author Ben Jalloun is seen through various stages in his personal geography, first that his childhood in Britain caused him to have a certain expectation of geography that caused difficulties for him in Fez, and then how cultural understanding is attained apart from one's formal education and often in relationship to personal geography. In other words, personal geography can be a powerful teacher, in some ways more than one's formal education. As our maps become more and more legible given advancing technologies, urban spatial organization becomes more abstract given the domination of capitalism and the need for abstractions to obscure reality. Campbell's work with the idea of the labyrinth works as both powerful image and relevant metaphor for understanding aspects of Moroccan reality and its reflection in literature.

Earlier mappings of territory are delineated in Ziad Bentahar's chapter on early relationships between Amazigh populations and the Islamic community as seen through Chraïbi's *La Mère du printemps*. Chraïbi's novel explains how early Muslims changed the landscape of Morocco and how they were changed in turn by the Amazigh residents of the land.

Naima Hachad discusses not the colonization of land but the colonization of the female body. Often shrouded in taboos and assigned to maternity or monstrosity, the female body is a site of challenge to many female authors who question and deconstruct its marginalization. They question the sanctity of the maternal body that silences women and subordinates them to their male relatives, including their own male children. They also deconstruct the association of the female body with monstrosity or deviation, resulting in an ambiguous figure that is both weak and hostile. Feminine Francophone literature has transformed the marginalized female body into discursive tools that transpose the dynamics of Moroccan politics and gender relationships.

Notes

1   Susan Gilson Miller and Rahma Bourquia, *In the Shadow of the Sultan: Culture, Power, and Politics in Morocco* (Cambridge: Harvard UP, 1999), 44.

2   Frantz Fanon, *The Wretched of the Earth*, trans. Constance Farrington (Harmondsworth: Penguin, 1990); Jarrod Hayes, *Queer nations: Marginal sexualities in the Maghreb* (Chicago: U Chicago P, 2000), 136.

CHAPTER 1

How the West Was Won:
The Arab Conqueror and the Serene Amazigh
in Driss Chraïbi's *La Mère du printemps*

Ziad Bentahar

The Moroccan author Driss Chraïbi (1926–2007), more than any other writer in the Maghreb, has portrayed Islam as a colonizing force and focused on the impact of the Arab conquest of North Africa on the original Amazigh (Berber) societies in the region. Although other North African authors, most notably the Algerian writer Kateb Yacine, have given importance to Amazigh characters and themes in their works, Chraïbi is distinctive because he explicitly addresses the arrival of Islam in North Africa through a fictionalized account of the Arab conquest of the region in the Seventh Century CE. *La Mère du printemps* is particularly noteworthy because it complements historical scholarship on this conquest and offers a literary perspective on Islamic identity in the Maghreb.[1]

Despite Chraïbi's warning, printed at the beginning of the book, in which he insists that it is indeed a novel and not a work of history, *La Mère du printemps* is nevertheless in dialogue with established historical narratives of the Islamic Empire's earliest westward expansions. In both cases the Arabian Peninsula and the Maghreb are seen as two initially separate places eventually brought together by religion. Islam's birthplace was, technically, the Hejaz in the Arabian Peninsula. Therefore, geographically, it is not a North African religion in origin. The original inhabitants of the Maghreb are an ethnic group different from the Arabs who brought Islam to North Africa. This geographical perspective, however, is limited. It is open to question whether or not the Arabian Peninsula at the time (as well as in the present day) was part of the same cultural space as Africa.

As Islam spread outside the Hejaz, it became, among other things, what could be considered a fully-fledged African religion, in view of the extent to which it was shaped by non-Arab practices on that continent. The historian David Robinson distinguishes between "Islamization" and "Africanization" to suggest that at least two processes were involved in the arrival of Islam in Africa:[2] while Islamization refers simply to the spread of the religion into the continent, Africanization indicates the particular way in which Islam was appropriated and influenced by African practices from both sides of the Sahara. In this view, the Africanization of Islam is an ongoing process that has involved a multitude of locations in both North and sub-Saharan Africa.

Robinson insists that there is nothing pejorative about his use of the term "Africanized Islam," because he is aware that the association of the religion with sub-Saharan Africa has in fact sometimes been perceived negatively, not only by colonizing Europeans but also by other Muslims.[3] The appropriation of this negative vision by Europeans and Arabs alike has endured, resulting in a latitude-based racial hierarchy in Islam that places North Africa closer to the center of the religious empire while pre-Arab components of the region are marginalized along with Islamic sub-Saharan Africa. According to Robinson, this view is traceable to the second century CE and to Ptolemy's climatic conception that Mediterranean societies, such as those of ancient Egypt, Greece, and Rome, constitute the center of civilization, while those of other regions are peripheral.[4] Robinson focuses on European attempts to rationalize the arrival of Islam in civilized climes.[5] These attempts range from waves of demonizing discourses regarding Islam following the conquest of the southern Iberian Peninsula to more recent French colonial efforts to distinguish between Muslims on both sides of the Sahara in order to undermine the formation of alliances between colonized peoples in the nineteenth and twentieth centuries.

Whereas historical narratives have tended to view the spread of Islam to the Maghreb chiefly as the Islamization/Arabization of Northern Africa and its Amazigh indigenous populations, Chraïbi, like Robinson, views the process as one in which the indigenous populations affected the religion, "Africanized" it, and shaped their ties to the Arab world. Furthermore, in Chraïbi's literary take on the subject, Islamic identity in the Maghreb as we think of it today – and indeed the very reason for the endurance of the religion in the region – is more Amazigh and less Arab than is generally perceived. As *La Mère du printemps* is intimately related to historical narratives, it is essential to start with an overview of these narratives to appreciate Chraïbi's text more fully.

From an historical perspective, the initial interest in the Maghreb after the Prophet's death came under the caliph ʿUmar ibn al-Khaṭṭāb who ruled for a period of ten years starting in 634 CE. The Islamic conquest of what was then still called Ifriqiya[6] was essentially a westward movement that started with the conquest of Egypt following the enthusiastic efforts of ʿAmr ibn al-ʿĀs in 640. Much of what is known today of the conquest of Egypt is owed to the ninth-century CE Egyptian scholar ʿAbd al-Raḥmān ibn ʿAbd al-Ḥakam (803–871 CE), who received most of his information from his father ʿAbd Allāh (771–c. 829 CE), an important figure of early Maliki law.[7] Ibn ʿAbd al-Ḥakam's account, entitled *Futūḥ Miṣr*, was edited on the basis of all the extant manuscripts and published by Charles Torrey in 1922.[8]

Egypt, once a part of the Byzantine Empire, came under Islamic control after a number of military campaigns by Arabs, followed by settlements in and about al-Fusṭāṭ and Alexandria. Two important moments stand out in these campaigns. The first consists of the capture in 641 CE of the fortress of Bab al-Yun (Babylon) at the southern tip of the Nile delta, where the city of Cairo is presently located. This area also comprised the city of Miṣr, which became the Arabic name for Egypt, and Heliopolis, the site of an important battle and currently a suburb of Cairo. The second moment was the surrender of Alexandria by treaty, which sealed ʿAmr's conquest of Egypt. Following the taking of Alexandria in 642 CE, Arabs conducted raids towards the West to maintain a hold on the Egyptian conquests. The priority was not to gain territory or booty as much as it was to protect achievements in Egypt against the potential threat of the Byzantines, who had possessions in the rest of North Africa.[9] Various campaigns followed, and within seven decades the Arabs had taken control over the entire North African coastline.

Stories about the source of ʿAmr's interest in Egypt and his persistence against all odds, including the caliph's doubts about his ability to conquer it, are romanticized to a considerable extent. These stories present the conquest as a divinely foretold, inevitable destiny. When ʿAmr expressed interest in conquering Egypt for the Islamic state, the caliph ʿUmar was hesitant. The caliph allowed ʿAmr to proceed on the condition that, if the caliph were to change his mind, he would send a messenger, and if a message reached ʿAmr before ʿAmr reached Egypt, he should return. ʿUmar did have second thoughts, and he did send a letter to ʿAmr, who guessed its contents and did not open it until he reached Egyptian territory, enabling him to proceed without breaking his promise to the caliph.[10]

ʿAmr's interest in Egypt seems to have been chiefly economic, as the following story related by Ibn ʿAbd al-Ḥakam suggests. Before the advent of Islam, ʿAmr had gone to Jerusalem to trade, and he came across a man half dead from thirst on a very hot day. ʿAmr gave him a drink, and the man lay down to sleep. While he was sleeping, a large snake came out of a hole next to him. ʿAmr saw it and killed it by shooting it with an arrow. When the man woke up and saw what had happened, he was grateful and convinced ʿAmr to come with him to his home town of Alexandria, where he would be able to reward him for saving his life twice, once from thirst and once from a deadly snake. It was then that ʿAmr was able to observe first-hand the wealth of Egypt.[11]

While the details of these mythologized stories usually call for little more than skepticism from today's historians, they are indicative of the construction of a discourse whereby the affiliation of North Africa to the Arab world is, in a sense, meant to be. The rhetoric of the conquests in Islamic historiographies can better inform us of the way in which this affiliation took place, starting with the very word by which these conquests are termed in Arabic: *futūḥāt*. As Bernard Lewis reminds us in *The Political Language of Islam*, although the ways in which early Islam spread have been called conquests, the Islamic tradition refers to them as *futūḥāt*, literally "openings."[12] For Lewis, the *futūḥāt* were seen not as conquests in the sense of forceful territorial acquisitions, but as the "opening" of impious people to the rightful new revelation. The usage of the trilateral root *ftḥ* (open) connotes the legitimacy of these Islamic advances. In addition to this semantic point and to the stories legitimizing ʿAmr's conquest of Egypt mentioned above, narratives of the conquest of Africa west of Egypt further illustrate the value of this kind of positive rhetoric in converting North Africa into Arab territory.

Just as the conquest of Egypt is associated with ʿAmr ibn al-ʿĀs, the conquest of the rest of North Africa is associated with ʿUqba ibn Nāfiʿ. ʿUqba was Amr's nephew, and he first joined the campaigns in the area that is present-day Libya, playing an important role in obtaining allegiance from the Lawata and Mazata Amazigh peoples around Tripoli in 661.[13] His most important act was the founding of the city of Kairouan in present-day Tunisia. Later on, ʿUqba led a number of campaigns in the interior and west of Kairouan, mostly avoiding the Byzantine-held coastline, and went as far as the Atlantic Ocean before making his way back east and dying in battle against an army led by Kusayla, an Amazigh leader whom he had previously defeated. In terms of conquest, ʿUqba's expeditions west of Kairouan were of little consequence. They consisted mostly of raids for booty and slaves, particularly female slaves who, according to the fourteenth-century CE scholar Ibn ʿIdhari al-Marrakushi,[14] were so astonishingly beautiful that they fetched a handsome price back east.[15] However, no arrangements were made for the collection of tributes or taxes or the establishment of outposts, and only two mosques – in Sus and Wadi Dra in Morocco – are attributed to him.[16] In fact, his raids may have actually impeded the progress of Arab invasions as they drove some of the Amazigh tribes to unite in resistance against the invaders, most notably under the leadership of Kusayla and that of the renowned al-Kāhina (The Priestess). It is only later that Arab presence in all of North Africa was cemented, largely through the efforts of leaders such as Ḥassan ibn al-Numan al-Ghassani and Musa ibn Nusayr starting in 698 CE. Islam in North Africa was ultimately consolidated through the conversion of Amazigh peoples, who, once converted, supported the conquests, and, in some instances, participated in them militarily as well.

The settlement of Tangiers circa 708 CE can be taken as a marker for the end of this first phase of Muslim settlement in North Africa if we look at the region with today's perspectives on national and continental borders. However, while the strait of Gibraltar may seem a logical frontier, it did not form a lasting obstacle, and the subsequent conquest of the southern Iberian Peninsula was part of the same, continuous movement, even though it was chiefly an Amazigh and not an Arab conquest; Andalusia then became tied to the same cultural and political spheres as the western parts of North Africa for several centuries.

In any case, the endurance of the mythical dimension attached to ʿUqba's expedition is significant, even if his role in converting North Africa to Islam was not substantial historically. As Hugh Kennedy has pointed out, ʿUqba is "credited in historical record and popular imagination with bringing Islamic rule to the Maghreb."[17] While some details surrounding ʿUqba's activities in North Africa have been the subject of thorough historical analyses, other stories about his North African campaigns have been noted but generally regarded as folk tales and dramatic embellishments of secondary importance. Yet these embellishments, which often occur in classical Arabic histories, reveal aspects that can be as informative as the purely historical dimension of these accounts.[18] In a typical example of such stories, ʿUqba miraculously discovers a subterranean spring and brings relief from a lack of water after performing the ritual Islamic prayer and invoking God.[19] These ornamental anecdotes, like those associated with ʿAmr's conquest of Egypt, contribute to the discursive claim of North Africa for the Arabs through the portrayal of ʿUqba as victoriously and triumphantly controlling the vast region and overcoming the obstacles it presented.

Several particular events stand out in this regard. One concerns the building of the settlement in Kairouan; another is the moment when ʿUqba reaches the Atlantic Ocean on his westbound campaign. Both of these events are narrated by Ibn ʿAbd al-Ḥakam in the fifth division of Futūḥ Miṣr and filtered into popular imagination as well as subsequent histories. The first event, the settlement of Kairouan and the building of its mosque, came out of a desire not to reside among the local population, but to build a new city which Muslims could inhabit.[20] When ʿUqba ordered his men to start building, however, they refused, complaining that the site he had chosen, strategically removed from the sea and safe against possible naval attacks, was infested with lions. ʿUqba then cried out to the beasts to leave his men alone out of respect for the members of his army who had been companions of the Prophet.[21] Ibn ʿIdhari al-Marrakushi narrates the event:

> [Uqba] yelled out: 'Listen, snakes and lions! We are the companions of the Messenger of God – Peace be upon him. So leave us, for we are settling here and whomever we find after this, we'll kill!' The people then witnessed an astonishing thing, as the lions came out of the scrub carrying their cubs in obedience, and the wolves and the snakes likewise carrying their young. The people of Ifriqya then lived forty years without seeing a single snake, scorpion or lion.[22]

The other event which shows ʿUqba as a victor in North Africa that has subsisted in the popular imagination is his arrival at the Atlantic shore. ʿUqba rode his horse into the ocean as far as he could, calling upon God to witness that he had gone as far as humanly possible to spread his religion.[23] The fact that his westward conquest could be stopped only by an impassable ocean underscores the divine will behind his endeavor. According to Ibn ʿIdhari al-Marrakushi:

> [ʿUqba] went on until he reached the ocean, and he entered it until the waters reached his horse's belly. He then raised his arms to the sky and said: "O God! Had the sea not prevented me, I would have continued on through the country unto the pass of Dhul Qarnayn [in the Quran, a figure who reached the setting place of the sun], defending Your faith and fighting whoever did not believe in You!"[24]

Such accounts of ʿUqba's glorified triumph over the North African environment serve to present the conquest as divinely sanctioned and emphasize the legitimacy of annexing North Africa to the Arab world. The westward spread of Islam is thus conceived as a Manifest Destiny, confirmed by divine signs – springs found miraculously, obedient lions, etc. – and therefore inevitable. From this perspective, whereas historical narratives have tended to view the spread of Islam to the Maghreb chiefly as the Islamization / Arabization of Northern Africa and its Amazigh indigenous populations, Chraïbi, like Robinson, views the process as one where the indigenous populations affected the religion, "Africanized" it, and shaped their ties to the Arab world. Furthermore, in Chraïbi's literary take on the subject, Islamic identity in the Maghreb as we think of it today – and indeed the very reason for the endurance of the religion in the region – is more Amazigh and less Arab than is generally perceived. If the imposition of the "Arab World" label on North Africa has been contested in Moroccan literature, it has never been as evident as in Driss Chraïbi's *La Mère du printemps* (*Mother Spring*), a novel published in 1982 and translated into English in 1989 by Hugh Harter.[25] By then, Chraïbi had already had a tremendous impact on Francophone literature in the Maghreb – indeed he shaped and defined it in many respects following the publication in 1954 of his first novel, *Le Passé simple*,[26] a book of such groundbreaking importance of that its publication can be considered a landmark even from a non-literary standpoint.[27] With his reputation already established, Chraïbi started showing a more explicit inclination towards topics regarding Islam and Morocco's Amazigh identity in the 1980s. *La Mère du printemps*, in which the author relates the story of ʿUqba ibn Nafi's arrival at the western edge of North Africa from a purely Amazigh point of view, is part of Chraïbi's so-called "Berber Trilogy" that explores the Arab conquest of Africa and Spain in the seventh century CE. Central to the trilogy is the fictionalized Amazigh clan of Aït Yafelman, from whose perspective history is retold.

The question of which novels make up the trilogy, however, is open to debate. Many critics, including Carine Bourget,[28] see the trilogy as consisting of the novels *Une enquête au pays* (1981), *La Mère du printemps*,[29] and *Naissance à l'aube* (1985) because they focus on the Aït Yafelman Amazigh clan, share some thematic elements, and have a few common characters whose descriptions are sometimes even copied verbatim from one novel to the other. However, although the Aït Yafelman are introduced in *Une enquête au pays*, that novel does not constitute a re-telling of Islamic history in the way the other two do. Rather, an important difference between this novel and the others is that *Une enquête au pays* is the debut of l'inspecteur Ali, an important character for a different phase of Chraïbi's work, whom the author revisits many times in later novels. Other evidence as well suggests that *Une enquête au pays* is not part of the trilogy: in a publisher's foreword to *Naissance à l'aube*, the novel is called the second rather than the third volume of a novelistic fresco ("une fresque romanesque") that started with *La Mère du printemps*.

If *La Mère du printemps* and *Naissance à l'aube* are indeed part of a trilogy, it would be more appropriate to pair them with a later work, *L'Homme du livre* (1995), which is a fictional biography of the Prophet Mohammed. This novel was announced to be in preparation when *Naissance à l'aube* was first published in 1985, and was then going to be entitled *L'Emir des croyants*, but came out only ten years later.[30] This delay, as well as the fact that *L'Homme du livre* was published by Eddif and Balland, whereas *Une Enquête au pays*, *La Mère du printemps*, and *Naissance à l'aube* were all published by Seuil, may have impacted opinions on which novels constitute the trilogy.

La Mère du printemps, however, is particularly important because this novel is the exemplar of a fictional account of the way in which North Africa was annexed to the Arab world following the Islamic conquest of the seventh century CE. While, as mentioned above, Chraïbi reminds readers in a warning note at the beginning of the novel that this is a work of fiction, not a historically accurate account, his inclusion of ʿUqba as a character makes a bold statement. As Bourget notes, the historical components in Chraïbi's work constitute a form of demystification of official histories that promote an Arab and Islamic culture at the expense of indigenous populations.[31]

The novel starts with a brief passage in the present day, with the character Raho Aït Yafelman pondering topics such as the past and destiny of Amazigh peoples and Islam in the world. The readers are then transported to the mouth of the Oum-Er-Bia River in Morocco in the seventh century CE, just before the arrival of the Arabs. This is the setting of most of the novel, which centers on the life of the Amazigh protagonist Azwaw Aït Yafelman and his strategies to avoid the extinction of his people as the Arabs gradually approach. After ʿUqba's successful conquest of all of North Africa toward the end of the novel, Azwaw converts to Islam; here the narrative mode of the novel changes, with Azwaw becoming the narrator as Imam Filani. This dual identity is ambiguous. While remaining antagonistic to the Arabs, he is also sincere in his new religion. However, he uses the Islamic call to prayer to send coded information to other Amazigh people, and the novel ends with him being discovered doing so and having his tongue cut out in punishment.

Fundamentally a story of cultural conflict, *La Mère du printemps* is a re-telling of the Arab conquest of North Africa from an Amazigh perspective.[32] The novel climaxes when Azwaw finally encounters the conquering ʿUqba at the moment when he rides into the Atlantic waters on his horse. As Violeta Baena Gallé notes,[33] the Arab army in *La Mère du printemps* is always defined in terms of its horses:

> The horse was everything: the friend, the brother, the father and the mother, the son and the ancestors. It was the pupil of the eye. The horse was taken care of first, before and after any battle. Whether in bivouac or at a halt, it was by his side that men slept. He was the most beautiful of all Creation: short ears, just like the pasterns and the tail; neck, legs, hips, and stomach long; the forehead, breast, and hips, wide.[34]

This attention to horses that accompanies descriptions of the Arabs in the novel offers a portrayal of the conquerors as "cowboys" riding into the sunset – literally into the "Far West," considering that this is precisely how the Maghreb is referred to in Arabic – and taming the "natives." Not surprisingly, Chraïbi dedicates his novel to the Native Americans (among other people), thereby solidifying this analogy. In this audacious parallel between the Arab conquest of Africa and the annihilation of many Native American peoples that accompanied European settlement in the Americas, the author assigns an evil role to the Arabs as colonizers, which enables him to question the hegemony of Arab accounts and their impact on the Maghreb. Here, the portrayal of 'Uqba stands in sharp contrast to the conventional historical accounts that memorialize him as a victor, such as *Al-Bayān al-mughrib fī akhbār al-Andalus wa al-Maghrib* by Ibn 'Idhari al-Marrakushi, where the Arab conqueror is, to all intents and purposes, celebrated for his Berber-killing skills.[35]

In the eleventh chapter of *Le Monde à côté*,[36] the second volume of his memoirs, Chraïbi relates briefly his initial interest in writing a fictional account of history in *La Mère du printemps*. While he gives us in his memoirs a clearer understanding of the novel's genesis, his laconic description is more indicative of his peculiar idiosyncratic style and quirky persona. He cryptically mentions the Islam of Ayatollah Khomeini and the socialism of French president François Mitterrand as the backdrop to a "vital" need he felt to look to the past to understand the present better. Chraïbi compares this need to distant music calling him back from his own past, that of the Oum-Er-Bia River that flows into the Atlantic Ocean by the town of Azemmour, which is quite near his own home town of El Jadida (previously known as Mazagan):

> I felt the vital need to go back in time, as far back in time as possible, in order to give a corporeal meaning to words and understand the present. It was like a throbbing music that called me from the depths of my past, that of the remembered Oum-Er-Bia, Mother of Spring … It is there and nowhere else that I set the action of my next novel, in the year 680 CE, at the very moment when, starting from the Tripolitanian desert at the head of the horsemen of Allah, the general Oqba Ibn Nafi would appear, genuine messenger of the new religion.[37]

The name of the river, Oum-Er-Bia, meaning "mother of spring" in Arabic, gives the novel its title. Although Chraïbi had already decided that the novel would be set by that river, and that it would be about 'Uqba's arrival from the east, he explains in *Le Monde à côté* that he was faced with writer's block. As he was struggling with this project, he went to bed one night after his wife had played a recording of Omar Naqishbendi playing the lute, only to wake up in the middle of the night with a case of insomnia. It was only after trying to go back to sleep by drinking several glasses of single-malt whisky that he realized, in a drunken epiphany, that music should be central to this novel. In fact, in the novel a character named Naqishbendi plays a lute as ʿUqba and his troops reach the Atlantic.

The importance of music in this novel, and in the work of Chraïbi in general, has been discussed by Stéphanie Delayre in *Driss Chraïbi, une écriture de traverse*.[38] According to Delayre,[39] Chraïbi explains that although in *Le Monde à côté* the inspiration for *La Mère du printemps* is attributed to Naqishbendi, as just noted, it actually comes from a piece entitled "La Mer" played by the Iraqi lute player Mounir Bachir. One important musical aspect of *La Mère du printemps* is the inclusion in the novel of musical notes on a staff, not only as the character Naqishbendi accompanies the arrival of ʿUqba on a lute, but also to render the *Chanson de la Pèche*, a fishing song whose lyrics were forgotten by the Amazigh character Yerma Aït Yafelman, and which became a wordless melody.

Music, then, as a mode of expression beyond words, takes on a new meaning. It not only serves to unlock the author's writing block, but also provides a metaphor for the continuation of an Amazigh voice after it is silenced by the Arabs' arrival. In addition to the symbolism of Yerma's forgetting the words to her song, a literal manifestation of this silencing occurs when Azwaw's tongue is cut out after his conversion to Islam, and he is reduced to wordlessness when he is discovered using the call to prayer to send coded messages to Amazigh peoples allied against the Arabs. Azwaw's heavily symbolic aphasia reinforces the notion that the Amazigh voice in North Africa's Islamic history and present identity has been silenced. Yet *La Mère du printemps* makes the point that both in early Islamic history and in the present, Amazigh presence is stronger than one cares to hear.

In the opening chapters of *La Mère du printemps*, Amazigh people in the present day are shown to understand their own practice of Islam to be inadequate and not quite as thorough as it should be. Raho Aït Yafelman considers that there is a hierarchical structure within Islam: "There were two Islams, one of the privileged and the other ..."[40] Raho clearly considers himself to belong to the "other" Islam. He blames his own uncivilized pagan forces when he declares that he has blasphemed. At the same time, he attempts to improve by self-discipline:

> [Raho] spit [sic] between his feet, to root out the Middle Ages that survived in him despite generations of Islam. He was not at all a Muslim worthy of the name, that's the truth of it! He still had to master his pagan forces ...[41]

Raho's acknowledgement of his situation as a Muslim not quite worthy of the name reflects the common derogatory views of Islamic religious practices in Africa in general, which imply that a singular, necessarily Arab, religious culture is valid, while all others are naïve and perpetually in the process of seeking to measure up to the ideal version of this imported system of belief.

Nevertheless, later in the novel and some centuries earlier, when Raho's homonymous ancestor warns his clan of the danger of the approaching Arab army, Azwaw accepts the inevitable with an odd serenity, "Yes, indeed, let the Arabs come! Standing in his boat, Azwaw awaits them. Everything is peaceful around him and inside him."[42] Rather than see the conquest as a defeat, Azwaw has the serene assurance that time is on his side. Through this character, Chraïbi reveals some of his theoretical insights into the repercussions of the Arab assimilation of North Africa to the Islamic identity of the region.

Earlier in the novel, Azwaw justifies his serenity upon hearing the news of the westward advance of the Arab conquerors by noting that they are only the latest of many waves of conquerors, including the Romans and the Phoenicians, who had failed to overcome Amazigh peoples in any permanent manner.[43] Yet, he realizes later that these new invaders are unlike earlier conquerors because they are driven by a religion:

> The other conquerors were interested in the earth and the riches of the earth, and I assure you that these Arabs are interested first and foremost in man, in what he is, and in what he can bring to them. They intermingle with the Berbers, in their blood, to found one single same tribe, the Oumma, as they call it.[44]

Azwaw remains serene nonetheless. He is confident that when Arabs accept Amazigh converts into their religious community, it is the Arab community more than that of the new converts that is affected. He supports this argument with a botanical metaphor: weeds, representing Amazigh peoples, in the long run take over a field at the expense of other seeds, which represent Arabs:

> We are going to occupy time's terrain. We are going to get inside these new conquerors, inside their very soul, into their Islam, their customs, their language, into everything that they know how to do with their hands and to say with their hearts. Into everything that is youthful, strong, and beautiful. We will slowly sap their vigour and then their life.[45]

In spite of an apparent Arab victory and the conversion to Islam that would ensue, the Amazigh will prevail because through miscegenation, both literal and cultural, these Arab colonizers will be assimilated into the people that they colonize rather than the other way around. Azwaw tells his clansmen:

> The Arabs may be happy with us, once we become Muslims like them. They will let their guard down and will let us live and procreate. We will doubtlessly never be their equals. It is the law of domination that makes things go ... Our sons will join with their daughters, and our daughters, with their sons. Every child that is born will be a Berber in blood and heart for us, even if he [doesn't carry] the name of his father ... As for our land, you all know it. You are its sons. It loves only its children. It is savage and beautiful, and very strong, stronger than all the invaders that wanted to dominate her in the past. She has been their cemetery. The Arabs will fatten it with their cadavers and the cadaver of Islam one day soon, in a few centuries. Their last descendants, if there are any, will only turn toward the past of their ancestors, and that day, we, the Imazighen, we will be the future.[46]

Therein is the novel's contribution not only to Islamic North African history but also to postcolonial theory. While historians have tended to quantify Amazigh contributions to the Arab victories in North Africa in terms of conversions and military deputation, Chraïbi sees these contributions rather as Arab losses, and gives credit to the Amazigh for Islam as we know it today in the Maghreb. If we view this from a postcolonial perspective, it is tempting to recall the well-worn concept of hybridity (especially in view of Chraïbi's choice of a botanical metaphor), and possibly view Amazigh Islam, at best, as a frail attempt at adopting an imposed Arab culture in which the colonized Amazigh "mimic" the colonizing Arabs by adopting their religion, language, and mores. Certainly, Chraïbi's portrayal of Raho praying reveals his view that present-day Amazigh Islam is perceived as a meek imitation of an imagined genuine article, necessarily different from it, and, in this case, undoubtedly inferior to it. Nevertheless, in Azwaw's outlook (and the source of his serenity), this imitation is declared as the transformation of the victor, effectively disarming the would-be conquerors. Affirming that the Amazigh will prevail within Islam implies that the Arabs will not.

The way that Chraïbi presents this process thwarts simplistic postcolonial readings of Islam's spread through the Maghreb. Instead of seeing the incorporation of an Amazigh component into a broader Islamic imperial project as the victory of Arab colonialism in which the colonized Amazigh inherit a crossbred cultural identity, he sees it as precisely the opposite: the ultimate continuation of an indigenous North African character through the inclusion of Amazigh elements within Islam. If the arrival of Islam in North Africa is an Arab colonial enterprise, annexing North Africa to the Arab world, then it constitutes a complete incorporation of the colonized subject's identity into the ideological discourse that dominates him – in this case the supremacy of Islam and Arab culture. This goes beyond the mere physical occupation of his land, because it is not erased by subsequent national or colonial projects such as French occupation. This dimension of the novel is particularly important because it complements historical scholarship, in which researchers have portrayed the assimilation of Amazigh peoples and their role in securing an Islamic presence in North Africa – namely in the settlements in Kairouan as well as in subsequent campaigns, including the conquest of Andalusia – mainly in terms of conversion and recruitment into Islamic armies,[47] rather than in terms of cultural contributions and transformations.

Chraïbi could be criticized for his essentialist representation of Amazigh peoples in *La Mère du printemps* and his other novels centering on Amazigh characters, and possibly for appropriating and trivializing Amazigh aspects of Morocco's cultural heritage, particularly considering that the emergence of French and Arabic language literatures in North Africa in the last century relegated Amazigh literatures, which mostly exist in the realm of oral expression, to a lesser standing. Nonetheless, in his treatment of Amazigh characters, Chraïbi brings out the significance of an insufficiently addressed dimension in the Islamic identity of North Africa. A good example of this debate can be found in an interview with Kacem Basfao that appeared in a special Chraïbi issue of the bilingual literary magazine *Lecture/Qirā 'āt* published after the author's death in 2007.[48] Kacem Basfao, professor at Aïn Chock University in Casablanca, a leading scholar on Chraïbi and longtime personal friend of the author, was asked about a possibly "occidental" perspective in novels such as *Une enquête au pays*, where small rural villages in Morocco are described as if they are isolated from the rest of the world.[49] In answer, Basfao argues that Chraïbi's description does not portray rural Morocco in an essentialist way, but that through his Amazigh characters he attempts to address humanist themes. Moreover, Basfao claims, Chraïbi's descriptions are not very far from a certain reality, as some rural areas in Morocco were in fact neglected by the political administration in the 1980s when *Une Enquête au pays* is set, and some villages in these areas suffered from a form of isolation similar to that portrayed in the novel.[50]

Although Chraïbi's use of Amazigh characters could indeed be read as a form of essentialism – be it an essentialist, reductionist view of Amazigh peoples, Morocco, the Maghreb at large, or Islam as a religion – it remains mainly an attempt to free North African identity from a marginalizing, Arab-centric view on Islam. Certainly, in view of the fact that Morocco's literary scene is too often reduced to two, mutually-exclusive linguistic spheres, one Arabic and the other Francophone, when Amazigh peoples are portrayed as anti-Arabs, especially by an author who writes in French, the picture that emerges can be read as anti-Arab, serving Arabophobe agendas. However, *La Mère du printemps* is also a literary attempt to rectify official North African histories that largely overlook the importance of Amazigh peoples, a crucial issue for revivalist cultural movements that, as Bruce Maddy-Weitzman has pointed out, prioritize memory work.[51] Through the inversion of official history, and a narration from an Amazigh perspective, Chraïbi reconstructs a cultural, national, and religious Amazigh element in an attempt to undermine the hegemony of the Arab component of North Africa's identity and reflect the complexity of the region. "Amazigh," then, is used conceptually as an indigenous African and pre-Islamic character, and put forth to validate a crucial aspect of North Africa not simply insofar as it is contrapuntal to an exogenous (Arab) religion, but as a factor in shaping the destiny of that religion in the region.

As the portrayal of the Islamization of North Africa in *La Mère du printemps* emphasizes an Africanization of Islam (or rather, to be precise, its "Amazighation" in this case), it reminds the reader that Islam in North Africa, which is thought of as exclusively Arab, is in fact largely Amazigh as well and remains engaged in a dynamic of ongoing configuration. The value of the Amazigh portrayal in *La Mère du printemps*, then, is its reminder that although the arrival of Islam in North Africa resulted in the region's being defined chiefly as a part of the Arab world, it is not exclusively Arab, as pre-Islamic and pre-Arab elements are in effect a crucial component of the character of North African peoples and are presented as fundamental to the vitality of the religion in the area.

By validating a non-Arab Islam, Chraïbi contributes to the formation of a Moroccan identity that remains relevant in circumstances of North African deviation from the Arab world. Such deviation can occur as a result of political events, such as shifting international alliances since the mid-Twentieth Century CE in contexts of the Cold War, oil crises and embargos, post-9/11 tensions, and conflicts in the Middle East. From a literary perspective, the rejection of imposed Arabic standards when they do not validate North African varieties of the language – incidentally, an issue particularly relevant to Chraïbi as well as to other authors from the Maghreb who write in French – can also foster anti-Arab sentiments. In these cases of North African deviation from the Arab world, the necessity of retaining Islam remains, if not because religion is foundational to national identity, or to avoid the real dangers of the legal and social repercussions of apostasy, then only out of sincere and genuine faith. From *La Mère du printemps* (and other works such as *L'Homme du livre*), it appears that Chraibi seems to lean towards the latter reason. Thus, he fits in the tradition of Muslim historians chronicling the Westward expansion of the religion, embellishing that narrative with his version of horse-back rides into the waves of the Atlantic, and marveling at the destiny of the land.

Notes

1   Driss Chraïbi, *La Mère du printemps* (Paris: Seuil, 2001).

2   David Robinson, *Muslim Societies in African History* (Cambridge: Cambridge UP, 2004), 27–59.

3   Ibid., 42.

4   Ibid., 74.

5   Ibid., 74–88.

6   A term referring initially to present-day Tunisia, coming from the Latin appellation of the southern Mediterranean coast; it was initially applied only to North Africa but the entire continent later took the name.

7   Jonathan Brockopp, *Early Mālikī Law: Ibn ʿAbd al-Ḥakam and his Major Compendium of Jurisprudence* (Leiden: Brill, 2000), 2.

8   Charles Torrey, *The History of the Conquest of Egypt, North Africa and Spain Known as the Futūḥ Miṣr of Ibn ʿAbd al-Ḥakam* (New Haven: Yale University Press, 1922).

9   Alfred Butler, *The Arab Conquest of Egypt and the Last Thirty Years of the Roman Dominion* (Oxford: Oxford University Press, 1978), 246; ʿAbd al-Wāḥid Dhannūn Taha, *The Muslim Conquest and Settlement of North Africa and Spain* (London: Routledge, 1989), 55.

10   Torrey, 56–57.

11   Ibid., 54.

12   Bernard Lewis, *The Political Language of Islam* (Chicago: The University of Chicago Press, 1988), 93.

13   Taha, 58.

14   Ibn ʿIdhari al-Marrakushi, *Al-Bayān al-Mughrib fī Akhbār al-Andalus wa al-Maghrib*, eds. G.S. Colin and E. Lévi-Provençal (Leiden: Brill, 1948).

15   Ibn ʿIdhari al-Marrakushi, 27.

16   Ibid., 27.

17   Hugh Kennedy, *The Great Arab Conquests: How the Spread of Islam Changed the World We Live In* (Philadelphia: Da Capo, 2007), 208.

18   E. Lévi-Provençal, "Un Nouveau récit de la conquête de l'Afrique du nord par les Arabes (A new story of the conquest of North Africa by the Arabs)," *Arabica* (Jan. 1954): 17–52, 26, 29.

19   Torrey, 195.

20   Kennedy, 209–210.

21   Torrey, 196.

22   Ibn ʿIdhari al-Marrakushi, 20.

23   Torrey, 199.

24   Ibn ʿIdhari al-Marrakushi, 27.

25   Driss Chraïbi, *Mother Spring*, trans. Hugh Harter (Washington, DC: Three Continents Press, 1989).

26   Driss Chraïbi, *Le Passe Simple (The Simple Past)* (Paris: Gallimard, 1954).

27   Pierre Vermeren. *Histoire du Maroc depuis l'indépendence (The History of Morocco since Independence)* (Paris: La Découverte, 2006), 111.

28   Carine Bourget, "L'Islam Syncrétique de Driss Chraïbi," *L'Esprit Créateur* 38.1 (Spring 1998): 57–68.

29   Paris: Seuil, 2001.

30   Jeanne Fouet. *Driss Chraïbi en marges* (Paris: L'Harmattan, 1999), 59.

31   Bourget, 57.

32   The sequel, *Naissance à l'aube*, is a re-telling of the conquest of Andalusia.

33   Violeta Baena Gallé. "L'Universalisation actantielle dans la trilogie tellurique de Driss Chraïbi." *Presence Francophone* 54 (2000): 41–64.

34   Chraïbi, 80.

35   Ibn ʿIdhari al-Marrakushi, 27.

36   Driss Chraïbi, *Le Monde à côté* (Paris: Gallimard, 2001).

37   Ibid., 190.

38   Stéphanie Delayre, *Driss Chraïbi, une écriture de traverse* (Bordeaux: Presses Universitaires de Bordeaux, 2006).

39   Delayre, 265, describing an interview Delayre conducted with Chraïbi on May 7th, 2001.

40   Chraïbi, 4.

41   Ibid., 4.

42   Ibid., 96.

43   Ibid., 89.

44   Ibid., 71.

45   Ibid., 73.

46   Ibid., 74.

47   Taha, 61–62, 76.

48   Kacem Basfao. "Interview. Hommage à Driss Chraïbi." *Special issue of Lecture/Qirā ʾāt* 1 (Nov 2007): 6–7.

49   Ibid., 6.

50   Ibid., 6–7.

51   Bruce Maddy-Weitzman, "Berber/Amazigh Memory Work," in *The Maghrib in the New Century: Identity, Religion, and Politics*, eds. Bruce Maddy-Weitzman and Daniel Zisenwine (Gainesville: University Press of Florida, 2007): 50–72, 51.

CHAPTER 2

Cultural Encounter in Moroccan Postcolonial Literature of English Expression

Mohamed Elkouche

Introduction

Ever since the publication of Edward Said's ground-breaking work *Orientalism* and the subsequent rise of postcolonial studies and discourses, literary scholars have applied his theory to various Western texts that represent or speak about the Orient. The vast majority of these studies have confirmed Said's central thesis that the East is in fact "Orientalized" and depicted negatively in these Western discourses – a systematic negative representation whose ultimate aim is the West's exertion and consolidation of its cultural and political hegemony over its Oriental Others.[1]

In this essay, however, the focus will be conversely on showing how the West or Occident is represented in Eastern discourses. This will be done through a brief study of some postcolonial Moroccan texts that deal with the theme of cultural encounter – that is to say, direct contact or meeting between Westerners and Easterners and the tensions or clashes that often ensue as a result of their belonging to two different civilizations with different sets of values and distinct worldviews. This chapter will attempt to raise and answer a number of pertinent questions including the following: What kind of images of the West and Westerners do Eastern writers produce? Are these images almost always uniformly negative, as is the case with the Orientalists' representation of the Orient and Oriental people? If so, can this practice be seen as a form of "writing back"; a counter-discourse that is intended to subvert or interrogate the constructions of Orientalist discourses? In other words, to what extent can these Eastern representations be stigmatized, by the same token, as Occidentalist? Do these "Occidentalist" discourses have any value or practical effects, especially when compared with the immense hegemonic function of Orientalist texts? Is there any way out of both Orientalist and Occidentalist discourses – a third alternative that can promote cosmopolitanism and fruitful intercultural dialogue between Easterners and Westerners?

Before answering these questions, it may be worth shedding some light on the discourse of Orientalism so as to provide the background for the exploration of what appears to be its stark antithesis: Occidentalist discourse. Accordingly, this study will be divided into two parts. The first attempts to define the term Orientalism and show how it operates discursively to construct its Others. The second focuses on discussing and illustrating how Moroccan postcolonial texts deal with the questions of Otherness and cultural encounter.

Orientalism and the Ideology of Otherness

In the first pages of *Orientalism*, Edward Said provides three definitions of the phenomenon he sets out to explore; he also puts these definitions in a nutshell in the following extract from his famous essay "Orientalism Reconsidered":

> As a department of thought and expertise Orientalism, of course, refers to several overlapping domains: first, the changing historical and cultural relationship between Europe and Asia, a relationship with a 4000-year-old history; second, the scientific discipline in the early nineteenth century, one specialized in the study of various Oriental cultures and traditions; and third, the ideological suppositions, images and fantasies about a currently important and politically urgent region of the world called the Orient.[2]

Orientalism, Said explains, usually conceives of "the East" and "the West" as two separate and monolithic entities; and this essentialist distinction is not so much "a fact of nature" as "a fact of human production" that can be well labeled "human geography."[3] This means that the Orient spoken about in Western texts is a mere linguistic creation and ideological construct that should by no means be associated with the Orient of concrete and objective reality. Given that discourse, as Michel Foucault puts it, has the power to produce rather than represent the things it speaks about, Orientalism can thus be seen as a discourse that characteristically constructs the Orient as Other with the aim of "dominating, restructuring, and having authority over [it]."[4]

Western literary texts have substantially contributed to this hegemonic Orientalist discourse. As a matter of fact, by systematically producing the image of the East or Easterner as a backward, inferior or savage Other, these texts have, in one way or another, helped to promote the West's colonial enterprise. The discourses that most readily come to mind as an illustration here are perhaps those of Rudyard Kipling, the British creative artist who can be considered an exemplary Orientalist. His famous poem "The Ballad of East and West" opens as follows: "Oh, East is East, and West is West, and never the twain shall meet, / Till Earth and Sky stand presently at God's great Judgment Seat ..."[5] These lines support and highlight quite superbly Said's notion of Orientalism as a discourse that is based on the dichotomy between the East and the West as two opposite worlds that seem to run parallel with each other. In his poem "The White Man's Burden," he bluntly urges his "White" (British/Western) people to venture out to "civilize" their cultural Others, described as "sullen peoples/Half devil and half child."[6] The ulterior motive of such so-called "civilizing mission" is of course the colonial domination and exploitation of these allegedly "inferior" people.

If one goes as far back as Shakespeare's age, one cannot also fail to find abundant literary texts that convey such ideology of Otherness. In his play *Othello, the Moor of Venice*, Shakespeare himself portrays his Moorish hero as a bestial Other who threatens to ruin and contaminate the Venetian social order through his decision to get married to Desdemona. The jealous Iago warns the latter's father in the following words:

> Iago: You'll have your daughter covered with a Barbary horse – You'll have your
> nephews neigh to you, you'll have coursers for cousins, and jennets for
> Germans.
> Brabantio: What profane wretch are thou?
> Iago: I am one, sir, that comes to tell you your daughter and the Moor are making
> the beast with two backs.[7]

Apart from the negative cultural connotation of the word Barbary – which refers here to Morocco and North Africa in general – this passage abounds in animal imagery that powerfully strips Othello of humanity, suggesting that he is a mere "horse" or despicable "beast." What is more, the passage implies that Desdemona herself will "go bestial" if she mates with him, and their children will turn out to be, and will behave like, animals! The underlying idea here is that there is something quite unnatural in this love relationship between the Moorish Othello and the fair Italian Desdemona, and that is why this relationship must be broken at all costs, lest it lead to the disruption of the normal and "human" conditions of the whole society.

In American literature too, one can find obvious traces of such Orientalist ideology that denigrates the Oriental Other and constructs him in the image of a savage and primitive creature. For example, in Paul Bowles' novel *The Spider's House*, which is set in Fez, the young Moroccan boy Amar is thus described from the perspective of the American tourist Polly:

> She sat there ... and stared at him ... A complete young barbarian, she thought, the antithesis of that for which she could have admiration. Looking at him she felt she knew what the people of antiquity had been like. Thirty centuries or more were effaced, and there he was, the alert and predatory sub-human, further from what she believed man should be like than the naked savage, because the savage was tractable, while this creature, wearing the armor of his own rigid barbaric culture, consciously defied progress.[8]

Needless to say, such words and phrases as "barbarian," "predatory sub-human," "naked savage," and "rigid barbaric culture" are highly expressive of how Amar – as a representative Moroccan native – is "othered" and "racialized" in Bowles' discourse. The reference to "the people of antiquity" and to the "thirty centuries or more" that separate Amar from contemporary civilization also stresses the immense, unbridgeable gap that exists between the civilized Westerners and their Eastern primitive Others.

The examples above reveal clearly how Orientalism functions as a discourse of Otherness. The East and the Easterner are systematically perceived as "Others" who can never be equal to the "self" (i.e. the West or Westerner). The two can also hardly meet because of the civilizational gap that separates them. If they ever meet, it is just in an attempt on the part of the benevolent Westerner to bring light and civilization to the helpless primitive Other. But when it comes to other kinds of relationship like marriage (as in the case of Othello and Desdemona) no good results can be expected. As one of Bowles' characters in *Let It Come Down* has put it, "only bad things can happen when Nazarenes and Moslems come together."[9]

Encountering the Other in Postcolonial Moroccan Texts

It is quite noticeable that the West and the Westerner(s) are conspicuously present in Moroccan texts written in English. Indeed, many of these texts dramatize situations that show different kinds of cross-cultural interaction and relationships between Moroccans and their Western counterparts, and the main setting for such encounters is either Morocco itself or some place in the Western world. But while it is true that the West/Westerner is usually perceived and represented as a cultural Other, it is important to note that its/his image is not characteristically negative, as is generally the case of the image of the East/Easterner in Orientalist literature. One can in fact find an amalgam of images that range from very positive to very negative representations, even if nearly all of these discourses remain fundamentally ambivalent, as will soon be illustrated.

The West often figures in Moroccan texts as an "other" world which is contrasted, whether directly or indirectly, with Morocco as a homeland. This world is clearly desired and sought out, whereas the native country is sometimes conceived of as a prison from which the protagonist(s) wishes to escape. For instance, in his autobiographical work entitled *Rewind*, Driss Temsamani writes: "I longed to flee my home country ... I left home to Miami, Florida; I knew I was gone for good ... In the USA, I had a window of opportunity, and I climbed through it."[10] Thanks to its promising prospects, America is readily accepted by the author, who wishes to stay there forever; in contrast, Morocco is abandoned and rejected because he regards it as "the land of no opportunity,"[11] the land of hungry children where there is "no future, no tomorrow."[12] Likewise, in his travel book *Alien ... Arab ... and Maybe Illegal in America*, Mohamed Fandi describes how the United States has fascinated him to the extent of his over-staying his visa and attempting to reside there for good. In his view, America is "the land of freedom, the land of business, the land where every day around the country many people become rich, millionaires ..."[13] It is, in short, "the best country of the world," and certainly "more than half of my country (and each country around the world) would be ready – anytime – to visit or stay in the States."[14]

Like the United States, Europe is also envisioned as a promised and promising land to which some Moroccans wish to emigrate at all costs. In Khalid Chaouch's play *Humble Odysseys*, for example, Abdou encourages Raghib to go to Spain, confirming that "in that country, it's so easy to get a job ... that country is a real paradise."[15] Lured by this vision, Raghib decides to get there even without having the necessary legal papers. Similarly, in Laila Lalami's *Hope and Other Dangerous Pursuits*, a group of young people take the risk of travelling illegally to Europe in an overcrowded inflatable boat. They all believe that if they manage to cross to this other world, their miserable lives will soon be transformed into ones of comfort, freedom and prosperity. Just as countless people from all over the world have crossed to the United States with the aim of tasting and enjoying "the American Dream", these emigrants also believe in the existence of "the European Dream"[16] in which they can equally share.

Such views about both Europe and America are obviously positive, and they contribute to painting a rosy picture of the West as a cultural Other. Nevertheless, one can notice in nearly all the works mentioned above a certain ambivalence that tends to undermine, or at least besmirch, the positive quality of the image reflected. Most emigrants fail to feel completely at ease in the land of the Other, as they often become disillusioned or nostalgic after some experience there. Temsamani, for instance, cannot help feeling nostalgic despite his former extreme enthusiasm about the American way of life. He explicitly expresses this feeling when he remarks, "I became nostalgic and started to reconnect with my roots, my home, Morocco."[17] What is more, he has now grown fed up with the materialistic and "crazy lifestyle"[18] of the United States, as one may infer from his statement, "We left our country to find a better life, but what we got is a gold-plated identity and a lot of debt."[19] He now realizes that real happiness cannot be achieved far away from one's native home and society: "The hell with the plastic life: give me one day with my family and friends and I will be happy for life."[20]

In Laila Lalami's novel, the characters who manage to make it to Spain are also disillusioned when their expectations fail to materialize. Faten has even found herself obliged to barter her virginity to be allowed to enter Spanish territory. She lets herself be deflowered by a Spanish officer, then goes on earn her living as a prostitute. Among her Spanish clients, Martin seems the most humane, as he appears willing to establish a special friendly relationship with her. But she soon discovers that he just wants to satisfy his sexual desire and exotic whims, and thus no room is left for any significant friendship between them.

In contrast, in Ahmed Radi's *Changing Times, Mobile Landscapes*, the protagonist Said – a Moroccan scholar who probably represents Radi himself and who goes to Wales to pursue his studies – succeeds in developing a real and meaningful relationship with a Western girl named Sarah:

> He was also lucky to come across and befriend a Scandinavian young girl. Despite their different colors and races and despite the huge distance separating the freezing north from the warm south, they were passionately in love with each other ... "You are my Ali Baba and my Andalousian knight." She made him feel proud of being an Arab, and also an African with his brown skin, so different from her snow whiteness, yet so complementary.[21]

This is a highly symbolic cultural encounter, wherein an Easterner and a Westerner seem to "complement" each other, despite all their differences. Yet Said soon realizes that this relationship cannot last long, as Sarah is motivated by passionate and romantic love, without ever thinking about the possibility of marriage. Said explains this in terms of the difference of perspectives between Easterners and Westerners: while the latter have a tendency "to enjoy to the full the ephemeral moment," the former rather "tend to establish something more solid and communal in the form of a social contract, with its obligations and responsibilities."[22] Thus their relationship seems doomed to sudden disruption from the very beginning.

In AnouarMajid's *Si Yussef*, however, the love and marital relationship between the Moroccan protagonist Si Yussef and the Spanish Lucia proves to be lasting and apparently successful. As a matter of fact, they have already been together for many years and their four children have already reached adulthood. This couple's love is reciprocal and very profound: while Lucia feels that "the meaning of her life was related to Si Yussef," who "gave her the satisfaction which no other person or institution had given her,"[23] her husband also believes that he is married to "the best woman in the world"[24] who "has given [him] the love of a thousand years."[25] Si Yussef prefers this Spanish woman to any from his home country because he does not want to entangle himself with the complexities of Moroccan customs and social bonds. As he confesses to Lamin, the narrator, he prefers to be free from "the whole mass of tradition and families that our women carry with them. A man here doesn't marry a woman but a whole tribe."[26] But in spite of all the comfort, happiness and satisfaction which his marriage to Lucia has offered to him, Si Yussef still feels that he is missing something vital in his life – namely, religious faith. Because of his Catholic Spanish wife, he has not only failed to perform his Islamic faith, but he also seems obliged to speak only Spanish in his home:

> And this is why I regret not having performed my prayers ... My good life didn't help me for any encounter with my creator. And this leads to the issue of my marriage to a woman who never accepted our faith. A man like me needs more than a good woman; he needs a Moslem. I mostly spoke Spanish at home; the pleasure to speak my soul was denied me all these years. As you know, the soul of man lives in his language.[27]

This passage really problematizes the question of cultural encounter between Easterners and Westerners. Although Lucia is portrayed very positively, it is clear that she has engendered an identity crisis for her husband. At bottom, he feels guilty of sacrificing both his religion and language, a fact which implies that he has partly lost two important components of his national and cultural identity. Since Lucia has retained her Catholic faith and imposed – whether directly or indirectly – the use of her Spanish language in their home, one can say that she appears symbolically as a dominant colonizer, while Si Yussef is the dominated and alienated colonized subject.

In his novel *A Chance*, Abderrahmane Sghir tells us a different story of such cross-cultural relations between a Moroccan and a Westerner. The narrative revolves around the sufferings of a young Moroccan man, called Brahim, who goes to work in America. He has already been working in a hotel in his native town and living happily with his native wife, but he is seduced by an American tourist named Amanda to travel with her to the United States. While there, Amanda does her best to prompt Brahim to renounce his wife and become her own lover, but in vain. When she gets desperate, she devilishly traps him in a bank problem that causes him to be imprisoned for ten years and causes a tragedy for the whole family.

Although this novel is very simple – or even simplistic – in its treatment of both theme and narrative techniques, it serves to cast some light on the kind of relationship that can exist between a Moroccan and a Westerner. Here, the Westerner is represented very negatively: Amanda is the image of a scheming, heartless and jealous lover who tries selfishly to "appropriate" another woman's husband.

In "A Woman From New York," Mohamed Mrabet presents us with another negative image of Americans. A group of Hippie men and women travel to Tangiers, and El Rifi – the young Moroccan protagonist, who may represent Mrabet himself – has some occasion to interact with them and witness their curious habits and behavior:

> Several Nazarene men with long hair sat nearby. Some Nazarene girls were squatting on the floor as they cooked something … El Rifi looked at the Nazarenes. The men had dandruff in their hair, and their skin was grey with dirt. Some of them had lice crawling in their beards. The girls had pimples and smelled stale, and their clothes needed to be washed and mended. A Moroccan had been cutting kif in the café that day, and they were smoking what he had thrown away.[28]

In this descriptive passage, Mrabet severely criticizes this group of American tourists and pokes fun at their unusual appearance and strange practices. Although, historically speaking, the Hippie was the latest mode at that time of the late 1960s, Mrabet raises the pertinent cultural question: How can such dirt, bad smell, and animalistic way of life be compatible with the ethics of a so-called civilized nation like the United States?

When El Rifi discusses the matter with one of these tourists (namely the Woman from New York referred to in the story's title), this American woman tries to defend the group, and she gets angry when the Moroccan criticizes her personally:

She was very angry. And you! She cried. Who are you? It's got nothing to do with me. I'm a Moslem. The poorest Moslem is cleaner than most Americans ... For instance, I think I'm better than you because I wash five times a day.[29]

Despite its simplicity and directness, this piece of dialogue is highly significant as it establishes a direct opposition between Islamic and Western civilizations. It suggests that Moslems are superior and much more civilized thanks to their Islamic religion which teaches them to be clean, both physically and spiritually. In contrast, American civilization is both implicitly and explicitly ridiculed and shown to be associated with dirt, bestiality and disease.

In "What Happened in Granada," Mrabet writes about another confrontation between him and some Westerners during his short visit to Granada. The story contains a number of significant scenes in which Mrabet openly clashes with these cultural Others, attempting to show them that he is not inferior, but rather superior, to them. For example, when he is offered wine during a family reunion, he decidedly refuses it in a conscious desire to stress his identity as a Moslem: "I don't drink, I said. I'll take a glass of water."[30] Once, he even threatens an English woman by brandishing "an Arab sword" and saying to her angrily: "I'm going to finish you off. You and your race! ... You're only an English whore and I'm a Riffian!"[31] In another scene, Mrabet is surrounded by a crowd of protesting Spaniards who want to blame him for his reckless and dangerous driving of a rented car. He responds, "I yelled at them: I shit on your ancestors and your whole race! I kept walking along, pushing through them. Barking dogs don't bite, I told them. A very fat woman came by. She called me a moro, and I called her a Christian pig."[32] In another scene, Mrabet even resorts to the Arabic language to insult some Spanish people by saying: "*Inaal din d'babakum* (God damn your father's religion)."[33]

In a less provocative counter-hegemonic stance, Abdellatif Akbib writes his travel book *Tangier's Eyes On America* to question some Western Orientalist stereotypes and suggest that the West itself can be easily made the object of an Easterner's criticism and ridicule. The title itself warns that America – and the whole Western world, by implication – is now subjected to representation under Tangier's Eastern eyes. The traditional roles are now subverted because it is no longer the West that is representing the East, but the other way around.

Like Mrabet, Akbib engages in a number of confrontations with different Americans, whom he represents as cultural Others. His technique consists in staging a series of encounters between him, as protagonist, and some Americans like the officer at the New York airport whom he skilfully represents as ignorant on the grounds that he is unable to speak any other language except his own. This ignorance is further stressed by his meeting with the American illiterate woman who stupidly asks him: "Whereabout is Morocco in the United States?"[34] While discussing with some Western intellectuals, the author is surprised at their ignorance and misunderstanding of the Others' culture and social reality, despite their academic background. One of the things he discovers, for instance, is that "Everything they knew about Islam was either exaggerated, distorted, or altogether wrong."[35] Akbib also recounts the story of his encounter with an angry American man who nearly kills him with his revolver. After narrowly escaping, the author says ironically that in America "the survival [is] for the quickest"[36] because there "weapons [are] sold like a gastronomic commodity."[37]

Such face-to-face encounters give Akbib the opportunity to express direct criticism of America and its people. He puts these latter in the position of cultural Others and depicts most of them as ignorant, shallow, or savage, just as the Oriental Other is depicted in Western hegemonic and Orientalist texts. These open confrontations between the protagonist and those Others permit him not only to subvert the traditional subject/object (or self/other) dichotomy but also to challenge many Western prejudices against Muslims or Orientals and to correct those misconceptions and cultural prejudices. In this way, it can be said that Akbib has succeeded in "writing back" to the West and problematizing its discourse of power and its ideology of Otherness.

The discourses of postcolonial Moroccan writers thus differ quite noticeably from the Orientalist ones. While the latter usually represent the Oriental Other negatively, these Moroccan texts include both positive and negative images of the West/Westerner as Other. In the majority of cases, they are ambivalent in their attitudes towards Otherness: the image is neither totally positive nor totally negative. Some writers tend to problematize this question of cultural Otherness. Anouar Majid chooses the third space of Tangiers to show that identity is unstable and that the forces of hybridity usually work to negate all notions of purity and fixedness. He also raises some problematic questions concerning the inevitability of cultural interaction between East and West. His narrator Lamin notes that, "There is nothing wrong if we are Europeanized or Americanized – up to a point. For wasn't the West also Orientalized? ... Their historians say that for ages they had borrowed our skills and knowledge. So what's wrong?"[38]

Some discourses like Akbib's and Mrabet's are so extreme in their negative representation of Otherness that they can be categorized as Occidentalist. They are obviously counter-hegemonic and counter-Orientalist. Yet, at least in the case of Akbib, this subversive strategy is used only as a means to an important end: to warn Westerners that Easterners are capable of "writing back" and producing the same cultural stereotypes against Westerners. This is what he implicitly means by stating that, "It is a misconception to suppose that only the West is capable of nourishing stereotypes vis à vis the East. We are capable of that, too. But as it is our duty to stem the tide of such negative attitudes, we can't afford to deal with the other by adopting what we want him to get rid of,"[39] His "tit for tat" strategy is therefore only a means to a mutually profitable end: the creation of a cosmopolitan inter-cultural dialogue which is fit to make us all transcend the ethnocentric ideology inherent in such binary categories as Occident/Orient, West/Rest, or Center/Peripheries.

Notes

1   Edward Said, *Orientalism* (London: Routledge, 1978).

2   Edward Said, "Orientalism Reconsidered," in *Literature, Politics and Theory*, ed. Francis Barker, et al (London, New York: Methuen, 1986), 211.

3   Edward Said, *Orientalism* (Harmondsworth: Penguin Books, 1978).

4   Ibid.

5   Rudyard Kipling, *A Choice of Kipling's Verse*, ed. T.S. Eliot (London: Faber and Faber, 1941), 111.

6   Ibid., 136.

7   William Shakespeare, *Othello, the Moor of Venice*, in *The Complete Works* (New York: Avenel Books, 1965), 1114.

8   Paul Bowles, *The Spider's House* (London: Abacus, 1991), 345.

9   Paul Bowles, *Let It Come Down* (Harmondsworth: Penguin, 2000), 284.

10   DrissTemsamani, *Rewind* (Bloomington: AuthorHouse, 2005), 19–20.

11   Ibid., 33.

12   Ibid., 122.

13   Mohamed Fandi, *Alien ... Arab ... And Maybe Illegal in America* (Charleston: BookSurge, 2006), 13.

14   Ibid., 14–15.

15   Khalid Chaouch, *Humble Odysseys: A Play in Five Acts* (Fez: Moroccan Cultural Studies Centre, 2002), 17–18.

16   Ibid., 9.

17   Driss Temsamani, *Rewind* (Bloomington: AuthorHouse, 2005), 162.

18   Ibid., 91.

19   Ibid., 106.

20   Ibid., 108.

21   Ahmed Radi, *Changing Times, Mobile Landscapes* (Marrakech: El Watanya, 2007), 42–43.

22   Ibid., 45–46.

23   AnouarMajid, *Si Yussef* (London: Quartet Books, 1992), 80.

24   Ibid., 139.

25   Ibid., 129.

26   Ibid., 139.

27   Ibid., 142.

28   Mohamed Mrabet, "A Woman From New York," *Mohamed Mrabet: Collected Stories*, trans. Bowles (Casablanca: Annajah Aljadida, 2004), 61.

29   Ibid., 62.

30   Mohamed Mrabet, "What Happened in Granada," *Mohamed Mrabet: Collected Stories*, 9.

31   Ibid., 19.

32   Ibid., 14.

33   Ibid., 21.

34   Abdellatif Akbib, *Tangier's Eyes On America* (Tangier: ADO Maroc, 2001), 37.

35   Ibid., 46–47.

36   Ibid., 30.

37   Ibid., 31.

38   Majid, 137.

39   Akbib, 85.

CHAPTER 3

Intersections: Amazigh (Berber) Literary Space

Daniela Merolla

The interaction of artistic productions with several languages, literary markets and media is crucial in the Amazigh literary space. Focusing on writers who use the Amazigh (Berber) language, this study addresses contemporary directions in Moroccan Amazigh (Berber) artistic works set against the historical and literary background of the Maghreb as well as the Amazigh diaspora in Europe. It also discusses Amazigh elements in Dutch novels and short stories published by writers of Riffian heritage. The term "Berber" will be used throughout this essay to indicate the historical continuity of the field of study.

Amazigh (Berber) Literary Space

As in the past, manifold genres, languages, and media constitute the Amazigh (Berber) literary space of today. Writers since the beginning of the twentieth century CE have contributed to a contemporary literature written in one of the Amazigh language variants, while other authors of Amazigh heritage have published novels in French and Arabic.[1] Novels and plays published in Dutch by writers originating from the Rif have received public acclaim, while some Berber authors have started to write in Spanish. New waves of migration and migration patterns have produced works by Berbers in Italian and English as well.

This is not to say that literacy was unknown in the past. The contemporary developments in written literature are not isolated from broader innovations in the literary market; some Amazigh writers, storytellers and singers were and are involved in multiple circuits of written and oral literary production. If most narratives and poetry until the last century were orally created and transmitted, Amazigh speakers since antiquity have known forms of script (Lybian, Tifinagh) while traders and religious leaders were well versed in the area's dominant languages.[2] Collections of tales and poems allow readers to enjoy elaborate oral literary traditions. Though some oral genres seem to disappear along with their contexts of production, new forms have also arisen. Increasingly, the overwhelmingly varied and enormously popular genre of "modern songs" incorporates "classical" musical styles with inspiration and instruments from around the world. For example, the songs of Hindi Zahra, who sings in English, and Chleuh Berber incorporate Chleuh sounds with blues, jazz, American folk, Egyptian music, and the influence of African singers such as Ali Farka Touré and Youssou N'Dour.[3] Another example is the music of the Tuareg band Tinariwen whose members play teherdent (lute), imzad (violin), tinde (drum) and electric guitar. Morgan[4] argues that they merge the Tuareg style of assouf ("solitude" or "nostalgia") with influences from Kabyle Berber contemporary songs, Malian blues, Algerian urban raï and Moroccan chaabi, pop, rock and Indian music.[5]

Another example may be seen in the revitalization of folktales in family settings and schools through films, novels, children's books, and cartoons. Not only are folktales documented in past collections, but they also represent a still vigorous oral heritage responding to the new contexts of school education and exposure to various media.[6] Thanks to international attention, storytellers again narrate folktales and perform comic pieces in town plazas. For example, Djamaa el-Fna Square in Marrakesh, where storytellers gather, was added to the UNESCO World Heritage List in 2001, while researchers, journalists, photographers and tour agencies have drawn attention to Arabic and Berber Moroccan storytelling in public squares and markets.[7] Told, sung, written, video-recorded, and spread online,[8] Amazigh oral literature is taking on a new life.

The notion of "literary space" can help us to understand long-term as well as more recent developments, which include multilingual, multimedia productions that intersect and interact with literatures produced in one of the vernacular forms of Amazigh (the Berber language).[9] Across languages of creation and variations in individual positions, we see numerous oral and written works marked by their authors' family language and by scenes and characters (partially) set in Amazigh environments. The nationalist critique in Morocco and Algeria[10] and the debate over the literary use of languages other than the author's "mother tongue"[11] notwithstanding, we see that the new political and intellectual climate of the Maghreb is leading to acceptance of the multilingualism that has resulted from long-term processes of expansion and migration. By recognizing the creative process that has resulted from interaction with other literatures and "literary spaces," the umbrella notion of "Amazigh (Berber) literary space" transcends the distinction between "Amazigh literature" – i.e. created in one of the Amazigh vernaculars – and literary works in other languages.

Tamazigh/ Amazigh/ Imazighen in the Maghreb

Some notes on the denomination and geographical spread of the Amazigh (Berber) language may be useful at this point. Since the 1990s, the term "Amazigh" (or Amazigh language) has seen widespread use.[12] It has gradually replaced "Berber" in daily use; and it is accepted in academic discourse.[13] Amazigh is used in the names of the institutes created to study the Amazigh language and culture in Algeria (Haut Commissariat à l'Amazighité, 1995) and in Morocco (Institute Royal de la Culture Amazighe, 2001). Other terms such as Tarifit, Tachelhiyt, Takbaylit and Tamashek describe some of the language variations spoken locally from Morocco to the Egyptian oasis of Siwa, along the Libyan border, and from the Mediterranean coast to Mauritania, Mali, Niger, Burkina Faso and northern Nigeria. In Morocco people speak Tarifit in the Rif mountains, Tamazight in the Middle Atlas, and Tachelhiyt (or Chleuh) further south in the Souss region. Amazigh people are estimated to number between 12 and 25 million, which makes Amazigh the second language of the Maghreb after Arabic.[14] As a consequence of migration, there are Amazigh (Berber) communities in France, Belgium, Spain, Italy, the Netherlands, Canada and the United States. An estimated two-thirds of Moroccan immigrants in the Netherlands speak Tarifit or come from a Berber-speaking region.[15]

We can speak of related Berber "languages" on account of the scattered nature of Amazigh linguistic communities in the Maghreb, the peculiarities of local variants, and because only a few speakers in the past were conscious of the linguistic unity of Amazigh. At the same time, scholars use the term Berber "language" to denote its unity at the meta-linguistic level and to indicate extended inter-comprehension.[16] Today, the terms Amazigh and Imazighen indicate a new awareness among Amazigh speakers of their linguistic unity and cultural specificity.

The present position of the Amazigh language in the Maghreb varies widely. Though their language is recognized as a national language in Mali and Niger, the once nomadic Tuaregs have borne the brunt of the creation of modern nation-states and their insurmountable borders.[17] The 2012 Tuareg-led rebellion and declaration of the independent state of Azawad in North Mali are linked to long-standing socio-economic marginalization.[18] In Kadafi's Libya, there was no room for language minorities, and the current situation remains far from clear.[19] More open attitudes have prevailed in Morocco and Algeria, where academic institutes have been founded committed to the study of Amazigh and Amazigh courses of study have been open at major universities. In Morocco, the pilot projects of alphabetization in Amazigh have been launched by the Moroccan Royal Institute for Amazighity, and the Amazigh language gained official status in the new Moroccan constitution of 2011. Nevertheless, Amazigh is not yet fully integrated into mass education, and contradictory policies affect government recognition of multilingualism.[20] Recent demonstrations in the Moroccan Rif in favor of economic, democratic and language rights have been met by military force.[21] Although the demonstrations were part of a broader national movement for democratization, they also revealed the enduring difficulties experienced by regional minorities within centralized states.

Amazigh Literary Space in Morocco and the Netherlands: Novels and Short Stories

References to Amazigh languages and communities appear in the French and Arabic works of renowned Moroccan writers such as Mohamed Khair-Eddine, Mohamed Choukri and Ahmed Toufiq.[22] Most known for its Chleuh setting is Khair-Eddine's *Légende et vie d'Agoun'chich*.[23] In the first part of this novel, the narrator discovers and describes an impoverished region and its inhabitants whose minority culture is threatened by colonial and post-colonial economic and political systems.[24] The narrator's deep attachment to the Chleuh language and land takes form in a narrative that reconstructs a forgotten past from the perspective of a Chleuh outlaw villager. The recreation of tales and myths in a poetic and oneiric style questions the homogenizing and manipulative vision of cultural identity promoted by centralized power and politics.[25] The initial narrator's voice recollects long-term continuity and "métissage" in Africa, while the narrative is marked by violence, local and international conflicts, and loss of personal and social identity.[26]

The tales of storyteller and painter Mohamed Mrabet present a particular form of oral-written interaction and take on an international, multilingual, and urban form in Paul Bowles' English translation and "recreation".[27] Mrabet's memories of the Rif and his attachment to his heritage are narrated in the first chapter of his autobiographical work with Eric Valentin.[28] More recently, we find elements of Khair-Eddine's oneiric approach in Mohamed Nadrani's visual representation of social and historical themes in the cartoons "The Sarcophagus of the Complex: Enforced Disappearances,"[29] on political repression in Morocco under King Hassan II, and "Emir Abdelkrim,"[30] on the Republic of the Rif, claiming independence from Spain and the Moroccan Sultan in 1921.

A number of authors from the Rif have achieved public and critical acclaim for their works in Dutch, including Abdelkader Benali, Khalid Boudou, Said El Haji, and Mustafa Stitou. Benali received major literary awards including the Geertjan Lubberhuizen Award in 1997, the Libris Prize in 2003, and the Best Foreign Novel in 1999 for the French translation of *Bruiloft aan zee* (*Wedding by the Sea*).[31] Khalid Boudou won the Gouden Ezelsoor Prize in 2002 for *Het schnitzelparadijs* (*The Schnitzel Paradise*),[32] while Mustafa Stitou received the prestigious VSB Poëzieprijs in 2004 for his poems *Varkensroze ansichten* (*Pink Pigs Postcards*).[33]

The written production in Amazigh has grown in recent years thanks to Chleuh and Riffian writers. Although academic institutions do not yet consistently support them, cultural associations across the territory have supported the publication of poems and novels in Amazigh.[34] Two of the oldest associations, AMREC (Association Marocaine de Recherches et Échanges Culturels) and ANCAP – Tamaynut (Association Nouvelle pour la Culture et les Arts Populaires – The New One), as well as the Agadir Summer University (AUEA), have played key roles in organizing cultural meetings for artists, activists, and scholars to discuss linguistic and literary themes. Since the 1970s, both AMREC and Tamaynut have published periodicals such as *Amud* (Seeds), *Anaruz* (Hope), *Arraten* (Documents), *Tamunt* (Togetherness), and *Tasafut* (Torch).[35] Nevertheless, contemporary written literature involves acute problems of marketing given the size of the reading public. Whereas theater and stand-up comedians are able to bridge the communication gap and attract larger audiences,[36] Amazigh novels and short stories are often self-financed and scattered across the small or ephemeral periodicals of cultural associations.

Chleuh

The first contemporary novel written in Chleuh was Mohammed Akunad's *Tawargit d imik* (*A Dream and a Little More*) published in 2002.[37] It addresses a "classical" dilemma of Islamic preaching in the Chleuh area: the need to use the language of the villagers to communicate religious ideas and values.[38] But unforeseen consequences explode when the cleric Si Brahim begins to preach in Chleuh. The villagers want him to speak about government land-grabbing and corruption. Understanding the sermon, women do not recognize themselves in the feminine images derived from classical texts and ask him to preach about their actual lives and present needs. Si Brahim, under pressure from political and religious authorities, faces a new dilemma: give up his initiative and preach in Arabic or abandon his position as fqih of the village.[39] By focusing on individual experience and avoiding didactic discussions of language rights, the novel joins a stream of Maghrebian works that explore the rural world. In contrast to the works of Khair-Eddine and Ahmed Toufiq, *Tawargit d imik* focuses on the contemporary time and world.

Before Akunad, Mohamed Moustaoui, Hassan Id Belqasm and Ali Sedki-Azayku and others had published collections of poems in Chleuh in the 1970s, while Ali Mimoun Essafi published the first Chleuh play in the 1980s.[40] According to several members of the writers' association Tirra (Writing),[41] there are discernible differences between older and younger generations of writers. Earlier authors, who usually began writing in Arabic and later switched to Chleuh, were influenced by Chleuh manuscripts and traditional poetry and rhythms. Younger generations tend to write in "standard" Amazigh, often in Latin or in Tifinagh characters, and make use of neologisms as well as the other Amazigh language variants of Morocco and Algeria. As there was no school curriculum in Amazigh, the acquisition of a "standard" written language is one of the effects of the remarkable activism of cultural associations that offered courses and information across the country. These younger generations do not necessarily follow Chleuh styles and rhythms, even though the language question is central in their work. The choice to write prose can also be seen as a significant departure from previous publications. One of the long-term debates on Amazigh has concerned the kind of language that could or should be used for literary, academic, and factual writing: a unified (non-existent in the spoken form) Amazigh, a standardized vernacular "purified" of loan words from Arabic and French (replaced by neologisms and outmoded terms), or a relatively standardized literary form close to the spoken language. The discussion becomes even more complex in the case of artistic expression since "working on the language" and innovation are themselves part of the literary project. Akunad's *A Dream and a Little More* seeks a difficult balance between vernacular and standardized literary forms.[42]

Currently there are some fifty novels and collections of short stories published in Chleuh, including *Muzya*[43] and *Amussu numalu*[44] by Lahacem Zaheur, *Ijjigen n tidi* by Mohamed Akunad,[45] *Ijawwan n tayri* by Brahim Lasri Amazigh,[46] and *Igdad n Wihran* by Lahoucine Bouyaakoubi.[47] Some of the titles seem to express, consciously or unconsciously, a position in the language debate since the writers choose neologisms and obsolete terms.[48] Bouyaakoubi suggests that the titles of the younger generation more generally signal literary intervention as they innovate on daily language use.[49]

If the language debate continues to inform chosen titles and themes, as in Akunad's first novel, new writers, under the influence of international poetry and philosophy, focus on urban life and topics.[50] For example, Brahim Lasri Amazigh's "The Siroccos of Love" treats the social censure of sexual relationships out of wedlock and the consequences for a young woman, symbolically named Tilelli (Freedom), when she gets pregnant and looks for someone to shelter her in the months preceding childbirth.[51] Bouyaakoubi explains that this subject, when spoken of openly, is usually off limits in Amazigh literature. Moreover, the language of sexuality and the body used by Lasri is both upsetting and a renewal; instead of using classical Arabic or French, he uses Chleuh terms for the body that are only used in private.[52]

Tarifit

Migration, travel, and memory are central themes in Riffian novels. There is significant continuity between the Rif and the diaspora in France, Belgium, Spain, and the Netherlands, with the first novels and short stories written in Tarifit appearing in Morocco, the Netherlands, and Spain. In the Netherlands, writers from the Rif who publish in Dutch have won public recognition, while those who choose to or are able to write in Tarifit are known among the activist circuit or in the larger Moroccan migrant community when they combine writing with theater and music. A number of short stories and collections of songs have appeared in Spanish thanks to Mohamed Toufali.[53] Many Riffian artists, in particular singers and musicians, are active in Melilla, the multilingual and multicultural Spanish outpost in Morocco.[54] Institutional support for Amazigh language, literature, and music is however lacking in Spain, which seems to indicate ignorance of, or disinterest for, the historical richness of reciprocal influences and the more recent colonial past.[55]

While Fouad Azeroual, theater-maker from Nador, wrote seven plays and a novel in the mid-1990s, the first novel published in Tarifit was Mohamed Chacha's *Reẓ ṭṭabu ad d teffegh tfukt*.[56] Chacha also published another novel and four collections of short stories and poems.[57] Mustafa Ayned, musician, singer, actor, and writer, brought out ironic and tender short stories in *Reḥriq n tiri*.[58] Other writers have produced both novels and theater pieces, including Mohamed Bouzaggou, *Jar u jar*,[59] and Said Belgharbi, *Aṣwaḍ yebuyebḥen!*.[60] Several collections of short stories have also been published in Arabic script by Bouzian Moussaoui and Mohammed Ouachikh.[61]

Among women writers, Fatima Bouziane has published several short stories in Arabic,[62] while *Tasrit n weẓru* by Samira Yedjis[63] is the first novel in Tarifit written by a woman.[64] Its title refers to an oral tale, the story of a young bride kidnapped by the jinns and transformed into a rock. This is largely a story seen through women's eyes though it also contains elements of a family saga spanning three generations. The first part concerns the village life and difficult marriage of Hniyya, the young female protagonist. The second describes the fighting spirit and military resistance of

Hniyya and her family during the war against Spain. The third part closes on a more optimistic note, following the difficulties experienced by the protagonist in adapting to urban life and her pain of separation from her children and grandchildren due to migration.[65]

Dutch

As mentioned above, authors of Riffian heritage have won critical acclaim in the Netherlands. Tarifit is present as a literary element in some of the works of authors such as Abdelkader Benali, Khalid Boudou, Said El Haji, and Mustafa Stitou. For example, "The Days of Satan" by Said El Haji addresses the lack of historical consciousness in the Rif.[66] In a satirical dialogue between Satan, the village imam and elderly immigrants from the Rif, the reader is made to understand that they have never heard of the Berber King Juba II or other figures of ancient history and that they have also forgotten Abdelkrim El-Khattabi,[67] the founder of the Republic of the Rif. "Nobody knew these names – and that said enough", concludes the scene.[68]

Abdelkader Benali's first novel *Weddings at Sea* takes on Rif migrants who try to cement their ties to their land of origin through marriage.[69] The main character, Lamarat, is a young man who goes to the Rif for the wedding of his sister and uncle.[70] His young uncle flees to a nearby town, and Lamarat is sent by his father to bring the bridegroom back, but the bridegroom's temporary refuge in the local bordello irreparably wounds the pride of the bride, Rebekka, leading to a paradoxical end. The story is woven around an intricate sequence of events, past and present, narrated during Lamarat's taxi ride from the house by the sea to the town. The inter-related themes that organize the narrative are introduced at the beginning of the novel: migration and the return to the "land of origin,"[71] men's fear of marriage, impoverished and degrading villages, and the cultural distance of returning migrants from their native villages represented by Lamarat's tourist-like gaze.[72] The family house built by Lamarat's father deteriorates over the course of the narrative; its final collapse coincides with the failure of the wedding and the impossibility of recovery from the consuming consequences of emigration/ immigration.[73] Different literary styles – childlike in some episodes and a stream-of-consciousness mode in others – submit the Dutch language to various forms of deterritorialization.

In Benali's novel, the stereotype of the Rif's backwardness is a recurrent theme treated with light irony. Lamarat's birth and the love story between his father and mother are reminiscent of rural folktales.[74] When Lamarat goes to Morocco, he discovers that he is the only one who does not understand his Tarifit-speaking grand-mother, and is therefore the ignorant ("illiterate") one in the family. The narrator playfully recollects a meeting between Lamarat and a Dutch salesman who wants to sell him plastic chairs. The vendor addresses Lamarat in a rather offensive mix of Berber, Arabic and Dutch, because he "knows" that he must address Berber high-landers in a "rustic" way. With Lamarat speaking standard Dutch and the Dutch salesman speaking coarse Arabic and Berber, the scene offers another ironic subver-sion of the expected ignorance of Riffian characters.[75]

As these examples show, the references to the Rif and the Amazigh language are not part of folkloric presentation, regionalism, or didactic teaching. These ele-ments are involved in the narrative of contradictory pulling forces through plays on words, irony, and an often phantasmagorical style, while the characters construct, de-construct, and re-construct their social and personal lives in the Netherlands as well as their memories from an elusive "home country". If deep "horseradish" roots[76] counter the estrangement of migration, in these texts Morocco tends to become a place for summer holidays.

Conclusion

The rich and diversified literary production included under the umbrella notion of "Amazigh literary space" gives us a glimpse of a world in transformation. Thanks to cultural baggage developed in the multiple languages learnt at home, school or in emigration, Amazigh writers develop their artistic creativity and give poetic form to the difficulty of daily living in rural and urban contexts; they portray, mix, and reconstruct socially and individually scathing issues. A common trait is that, whether the setting of the works is an Amazigh region or not, the reference to the Amazigh language is not ethnographic or didactic, but rather integrated in the characterization and the narrative. The main difference occurs when migrant writers, such as those writing in Dutch, adopt a tourist gaze. Within the Amazigh literary space, there is a definite effort to create a written literature in Amazigh. Writers build on the experience of their predecessors, whether they used Amazigh, French, or Arabic. As the production of novels in Amazigh becomes increasingly "normal," the language question is less and less explicitly treated. We also see that artistic effervescence – the myriad of cultural, journalistic, and academic activities together with the personal effort of diffusion – encounters difficulties known to all literary writing in Morocco.[77] However, these difficulties are made more acute by the extreme limitation of audience and the scarce funds for Amazigh publishing houses. In this respect, the situation does not appear to have changed over the last decade: songs and theater in Tarifit are widespread at the popular levels, and while the increasing use of new media – whether radio, television or the Internet – is certainly important, it does not yet fully support the publication of artistic writing in Amazigh.

Notes

1 Among others, Mouloud Feraoun, the Amrouche family, Mouloud Mammeri, Nabile Farès (in French) and Belaïd Ali Ait, Aliche, Si Amar-ou-Saïd Boulifa, Saïd Said and Amer Mezdad (in Kabyle) from Algeria; the poet Hawad (in Touareg and French) from Niger; and the novelist Ibrahim Al-Koni (Arabic) from Libya.

2 Bilingual stelae (Libyan / Punique or Latin) date from the sixth century BCE. The famous writer Apuleius wrote in Latin but was born in the Berber town of Madaura (M'daourouch in Algeria today) about 123-125 CE. The themes of Berber folktales have also been found in manuscripts written in Arabic and in Berber traced back to the sixteenth century CE (Henri Basset, *Essai sur la littérature des Berbères*, Carbonel, Algiers, 1920. Repr. Awal – Ibis Press 2001, 55 note 3; Abdellah Bounfour, Manuscripts berbères en caractères arabes, *Encyclopédie Berbère*, 30, 2010: 4554–4563; Gabriel Camps, Avertissement. Etre berbère, *Encyclopédie Berbère*, Vol. I, 1984:7–48; Salem Chaker, Libyque: écriture et langue, *Encyclopèdie Berbère* 28–29, 2008: 4395–4409; Emile Dermenghen, Le mythe de Psyché dans le folklore nord-africain, *Revue Africaine*, 1945: 41–81; Lionel Galand, Les alphabets libyques, *Antiquités Africaines 25* (1989): 69–81; Paulette Galand-Pernette, Littératures berbères, des voix, des lettres, Paris: PUF, 1998, 26–27; Jean-Pierre Laporte, Manuscripts latins d'Afrique, *Encyclopédie Berbère*, 30, 2010: 4563–4568; Tadeusz Lewicki, Quelques textes inédits en vieux berbère, *Revue des études Islamiques*, 1934, 3: 275–296, 282, 288; Ouahmi Ould-Braham, Lecture des 24 textes berbères médiévaux extraits d'une chronique ibadite par T. Lewicki, *Littérature orale arabo-berbère*, 1987: 87–125). Historical overview in Michael Brett and Elizabeth Fentress, *The Berbers*, Blackwell, Oxford, 1996. Other languages known among Amazigh speakers in Morocco today are dialectal Arabic, French, and Spanish. French and Spanish spread in the Maghreb through European expansionism and colonization.

3 See the interview with Hindi Zahra published on *Aujourd'hui le Maroc*: "Je m'intéresse à toutes les cultures et j'ai envie que ma musique soit universelle et réunisse des gens de divers horizons. Je voudrais qu'elle s'inscrive dans la pluralité [All cultures interest

me; I want my music to be universal and unite people from various backgrounds. I hope my music belongs to all]" (Amine Harmach, Interview with Zahra Hindi: "J'ai envie de promouvoir l'amazigh à travers mon chant [I want to promote the Amazigh through my music]," *Aujourd'hui, Le Maroc* (Jan. 29, 2009), http://www.aujourdhui.ma/maroc -actualite/magazine/zahra-hindi-j-ai-envie-de-promouvoir-l-amazigh-a-travers -mon-chant--61657.html; See also Samriddhi Tanti, Hindi Zahra – Music for the Soul, *EF News International* (21 September 2011), http://www.efi-news.com/2011/09/hindi -zahra-music-for-soul.html.)

4   Andy Morgan, *Tinariwen – Sons of the desert*. In *Andy Morgan writes …* (Website, January 6, 2011) (http://www.andymorganwrites.com/tinariwen-sons-of-the-desert/), first published in *Songlines* 29, 2007.

5   See also Peter Culshaw, "Desert Storm [Tinariwen]," *Songlines* 42 (March–April, 2007): 20–25. www.eyefortalent.com/eft-press/T-N%20SonglinesMarApr07.pdf; *Tinariwen, Aman Iman*, Documentary, Berber/French, www.youtube.com/watch?v=iOu4fdlPiWI

6   Daniela Merolla, *De l'art de la narration tamazight (berbère). 200 ans d'études: état des lieux et perspectives* (The art of Amazigh storytelling; Two-hundred years of research: the current status and perspectives) (Paris/Leuven: Peeters, 2006).

7   On the Djamaa el-Fna Square, see the UNESCO World Heritage List, 2001. http://www .unesco.org/bpi/intangible_heritage/morroco.htm. See also Thomas Ladenburger, *Al-Halqa: In the storyteller's circle*, Documentary, Germany 2010, 90min, http://www.alhalqa .com, and Thibaut Danteur, *L'authenticité par la mise en scène. Analyse dialogique des activités touristiques et culturelles de la place Jemaa el Fna, Via@, Les imaginaires touristiques*, n°1, 2012. URL: http://www.viatourismreview.net/Article7.php; Rachele Borghi and Claudio Minca, Le lieu, la place, l'imaginaire: discours colonial et littérature dans la description de la Jamaa el Fna, Marrakech, *Expressions Maghrebins* 2: 155–174, 2003; Ahmed Skounti and Ouidad Tebbaa, 2005, *La place Jemaa El Fna: patrimoine culturel immatériel de Marrakech, du Maroc et de l'Humanité* (Rabat: Éditions de l'UNESCO).

8   Daniela Merolla, Digital Imagination and the 'Landscape of Group Identities': the Flourishing of Theatre, Video and 'Amazigh Net' in the Maghrib and Berber Diaspora, *Journal of North African Studies* 7.4 (2002): 122–131; Mena Lafkioui and Daniela Merolla, eds., *Oralité et nouvelles dimensions de l'oralité: Intersections théoriques et comparaisons des matériaux dans les études africaines* (Orality and new dimensions in orality: intersections and theoretical comparisons in African studies) (Paris: Inalco, 2008).

9   See Merolla *De l'art*, 71–74, 183–195. Tamazight, the feminine and singular form, means "Amazigh woman" and the vernacular spoken in the Moroccan Middle Atlas. As languages are usually feminine in Berber, "Tamazight" also indicates the "Amazigh language" as a whole. In Morocco, the masculine form Amazigh (instead than the femi-

nine form Tamazight) is used, to avoid confusion with the Middle Atlas vernacular. I follow this use in the present article.

10   The nationalist critique saw many "Berber" characterizations as regrettable forms of French acculturation, and these works were often accused of lacking patriotism. See Mostefa Lacheraf, La Colline oubliée ou la conscience anachronique, in Philippe Lucas and Jean-Claude Vatin, eds., *L'Algérie des anthropologues* (Paris: Maspero, 1975), 231–232, texte 65, first published in *Le Jeune Musulman* (13 February, 1953); See also Christiane Achour, Littérature et apprentissage scolaire de l'écriture: influences réciproques, *Littératures du Maghreb, Itinéraires et Contacts de cultures* 4–5 (Paris: Centre d'Etude des Nouveaux Espaces Littéraires, 1984): 15–56; Jacqueline Kaye and Abdelhamid Zoubir, *The ambiguous compromise: Language, literature, and national identity in Algeria and Morocco* (London and New York: Routledge, 1990); Mohamed Saïd El Zemouri, *Berbérisme dans la littérature maghrébine d'expression française (les cas de Driss Chaïbi, Mohamed Khaïr Eddine, Yacine Kateb, Nabil Farès)* (Tétouan: Faculté des Lettres et des Sciences Humaines, 1997).

11   Jean Déjeux, Francophone literature in the Maghreb: the problem and the possibility, *Research in African Literatures* 23.2 (1992): 5–19; Mouloud Mammeri, *Littérature berbère orale, Les Temps modernes* 33.375 (Oct. 1977): 407–418; Mouloud Mammeri, *Poèmes kabyles anciens* (Paris: Maspero, 1980); Albert Memmi, *Portrait du colonisé, précédé du portrait du colonisateur* (Paris: Buchet/Chastel, 1957); ObiajunwaWali, The Dead End of African Literature, *Transition* 10, (1963): 330–335.

12   In Arabic and European languages, the terms "Berber / Barbar / Breber" have been known since the Eighth and Sixteenth Centuries CE respectively. The term "Berber" became established under the impetus of colonial ethnography of the nineteenth century CE. It is increasingly rejected in North Africa because "Berber" derives from the Greek βάρβαρος and the Latin barbarus, and meaning "uncivilized." See also Chantal de la Veronne, Distinction entre arabes et berbères dans les documents d'archives européennes des XVIe et XVIIe siècles concernant le Maghreb, *Actes du premier congrès d'études des cultures méditerranéennes d'influences arabo-berbères* (Algiers: SNED, 1973), 261–265.

13   Amazigh is the singular form of Imazighen, usually translated as "free (noble) men" and is also used as an adjective (Amazigh language). The term Amazigh was known in Morocco and Libya and is nowadays accepted in Algeria and in areas where it was not previously used. Linguistically, Amazigh belongs to the Afro-Asiatic family along with languages such as Arabic, Hebrew, Amharic, Hausa, Oromo, and ancient Egyptian. See also Salem Chaker, Amazigh (le/un) Berbère, *Encyclopèdie Berbère* 4 (1987): 562–568.

14   Its speakers number between 30 and 40% of the Moroccan population (Rif, Middle and High Atlas, Sous). In Algeria, between 14 and 25% of the population speaks local

forms of Amazigh (Kabylia, Aurès, Mzab). The Tuaregs, who live in a wide Saharan and sub-Saharan area across Algeria, Libya, Mali, Niger, Burkina Faso, and Nigeria, are estimated to have around two million speakers. In Tunisia there are small pockets of Berber speakers on the Isle of Djerbaa and in the south (Chenini, Douz, Tozeur), while larger communities live in Libya (an estimated 3% of the Libyan population). The range of estimates indicates that censuses, when taken at all, have not inquired about language use, and any existing sources are old or unreliable. See also Salem Chaker, Le berbère, in Bernard Cerquiglini, ed., *Les langues de France*. (Paris: PUF, 2003), 215–227; Joseph H. Greenberg, Studies in African linguistic classification: IV, Hamito-Semitic, *Southwestern Journal of Anthropology* 6 (1950): 47–63; M. Paul Lewis, ed., *Ethnologue: Languages of the World* (Dallas: SIL International, 2009), Online version: http://www.ethnologue.com/; Lamara Bougchiche, *Langues et littératures berbères des origines à nos jours. Bibliographie internationale*, (Paris: Ibis, 1997).

15   Abderrahman El Aissati and Petra Bos, Arabic and Berber in the Netherlands and France, in Guus Extra and Jeanne Maartens, eds., *Multilingualism in a multicultural context. Case studies on South Africa and Western Europe. Studies in Multilingualism* 10. (Tilburg: Tilburg UP, 1998), 179–195; Salem Chaker, La langue berbère en France, in Mohamed Tilmatine, ed., *Enseignement des langues d'origine et immigration nord-africaine en Europe: langue maternelle ou langue d'Etat?* (Paris: Inalco, 1997), 15–30; Mohamed Chafik, *Amazighen* (Amsterdam: Bulaaq, 1989); Magreet Dorleijn and Jacomine Nortier, Van de hand en de handschoen, in Ad Backus, et al., *Artikelen van de Zesde Anéla-conferentie* (Delft: Eburon, 2009), 83–92; Guus Extra and Jan Jaap de Ruiter, eds., *Babylon aan de Noordzee: Nieuwe talen in Nederland* (Amsterdam: Bulaaq, 2001), 60–77; Guus Extra and Jan Jaap de Ruiter, The sociolinguistic status of the Moroccan community in the Netherlands, *Indian Journal of Applied Linguistics* 20.1–2 (1994): 151–176.

16   Kossmann (1999) indicates two (northern and southern) Berber "dialect continua." See Maarten Kossmann, *Essai sur la phonologie du proto-berbère* (Cologne: Rüdiger Köppe Verlag, 1999); See also Salem Chaker, Unité et diversité de la langue berbère, *Unité et diversité de tamazight*, Actes du Colloque international (Ghardaïa 20–21 avril 1991), Tizi-Ouzou, FNACA, 1992, 129–142; Jeannine Drouin, Unité et pluralité littéraires dans les sociétés berbérophones, CIUDT 1 (1992): 115–128; Lionel Galand, La langue berbère existe-t-elle? in Christian Robin, ed., *Mélanges linguistiques offerts à Maxime Rodinson* (Paris: Geuthner, 1985), 175–184; Miloud Taïfi, Unité et diversité du berbère: Détermination des lieux linguistiques d'intercompréhension, *Études et Documents Berbères* 12 (1994), 119–138.

17   Hélène Claudot-Hawad, *Le Touaregs: portait en fragments* (Aix-en-Provence: Edisud, 1993); Hélène Claudot-Hawad, ed., *Berbères ou Arabes? Le tango des specialists* (Paris: Irenam,

2006). Tuaregs live in a vast area across Algeria, Libya, Mali, Niger, northern Burkina Faso and northern Nigeria.

18   Tuareg-led rebellion in north Mali, *Aljazeera Explainer* (03 April, 2012), www.aljazeera.com/indepth/features/2012/03/201232211614369240.html; Mali Tuareg rebels' call for independence rejected, *BBC News* (03 June, 2012), www.bbc.co.uk/news/world-africa-17640223; see also the Tuareg site of the MLNA, Mouvement National de libération de l'Azawad, www.mnlamov.net/english.html.

19   See, for example, Peter Fragiskatos, Will Gadhafi defeat bring new freedom for Berbers in Libya?, CNN *Opinion* (26 August, 2011), http://articles.cnn.com/2011-08-26/opinion/fragiskatos.berber.language_1_tamazight-berber-minority-berber-culture?_s=PM: OPINION; Christopher John Chivers, Amid a Berber reawakening in Libya, fears of revenge, *The New York Times* (8 August, 2011), http://www.nytimes.com/2011/08/09/world/africa/09berbers.html?pagewanted=all; Christopher John Chivers, Libya clashes: "at least 14 dead" around Zuwara, *BBC News* (3 April, 2012), http://www.bbc.co.uk/news/world-middle-east-17602343; Glen Johnson, In post-Kadafi Libya, Berber minority faces identity crisis, *Los Angeles Times* (22 March, 2012), http://articles.latimes.com/2012/mar/22/world/la-fg-libya-identity-20120323.

20   A commission in Morocco proposed the Amazigh language as an official national language only after the 2011 "Arab Spring" in which Berber speakers participated in Libya and across the Maghreb.

21   On protests in the Rif area in March 2012 see, for example, Paul Schemm, Protests spread in Morocco's north Rif mountains, *The Guardian* (3 December, 2012), http://www.guardian.co.uk/world/feedarticle/10139625; Abdelhafid Marzak, Province d'Al Hoceïma, Casseurs en uniforme, *Actuel* 133 (16 March, 2012), www.actuel.ma/Societe/Province_dAl_Hoceima_Casseurs_en_uniforme/955.html; Pedro Canales, El Rif marroquí se rebela contra el abandono, *El Imparcial* (13 Mar, 2012), http://www.elimparcial.es/contenido/100992.html.

22   Mohamed Choukri, *For Bread Alone*, trans. Paul Bowles (London: Peter Owen, 1974); Mohamed Choukri, *Zoco Chico*, trans. Mohamed El Ghoulabzouri (Paris: Didier Devillez, 1996); Ahmed Toufiq (also transcribed as Al-Tawfiq), *Shajarat al-hinna ' wa-al-qamar / L'arbre et la lune (The tree and the moon)*, trans. Philippe Vigreux (Paris: Phébus, 2002).

23   Mohammed Khaïr-Eddine, *Légende et vie d'Agoun'chich (The Legend and Life of Agoun'-chich)* (Paris: Seuil, 2010).

24   "Quand vous débarquez dans un pays que vous n'avez jamais vu ou que vous avez déserté depuis longtemps, ce qui vous frappe avant tout, c'est la langue ... Eh bien! le Sud, c'est d'abord une langue: la tachelhït (When you land in a new country or one you left long ago, what strikes you first and foremost is the language ... Well! In the

south, there is one primary language, Tashelhit)" Khaïr-Eddine (1984/2010), 3; "Cela [le problème de la pérennité culturelle] touche essentiellement les cultures de tradition orale, les langues minoritaires dont la richesse s'estompe faute de pouvoir échapper à l'oubli par simple retranscription ... En dehors du Sénégal, qui commence à codifier ses quatre langues nationales, les autres pays d'Afrique ont tendance à dédaigner leurs attaches (The problem of cultural continuity primarily affects oral cultures, whose wealth is unable to escape oblivion by simple transcription ... Outside of Senegal, where the four national languages have begun to be codified, many African countries have a tendency to show disdain for their languages)" Khaïr-Eddine (1984/2010), 7.

25   Zohra Mezgueldi, Légende et vie d'Agoun'Chich, Itinéarires et contact de cultures 15–16.1–2 (1992): 121–126; Zohra Mezgueldi, Oralité et stratégies scripturales dans l'œuvre de Mohammed Khaïr-Eddine, Thesis, Université Lumière-Lyon 2 (2001), Dir. Charles Bonn and Marc Gontard; See also Ali Chibani, Légende et vie d'Agoun'chich. L'effacement, http://la-plume-francophone.over-blog.com/article-31308167.html (12 May 2009).

26   "[La ville] C'est le point de convergence heureuse de deux cultures, la berbère et la négro-africaine. Cet art ce manifeste dans les moindres choses, les plus infimes gestes ... À travers lui, on discerne le génie de ces peuples qui essayent d'oublier la haine, la traite ancienne et actuelle et qui pratiquent le métissage biologique et culturel sans arrière-pensée [The town is the point of convergence for two happy cultures, the Berber and the Black African; Here art manifests itself in the smallest gestures ... Here we discern the spirit of people who are trying to forget hatred, who are trying, without reservation, to understand their past and present conditions, both biological and cultural]" Khaïr-Eddine (1984/2010), 16.

27   Critical analysis of the artistic "collaboration" between Bowles, Choukri, and Mrabet is discussed in Khalid Amine, Paul Bowles' Tangier: An Ambiguous Compromise, in Ralph M. Coury and R. Kevin Lacey, eds., Writing Tangier (New York: Peter Lang, 2009), 59–74; R. Kevin Lacey, The Writers/Storytellers of Morocco and Paul Bowles: Some Observations and Afterthoughts, in Ralph M. Coury and R. Kevin Lacey, eds., Writing Tangier (New York: Peter Lang, 2009), 75–94; Salah Moukhlis, Localized identity, universal experience: celebrating Mohamed Choukri as a Moroccan writer, in Ralph M. Coury and R. Kevin Lacey, eds., Writing Tangier (New York: Peter Lang, 2009), 21–34.

28   Mohamed Mrabet and Eric Valentin, Mémoires fantastiques (Paris: Rouge Inside, 2011).

29   2005.

30   2008.

31   Saïd Belgharbi, Aṣwaḍ yebuyebḥen! (The Hoarse Look!) (Berkane: Trifagraph, 2006).

32   Khalid Boudou, Het schnitzelparadijs (The Schnitzel Paradise) (Amsterdam: Vassallucci, 2001).

33 Mohamed Stitou, *Varkensroze ansichten (Pink Pigs Postcards)* (Amsterdam: De Bezige Bij, 2003).

34 Louisa Dris-Aït-Hamadouche and Yahia Zoubir, The Maghreb: Social, Political and Economic Developments, in Mehdi Parvizi Amineh, ed., *The Greater Middle East in Global Politics* (Brill: Leiden, 2007), 249–278; Moha Ennaji, *Multilingualism, Cultural Identity, and Education in Morocco* (USA: Springer, 2005), 73; Abderrahmane Lakhsassi, État de la culture Amazighe après 50 ans d'indépendance: Théâtre, Cinéma-Vidéo, Roman, Poésie, in Mohamed Tozy, *50 ans de développement humaine & Perspectives 2025*, Rapport Thématique, Cinquantenaire de l'Indépendance du Royaume du Maroc (2006), 113–129, http://www.rdh50.ma/fr/pdf/contributions/GT9--6.pdf; Bruce Maddy-Weitzman, *The Berber Identity Movement and the Challenge to North African States* (Austin: University of Texas Press, 2011); Merolla, Digital Imagination 122–131.

35 See also the conference proceedings of the AUEA. The first associations were located at Sous, Rabat, Casablanca and in the Rif (Al-intilâqa). The local or regional associations Izuran (Roots) at Ouarzazate, Tilelli (Liberty) at Goulmima, Ilmas (Source) at Nador and Numidya at Al Hoceima are more recent. They participated in the "Agadir Charter for Linguistic and Cultural Rights" in 1991. Some of these groups belong to the umbrella organization CMA (Congrès Mondial Amazigh/ Amazigh World Congress). Currently some 40 associations are active in Morocco. See: http://www.europemaroc.com/assoc .html.

36 On theater see Abderrahmane Lakhsassi, État de la culture Amazighe après 50 ans d'indépendance: Théâtre, Cinéma-Vidéo, Roman, Poésie, in M. Tozy, *50 ans de développement humaine & Perspectives 2025*, Rapport Thématique, Cinquantenaire de l'Indépendance du Royaume du Maroc (2006): 113–129, http://www.rdh50.ma/fr/pdf/ contributions/GT9--6.pdf; See also Merolla, Digital Imagination; Daniela Merolla, De la parole aux vidéos. Oralité, écriture et oralité médiatique dans la production culturelle amazigh (berbère). *Afrika Focus* 18.1–2 (2005): 33–57; Merolla, De l'art.

37 Mohammed Akunad. *Tawargit d imik (A Dream and a Little More)* (Rabat: Tizrigin Bouregreg, 2002).

38 Nico Van den Boogert, *Muhammad Awzal and the Berber literary tradition of the Sous*, Leiden (thèse), 1995.

39 Mohammed Akunad. *Un youyou dans la mosquée, Tawargit d imik*, trans. Lahcen Nachef (Maroc: Edilivre, 2012); M. Akunad, *Un youyou dans la mosquée*, traduit de l'amazigh par Lahcen Nachef (Maroc: Edilivre, 2012); Afulay 2003, www.mondeberbere.com/ littérature/akunad/indexc.htm. A *fqih* or *faqih* is an expert in religious law, or a person with religious knowledge.

40 Moustaoui's first collection was *Iskraf* (1976); Ali Mimoun Essafi's pieces are *Ussan sem-*

miɣnin (Cold Days) (Casablanca, 1983) and Tighrit tabrat (Reading a letter) (Casablanca, 1994); An overview of Amazigh publications in Morocco is in Lakhsassi: http://www .rdh50.ma/fr/pdf/contributions/GT9--6.pdf; An anthology of Amazigh poetry is in Abdellah Bounfour and Amar Ameziane, *Anthologie de la poésie berbère traditionnelle* (Harmattan: Paris, 2010).

41 Interview with Mr. Akunad, Mr. Arejdal, Mr. Bouyaakoubi, Mr. Lahacem, and Mr. Oussous at the Hotel Aferni, Agadir (18 July, 2010). I would like to thank Lahoucine Bouyaakoubi, a young researcher and writer, for his help.

42 Interview with the author in 2002.

43 Lahacem Zaheur, *Muzya* (Agadir, 1994).

44 Lahacem Zaheur, *Amussu n umalu* (The Movement of the Shadow) (Agadir: Aqlam, 2008).

45 Mohammed Akunad, *Ijjigen n tidi* (Flowers of Toil) (Agadir: Aqlam, 2007).

46 Brahim Lasri Amazigh, *Ijawwan n tayri* (The Siroccos of Love) (Marrakech: Association Imal, 2008).

47 Lahoucine Bouyaakoubi, *Igdad n Wihran* (Birds of Oran), (France: privately printed, 2010).

48 'Une autre catégorie [qui] se caractérise par l'emploi de néologismes ou de mots tombés en désuétude dans la langue amazighe, tels *Imula n tmekwtit* (Ombres de mémoire) d'El Khatir Aboulkacem-Afulay ou *Aggad n tidt* (Ovaire de vérité) de Taieb Amgroud' [A category characterized by the use of words or neologisms fallen into disuse in the Amazigh language, such as Shadow memory (El-Khatir Aboulkacem Afulay) or Ovary truth (Taieb Amgroud)], Lahoucine Bouyaakoubi, *Ijawwan n tayri* de Brahim Lasri Amazigh. Un sujet tabou dans une langue taboue [A taboo subject in a taboo language] (2009), http://www.amazighnews.net/20090109289/Ijawwan-n-tayri-de-Brahim-Lasri -Amazigh.html.

49 Bouyaakoubi (2009) writes: "Depuis le début des années 1990 … [le titre] ne tire pas son authenticité de l'héritage culturel commun mais de 'l'étrangeté' de la combinaison des mots. Il apparaît comme une expression littéraire formulée de façon à s'éloigner du langage courant; 'Ijawwan n tayri' se compose de deux mots connus dans l'air tachelhit. Ijawwan (Siroccos) et tayri (Amour) liés par la préposition 'n' (de). Dans cette combinaison de mots qui n'est pas courante, cette expression apparaît comme une pure invention littéraire pas très éloignée du langage quotidien sans pour autant lui appartenir [Since the early 1990s, the title has not determined authenticity but rather the common cultural heritage of 'foreignness' in certain combinations of words. This appears as a literary expression, formulated to depart from contemporary language … 'Ijawwan n tayri' consists of two known words in Tachelhit: *Siroccos* and *Tayri* (love) linked by the preposition "n" (of). In this rare combination of words, the expression is purely literary invention: not far from everyday language yet not belonging to it]."

50 See book reviews by Bouyaakoubi at http://www.amazighnews.net/20080802227/
L-Histoire-contemporaine-de-Souss.html; http://www.amazighnews.net/2007063021/
Ijjigen-n-tidi-de-Mohammed-Akunad.html; and www.akunad.com/net/.

51 Brahim Lasri Amazigh, *Ijawwan n tayri (The Siroccos of Love)* (Marrakech: Association Imal,
2008).

52 Lahoucine Bouyaakoubi, Ijawwan n tayri de Brahim Lasri Amazigh: Un sujet tabou
dans une langue taboue (2009), http://www.amazighnews.net/20090109289/Ijawwan-n
-tayri-de-Brahim-Lasri-Amazigh.html.

53 Mohamed Toufali, *Escritores Rifeños Contemporáneos. Una Antología de Narraciones y Relatos de Escritores del Rif*. (Editorial Lulu, 2007), www.Lulu.com. Toufali published five
short stories written in Spanish by himself, Karima Toufali, and Mohamed Lemrini El
Ouahhabi. He mentions Abdelkader Ouariachi and Mohamed Temsamani as the pre-
cursors of Castilian literature of the Rif, 8. See also Mohamed Toufali, Literatura Rifeño-
Andaluza …? (Reflexiones sobre la existencia de una literatura rifeña de expresión castellana), *Volubilis, revista de Pensamiento*, UNED 7 (March 1999): 114–124; Mohamed Toufali,
Igennijen ed Izran en Arrif (Canciones y versos del Rif). (Mrtich, 2011).

54 Melilla, geographically in North Morocco, is part of Spain but obtained Autonomous
City Status in 1995. Its 65,000 inhabitants include Christian, Muslim, Jewish, and (small)
Hindu communities. Besides Spanish, many residents also speak Arabic and Tarifit.

55 Until recently, Spanish literary criticism paid little attention to African writing in
Spanish, see Sabrina Brancato, "Voices Lost in a Non-Place: African Writing in Spain,"
in Elisabeth Bekers, Sissy Elff and Daniela Merolla, eds., *Transcultural Modernities, Narrating Africa in Europe* (Amsterdam: Rodopi, 2009), 3–17.

56 Mohamed Chacha, *Reẓ ṭṭabu ad d teffegh tfukt* (Breaking the Taboo and Let the Sun
Appear) (Amsterdam: Izaouran, 1997).

57 Chacha also published another novel and four collections of short stories and poems.
His first attempt at writing was in Arabic before he arrived in the Netherland as a
refugee in the 1970s.

58 Mustafa Ayned, *Reḥriq n tiri* (The Pain of the Shadow) (Amsterdam: Izaouran, 1996).

59 Mohamed Bouzaggou, *Ticri x tama n tsarrawt (Walking on the Edge of the Lace)* (Berkane:
Trifagraph, 2001); M. Bouzaggou, *Jar u jar (Between the Two)* (Berkane: Trifagraph, 2004).

60 Saïd Belgharbi, *Aṣwaḍ yebuyebḥen! (The Hoarse Look!)* (Berkane: Trifagraph, 2006).

61 Abderrahman El Aissati and Yahya E-rramdani, "Berbers," in Guus Extra and Jan Jaap
de Ruiter, eds., *Babylon aan de Noordzee: Nieuwe talen in Nederland* (Amsterdam: Bulaaq,
2001), 60–77.

62 Personal interview, 2005. Toufali (2007) published, among others, a Spanish translation
of a short story by Fatima Bouziane, "Normal," in Mohamed Toufali, *Escritores Rifeños*

Contemporáneos: Una Antología de Narraciones y Relatos de Escritores del Rif (Editorial Lulu, 2007), 14–17, www.Lulu.com.

63   Samira Yedjis n Idura n Arrif (pseudonym), *Tasrit n weẓru* (The Bride of the Rock) (Oujda: Anakhla, 2001).

64   Though two chapters of Fatima Merabti's Kabyle novel *Yir Tagmat* (*Bad Brotherhood*) were published in 1997 and 1998 by the journal *Tizir*, the novel remains unpublished: Fatima Merabti, *Yir Tagmat* (*Bad Brotherhood*), *Tizir* (Nov. 1997): 36–40 et (Jan. 1998): 35–38; the first novel published in Taqbaylit by a woman writer is Lynda Koudache, *Aâecciw n tmes* (*The Fire Shelter*) (Tizi-Ouzou: Editions Tasekla, 2009); many novels and poems by women writers from Kabylia (Algeria) have appeared in French, among them the well-known autobiography of Fadhma Amrouche and four novels by her daughter Taos Marguerite Amrouche.

65   Abdel Mottaleb Zizaoui, L' écriture et le défi dans le roman "*Tasrit n weẓru*," *Ayamun Cy-berRevue de littérature berbère* 34 (July, 2008), http://www.ayamun.com/Juillet2008.htm.

66   Saïd El Haji, *De dagen van Sjaitan* (*The Days of Satan*) (Amsterdam: Vassallucci, 2000).

67   "Abdelkrim El-Chattibi" in the text by El Haji *De dagen*, 143.

68   Saïd El Haji *De dagen*, 144.

69   Abdelkader Benali, *Bruiloft aan zee* (*Wedding by the Sea*) (Amsterdam: Vassallucci, 1996).

70   Writer and scholar Fouad Laroui notes that this is a quite unusual marriage for Moroccan customs (personal communication); it can be interpreted as pointing to the author's lack of knowledge of Moroccan marriage mores or to his voluntary "unsettling" choice.

71   "The taxi driver … [could have told] that the young man was linked to the region in a certain way, a kind of fat horseradish that oddly enough only got fatter the further it grew up from the root and tenaciously went on growing in a landscape that was otherwise bone-dry" (Benali, *Bruiloft* 5). This and following quotations are Daniela Merolla's translation.

72   Distance is signaled for example by Lamarat's inability to recognize the sounds of cicadas and local customs, such as the rear-view mirror placed in a downward position as a form of respect to one's passengers.

73   "In this town Lamarat's father … had ordered a house to be built, a house with five pillars and a water pipe that soon clogged with cockroaches and crumbling mortar" (Benali *Bruiloft*, 6). "But ten years later, when Lamarat came back to the region … he was told by everyone that after his house had fallen down many others had followed, everything is empty, the houses are in ruins and everybody is busy in the town (which is much more enjoyable, with all those casual contacts, etc.)" (Benali *Bruiloft*, 160).

74 "Lamarat ... had been born one sunny Saturday to a father and mother who, before they were married, had lived in two houses one on top of the other in the centre of the village of Touarirt on the Mediterranean coast; at a faraway time for the one and only yesterday for the other, but far, far, far away from Thalidomide children and birth control" (Benali *Bruiloft*, 7).

75 "Salaam mulaykum, keen bak vie dhar!" "What you mean is that I should understand Arabic," Lamarat said, thinking out aloud, "but unfortunately I do not understand that language of yours." "Well, then, I'll put it another way: ehlel ye sehlel ouid wewesch e mis n tefkecht" (freely translated from Berber to Dutch: Good morning, go fetch your father, son of a king-sized portion of spite). "Floor knew that you should always treat Berbers insolently, rudely, otherwise you do not get your message across" (Benali *Bruiloft*, 65).

76 Benali, *Bruiloft*.

77 Fouad Laroui, *Le drame linguistique marocain* (Casablanca: Le Fennec, 2011).

Works Cited

Achour, Christiane, Littérature et apprentissage scolaire de l'écriture: influences réciproques, *Littératures du Maghreb, Itinéraires et Contacts de cultures 4–5*, Paris: Centre d'Etude des Nouveaux Espaces Littéraires, 1984: 15–56.

Aissati (El), Abderrahman and Petra Bos. Arabic and Berber in the Netherlands and France. In Guus Extra and Jeanne Maartens (eds.) *Multilingualism in a multicultural context. Casestudies on South Africa and Western Europe. Studies in Multilingualism 10.* Tilburg: Tilburg University Press, 1998: 179–195.

Aissati (El), Abderrahman and Yahya E-rramdani, "Berbers". In Guus Extra and JanJaap de Ruiter (eds.) *Babylon aan de Noordzee: Nieuwe talen in Nederland*, Amsterdam: Bulaaq, 2001: 60–77.

Akunad, Mohammed. *Ijjigen n tidi* (Flowers of Toil), Agadir: Aqlam, 2007.

Akunad, Mohammed. *Tawargit d imik* (A Dream and a Little More), Rabat: Tizrigin Bouregreg, 2002.

Akunad, Mohammed. *Un youyou dans la mosquée*, (Tawargit d imik), Trans. by Lahcen Nachef, Maroc: Edilivre, 2012.

Aljazeera, Explainer: Tuareg-led rebellion in north Mali, 03-04-2012; www.aljazeera.com/indepth/features/2012/03/20123221161436924o.html;

Amine, Khalid. Paul Bowles' *Tangier: An Ambiguous Compromise.* In Ralph M. Coury and R. Kevin Lacey (eds.) *Writing Tagier*, New York: Peter Lang, 2009: 59–74.

Ayned, Mustafa. Reíriq n tiri (The Pain of the Shadow), Amsterdam: Izaouran, 1996.

Basset, Henri. *Essai sur la littérature des Berbères*, Algiers: Carbonel, 1920. Repr. Awal – Ibis Press 2001.

BBC News, Mali Tuareg rebels' call on independence rejected, 06-03-2012 www.bbc.co.uk/ news/world-africa-17640223

BBC NEWS, Libya clashes: "at least 14 dead" around Zuwara, 3 April 2012, http://www.bbc.co .uk/news/world-middle-east-17602343

Belgharbi, Saïd. Aṣwaḍ yebuyebḥen!, (The Hoarse Look!), Berkane: Trifagraph, 2006

Benali, Abdelkader. *Bruiloft aan zee*, (Wedding by the Sea), Amsterdam: Vassallucci, 1996.

Borghi, Rachele and Claudio Minca, Le lieu, la place, l'imaginaire: discours colonial et littéra-ture dans la description de la Jamaa el Fna, Marrakech, *Expressions Maghrebins* 2: 155–174, 2003

Boudou, Khalid. *Het schnitzelparadijs*, (The Schnitzel Paradise), Amsterdam: Vassallucci, 2001.

Bougchiche, Lamara. Langues et littératures berbères des origines à nos jours, Bibliographie internationale, Paris: Ibis, 1997.

Bounfour, Abdallah. Manuscripts berbères en caractères arabes, *Encyclopédie Berbère*, 30, 2010: 4554–4563.

Bounfour, Abdallah and Amar Ameziane, *Anthologie de la poésie berbère traditionnelle*, Paris: L'Harmattan, 2010.

Bouyaakoubi, Lahoucine. Ijawwan n tayri de Brahim Lasri Amazigh. Un sujet tabou dans une langue taboue, 2009, http://www.amazighnews.net/20090109289/Ijawwan-n-tayri-de -Brahim-Lasri-Amazigh.html.

Bouyaakoubi, Lahoucine (Anir). *Igdad n Wihran*, Birds of Oran, France: privately printed, 2010.

Bouzaggou, Mohamed. *Ticri x tama n tsarrawt* (Walking on the Edge of the Lace), Berkane: Trifagraph, 2001.

Bouzaggou, Mohamed. *Jar u jar*, (Rumor – lit. "Between the Two"), Berkane: Trifagraph, 2004.

Bouziane, Fatima. "Normal". In Toufali Mohamed, (ed.) *Escritores Rifeños Contemporáneos. Una Antología de Narraciones y Relatos de Escritores del Rif*, Editorial Lulu, 2007: 17–14. www.Lulu .com.

Brancato, Sabrina. "Voices Lost in a Non-Place: African Writing in Spain." In Elisabeth Bekers, Sissy Elff and Daniela Merolla, (eds.) *Transcultural Modernities, Narrating Africa in Europe*, Amsterdam: Rodopi, 2009, 3–17.

Brett, Michael, and Elizabeth Fentress. *The Berbers*, Oxford: Blackwell, 1996.

Camps, Gabriel. Avertissement. Etre berbère, *Encyclopédie Berbère*, Vol. I, 1984:7–48.

Canales, Pedro. El Rif marroquí se rebela contra el abandono, *El Imparcial* 13-03-2012, http:// www.elimparcial.es/contenido/100992.html.

Chacha, Mohamed. *Reå „abu ad d teffegh tfukt* (Breaking the Taboo and Let the Sun Appear), Amsterdam: Izaouran, 1997.

Chafik, Mohamed. *Amazighen*, Amsterdam: Bulaaq, 1989.

Chaker, Salem. Amazigh (le/un) Berbère, *Encyclopèdie Berbère*, 4, 1987: 562–568.

Chaker, Salem. *Berbères aujourd'hui*, Paris: L'Harmattan, 1989.

Chaker, Salem. Unité et diversité de la langue berbère, *Unité et diversité de tamazight*, Actes du Colloque international (Ghardaïa 20–21 avril 1991), Tizi-Ouzou: FNACA, 1992, 129–142.

Chaker, Salem. La langue berbère en France. Ed. M. Tilmatine. Enseignement des langues d'origine et immigration nord-africaine en Europe: langue maternelle ou langue d'Etat? Paris: Inalco, 1997: 15–30.

Chaker, Salem. Le berbère. Ed. B. Cerquiglini. *Les langues de France*. Paris: PUF, 2003: 215–227.

Chaker, Salem. Libyque: écriture et langue, *Encyclopèdie Berbère* 28–29, 2008: 4395–4409.

Chibani, Ali. Légende et vie d'Agoun'chich. L'effacement, http://la-plume-francophone.over-blog.com/article-31308167.html (*12 May 2009*).

Chivers, Christopher John. Amid a Berber reawakening in Libya, fears of revenge, *The New York Times*, 8 August 2011 http://www.nytimes.com/2011/08/09/world/africa/09berbers.html?pagewanted=all

Choukri, Mohamed. *For Bread Alone*, Trans. and Introduction by P. Bowles. London: Peter Owen, 1974.

Choukri, Mohamed. *Zoco Chico*, French Trans. Paris: Didier Devillez, 1996

Claudot-Hawad, Hélène. *Le Touaregs: portait en fragments*. Aix-en-Provence: Edisud, 1993.

Claudot-Hawad, Hélène, (ed.), Berbères ou Arabes? Le tango des specialists. Paris: Irenam, 2006.

Culshaw, P. Desert Storm [Tinariwen], *Songlines*, 42, March–April, 2007: 20–25. www.eyefortalent.com/eft-press/T-N%20SonglinesMarApr07.pdf

Danteur, Thibaut. L'authenticité par la mise en scène. Analyse dialogique des activités touristiques et culturelles de la place Jemaa el Fna, *Via@*, *Les imaginaires touristiques*, n°1, 2012. URL: http://www.viatourismreview.net/Article7.php

De La Veronne, C. Distinction entre arabes et berbères dans les documents d'archives européennes des XVIe et XVIIe siècles concernant le Maghreb, *Actes du premier congrès d'études des cultures méditerranéennes d'influences arabo-berbères*, Algiers: SNED, 1973, 261–265.

Déjeux, Jean, Francophone literature in the Maghreb: the problem and the possibility, *Research in African Literatures*, 23, 2, 1992: 5–19.

Dermenghen, Emile. Le mythe de Psyché dans le folklore nord-africain, *Revue Africaine*, 1945: 41–81.

Dorleijn, Magreet and Jacomine Nortier, Van de hand en de handschoen: code en stijl als tweetalige opties voor jongeren met een Turkse en Marokkaanse achtergrond. In Ad Backus et al. *Artikelen van de Zesde Anéla-conferentie*. Delft: Eburon, 2009, 83–92.

Dris-Aït-Hamadouche, Louisa and Yahia Zoubir. The Maghreb: Social, Political and Economic Developments. In Mehdi Parvizi Amineh, (ed.), *The Greater Middle East in Global Politics*. Leiden: Brill, 2007: 249–278.

Drouin, Jeannine. Unité et pluralité littéraires dans les sociétés berbérophones. CIUDT 1, 1992: 115–128.

Extra, Guus and Jan Jaap de Ruiter. The sociolinguistic status of the Moroccan community in the Netherlands, *Indian Journal of Applied Linguistics*, 20(1–2), 1994: 151–176.

http://www.letterkundigmuseum.nl/Literaircentrum/Literaireprijzen/tabid/99/ AwardYearID/2177/Mode/DetailsAwardYear/Default.aspx

El Haji, Saïd. *De dagen van Sjaitan* (The Days of Satan). Amsterdam: Vassallucci, 2000.

El Zemouri, Mohamed Saïd. Berbérisme dans la littérature maghrébine d'expression française (les cas de Driss Chaïbi, Mohamed Khaïr Eddine, Yacine Kateb, Nabil Farès). Tétouan: Faculté des Lettres et des Sciences Humaines, 1997.

Ennaji, Moha. Multilingualism, Cultural Identity, and Education in Morocco, USA: Springer, 2005.

Essafi, Ali Mimoun, *Ussan semmidnin* (Cold Days). Casablanca, 1983.

Essafi, Ali Mimoun, *Tighiri ntebrat* [Reading a letter]. Casablanca, 1994.

Fragiskatos, Peter. Will Gadhafi defeat bring new freedom for Berbers in Libya?, CNN *Opinion*, 26 August 2011, http://articles.cnn.com/2011-08-26/opinion/fragiskatos.berber.language _1_tamazight-berber-minority-berber-culture?_s=PM:OPINION

Galand, Lionel. La langue berbère existe-t-elle? in Ch. Robin (Ed.), *Mélanges linguistiques offerts à Maxime Rodinson*. Paris: Geuthner, 1985: 175–184.

Galand, Lionel. Les alphabets libyques, *Antiquités Africaines* 25 (1989): 69–81.

Galand-Pernette, Paulette. Littératures berbères, des voix, des lettres, Paris: PUF, 1998.

Greenberg, Joseph H. Studies in African linguistic classification: IV. Hamito-Semitic, *Southwestern Journal of Anthropology* 6 (1950): 47–63.

Harmach, Amine. Interview, Zahra Hindi: "J'ai envie de promouvoir l'amazigh à travers mon chant", 29-01-2009, *Aujourd'hui, Le Maroc*, http://www.aujourdhui.ma/chronique -judiciaire-details66707.html

Johnson, Glen. In post-Kadafi Libya, Berber minority faces identity crisis, *Los Angeles Times*, 22 March 2012, http://articles.latimes.com/2012/mar/22/world/la-fg-libya-identity -20120323.

Kaye, Jacqueline and Abdelhamid Zoubir. The ambiguous compromise: Language, literature, and national identity in Algeria and Morocco, London and New York: Routledge, 1990.

Khaïr-Eddine, Mohammed. *Légende et vie d'Agoun'chich*. Paris: Seuil, 2010.

Koudache, Lynda. *Aâecciw n tmes* (The Fire Shelter). Tizi-Ouzou: Tasekla, 2009.

Kossmann, Maarten. *Essai sur la phonologie du proto-berbère*. Cologne: Rüdiger Köppe Verlag, 1999.

Lacey, R. Kevin. The Writers/Storytellers of Morocco and Paul Bowles: Some Observations and Afterthoughts. In R.M. Coury and R.K. Lacey (eds.) *Writing Tangier*. New York: Peter Lang, 2009: 75–94.

Lacheraf, Mostefa. La Colline oubliée ou la conscience anachronique. In Lucas, Ph. and J.C. Vatin, *L'Algérie des anthropologues*, Paris: Maspero, 1975, texte 65. First Published in *Le Jeune Musulman*, 13 February, 1953.

Lacoste-Dujardin, C. *Le conte kabyle*. Paris: Maspero, 1970.

Lafkioui, Mena and Daniela Merolla (eds.). Oralité et nouvelles dimensions de l'oralité. Intersections théoriques et comparaisons des matériaux dans les études africaines, Colloques Langues O'. Paris: Inalco, 2008.

Ladenburger, Thomas. *Al-Halqa: In the storyteller's circle*, Documentary, Germany 2010, 90min, http://www.alhalqa.com

Lakhsassi, Abderrahmane. État de la culture Amazighe après 50 ans d'indépendance. Théâtre, Cinéma-Vidéo, Roman, Poésie. In Tozy, M. *50 ans de développement humaine & Perspectives 2025*, Rapport Thématique, Cinquantenaire de l'Indépendance du Royaume du Maroc, 2006: 113–129, http://www.rdh50.ma/fr/pdf/contributions/GT9--6.pdf

Laroui, Fouad. *Le drame linguistique marocain*. Casablanca: Le Fennec, 2011.

Laporte, Jean-Pierre. Manuscripts latins d'Afrique, *Encyclopédie Berbère*, 30, 2010: 4563–4568.

Lasri Amazigh, Brahim. *Ijawwan n tayri* (The Siroccos of Love). Marrakech: Association Imal, 2008.

Lewicki, Tadeusz. Quelques textes inédits en vieux berbère, *Revue des études Islamiques*, 1934, 3: 275–296.

Lewis, M. Paul (ed.). *Ethnologue: Languages of the World*. Dallas: SIL International 2009. Online version: http://www.ethnologue.com/

Littérature orale arabo-berbère, 26, 1998.

Maddy-Weitzman, Bruce. The Berber Identity Movement and the Challenge to North African States. Austin: University of Texas Press, 2011.

Mammeri, Mouloud., Littérature berbère orale, *Les Temps modernes* 33.375 (Oct. 1977): 407–418.

Mammeri, Mouloud. *Poèmes kabyles anciens*. Paris: Maspero, 1980.

Marzak, Abdelhafid. Province d'Al Hoceïma, Casseurs en uniforme, *Actuel* 133, 16-03-2012. www.actuel.ma/Societe/Province_dAl_Hoceima_Casseurs_en_uniforme/955.html

Memmi, Albert., Portrait du colonisé, précédé du portrait du colonisateur, Paris: Buchet/ Chastel, 1957.

Merabti, Fatima. Yir Tagmat, *Tizir* (Nov. 1997): 36–40; et (Jan. 1998): 35–38.

Merolla, Daniela. Digital Imagination and the "Landscape of Group Identities": the Flourishing of Theatre, Video and "Amazigh Net" in the Maghrib and Berber Diaspora. *Journal of North African Studies* 7.4 (2002): 122–131.

Merolla, Daniela. De la parole aux vidéos. Oralité, écriture et oralité médiatique dans la production culturelle amazigh (berbère). *Afrika Focus* 18.1–2 (2005): 33–57.

Merolla, Daniela. *De l'art de la narration tamazight (berbère)*. 200 ans d'études: état des lieux et perspectives. Paris/Leuven: Peeters, 2006.

Mezgueldi, Zohra. Légende et vie d'Agoun'Chich. *Itinéarires et contact de cultures* 15–16.1–2 (1992): 121–126.

Mezgueldi, Zohra. *Oralité et stratégies scripturales dans l'œuvre de Mohammed Khaïr-Eddine*. Thesis, Université Lumière-Lyon 2, 2001, Dir. C. Bonn and M. Gontard.

MLNA Tuareg site, *Mouvement National de libération de l'Azawad* www.mnlamov.net/english.html.

Morgan, Andy. Tinariwen – Sons of the desert. In *Andy Morgan writes ...* (Website), January 6, 2011 (http://www.andymorganwrites.com/tinariwen-sons-of-the-desert/), First published in *Songlines*, 29, 2007.

Moukhlis, Salah. Localized identity, universal experience: celebrating Mohamed Choukri as a Moroccan writer. In Ralph M. Coury and R. Kevin Lacey (eds.) *Writing Tangier*. New York: Peter Lang, 2009: 21–34.

Mrabet, Mohamed and Eric Valentin, *Mémoires fantastiques*. Paris: Rouge Inside, 2011.

Ould-Braham, Ouahmi. Lecture des 24 textes berbères médiévaux extraits d'une chronique ibadite par T. Lewicki, *Littérature orale arabo-berbère*, 1987: 87–125.

Schemm, Paul. Protests spread in Morocco's north Rif mountains, *The Guardian*, 12-03-2012, http://www.guardian.co.uk/world/feedarticle/10139625.

Skounti, Ahmed and Ouidad Tebbaa. *La place Jemaa El Fna: patrimoine culturel immatériel de Marrakech, du Maroc et de l'Humanité*, Rabat: Éditions de l'UNESCO, 2005.

Stitou, Mustafa. *Varkensroze ansichten*, (Pink Pigs Postcards). Amsterdam: De Bezige Bij, 2003.

Taïfi, Miloud. Unité et diversité du berbère: Détermination des lieux linguistiques d'intercompréhension, *Études et Documents Berbères* 12 (1994): 119–138.

Tanti, Samriddhi. Hindi Zahra – Music for the Soul, *EF News International*, 21 September 2011, http://www.efi-news.com/2011/09/hindi-zahra-music-for-soul.html

Tinariwen, Aman Iman, Documentary, Berber/French, www.youtube.com/watch?v=iOu4fdlPiWI

Toufali, Mohamed. Literatura Rifeño-Andaluza ...? (Reflexiones sobre la existencia de una literatura rifeña de expresión castellana), *Volubilis, revista de Pensamiento*, UNED, No. 7 March 1999: 114–124.

Toufali, Mohamed. Escritores Rifeños Contemporáneos. Una Antología de Narraciones y Relatos de Escritores del Rif. Editorial Lulu, 2007, www.Lulu.com.

Toufali, Mohamed. Igennijen ed Izran en Arrif (Canciones y versos del Rif). Mrtich, 2011.

Toufiq, Ahmed. Shajarat al-hinna' wa-al-qamar (The Tree and the Moon), 1998, French Trans.: L'arbre et la lune, Paris: Phébus, 2002.

UNESCO World Heritage List 2001. http://www.unesco.org/bpi/intangible_heritage/morroco.htm.

Wali, ObiajunwaWali., The Dead End of African Literature, *Transition* 10, 1963: 330–335.

Van den Boogert, Nico. Muhammad Awzal and the Berber literary tradition of the Sous, Leiden (thèse), 1995.

Yedjis n Idura n Arrif, Samira. *Tasrit n weẓru (The Bride of the Rock)*, Oujda: Anakhla, 2001.

Zaheur, Lahacem. *Myuzya*. Agadir, 1994.

Zaheur, Lahacem. *Amussu n umalu* (The Movement of the Shadow). Agadir: Aqlam, 2008.

Zizaoui, Abdel Mottaleb. L' écriture et le défi dans le roman "*Tasrit n weẓru*", *Ayamun CyberRevue de littérature berbère*, No. 34, July 2008, http://www.ayamun.com/Juillet2008.htm

Writing in the Feminine: The Emerging Voices of Francophone Moroccan Women Writers

Touria Khannous

Despite extensive scholarly work on Francophone women authors, little has been written about Francophone women writers from Morocco. While authors such as Fatima El Bouih and Malika Oufkir are well known outside Morocco, since their work has been translated into English and other languages, authors such as Siham Benchekroun, Touria Oulehri, Houria Boussejra, Rita Al Khayat, and Noufissa Sbai, among others, lack a wider audience. Their novels have been published only in Morocco and thus have yet to be exposed to a larger audience. Francophone Moroccan literature has existed since the 1960s, but it is only in the early 1980s that a new wave of Francophone women writers has emerged onto the literary scene. Early authors of this generation include Halima Ben Haddou, *Aicha Le Rebelle* (1982); Farida Elhany Mourad, *La Fille aux Pieds Nus* (1985); Badia Hadj Nasser, *Le Voile mis a nus* (1985); the second group of writers began writing in the 1990s and include Houria Boussejra, Siham Benchekroun; Touria Oulehri, Malika Oufkir, and Aicha Chenna. Their works encompass fiction such as novels, plays and poems, as well as non-fictional testimonials. The thematic links between their fictional and testimonial works are clear, since they both constitute a literature of protest and resistance.

Recognizing new developments in feminist consciousness and feminist activism in Morocco, the present study encompasses select examples of novels and testimonials written by Francophone Moroccan women writers. Authors whose work is analyzed here include Siham Benchekroun, Houria Boussejra, Touria Oulehri, and Malika Oufkir. Drawing on works published between 1999 and 2004, I examine these women's texts as engaged implicitly or explicitly with social and political concerns – the common concerns of the Habermasian public sphere of challenging prevailing patriarchal ideologies and questioning national politics. I thus situate these women's texts within the socio-political reality of Morocco, which necessitates a vigorous critique of the socio-political issues facing the country. The authors' socio-oriented work reveals a harsh critique directed not only against socio-cultural patriarchy, traditions and practices that have denied women agency within rigid gendered stratifications, but also against the larger political system and the economic asymmetries which characterize Moroccan society. Their multi-faceted critique is understandable given the political landscape of Morocco at the time they wrote their novels.

In his book *Ecritures féminines au Maroc: continuité et evolution* (*Female writers in Morocco: Continuity and Evolution*), Najib Redouane argues that the Francophone women writers who burst upon the literary scene in Morocco in the 1990s have been an influential force, decrying women's conditions in Moroccan society: "The literary word constitutes for these women a militant act, an original form of commitment, and a re-appropriation of oneself in a society in which women are reduced to silence."[1] What emerges most powerfully in their texts is the desire to construct self-defined images of womanhood, a breaking away from fixed notions of gender identity and feelings of inferiority imposed by a patriarchal society with its accompanying religious and legal restrictions. Despite the fact that these writers may have little knowledge of feminist theories produced in academe in Africa, Europe, or the United States, their narratives demonstrate important feminist principles.

Valerie Orlando argues that Francophone Moroccan women's writing falls within a tradition described by Sartre as engaged literature: "Like Sartre and the activist engagés authors writing on the French left in the aftermath of Europe's decimation, Moroccan authors feel that it is their duty to write and produce for their society in order to effectuate change."[2] Moroccan critic Farida Bouhassoune explains that this revolutionary bent lies at the root of the feminist strategies deployed by women writers, and explains their desire to attack masculine structures of power, and oppressive cultural icons of femininity such as motherhood. Such resistance is also manifested in their rejection of the political system and their call for reform. Thus, their texts are socially engaged narratives, entangled with questions of gender within a broad socio-political context of egregious violations of women's rights by the institutions of power that are controlled by men.[3] Female Moroccan writer Siham Benchekroun argues along the same lines as Farida Bouhassoune when she asserts that Moroccan women's literature is a literature of revolution: "My writing is clearly my way of engaging in militant actions ... to defend my values ... to fight against what I question: extreme poverty, injustice, violence against women, social hypocrisy, and the glorification of money and appearances."[4] Such revolutionary writing emerges from a radical feminist stance which seeks irrevocable change not only in gender relations but also in the political sphere.

Subversive Feminine Writing

In her essay entitled "ÊTRE Une Femme, ÊTRE Marocaine, Ecrire," Siham Benchekroun addresses the common questions she receives from journalists about how women can fit into the writing tradition, given the fact that literature has been dominated by men until recently. While she insists that she is a writer first and foremost before being a woman writer, she admits that gender remains a major component of her writing. Benchekroun describes Moroccan feminine writing as transgressive in many ways because it unveils the private and what is taboo. The unveiling of such taboos provokes the experience of shame caused by the public exposure of writing: "The sense of shame provoked not only by a woman's act of writing, but by any kind of expressions of self, as soon as they extend beyond the private, domestic sphere, to be visible, audible, legible, within the public sphere."[5] Writing therefore is more problematic for the female writer whose work exposes her to untenable public scrutiny. When taboos are unmasked, the public is shocked by the authors' deliberate subversions of social convention. To Benchekroun, feminine writing is a violation of the prevailing ideologies that regulate masculine and feminine behavior: "Indeed, writing is a mere breach, among others, of an atavistic rule that confines women to a cloistered, supervised space. This is the reason why their act of speech in public space ... their writing intervention can be perceived, in the collective unconscious ... as a transgression."[6] This breaking of taboos is relevant not only to writing, but to other professions held by women as well. Benchekroun draws parallels between women writers and the professional groups of women lawyers, politicians, and doctors who are conquering public space. She compares producers of female culture through art and writing with those engaged in the production of services for the broader society in education, health, politics, and administration:

> The development of women's literature in Morocco corresponds to the growing role assumed by women in the public arena. It partakes of the same evolution, the same change of behavior, of status and public relations: some women hold positions of responsibility and power; they assume roles which were exclusively male in times past, while other women contribute to society's development through their writing.[7]

Thus, the act of writing becomes a hallmark of women writers' self-assertion and intervention in the public sphere.

Radical Critiques of Patriarchy

The novels studied here, in which the female voice is an important part of the narrative, signal a notable change in the representation of women's relationship to patriarchal power. For the woman writer inscribing female characters outside patriarchal hierarchy entails reinventing language and narrative strategies for the purpose of articulating femininity outside phallocentric discourse. Writing itself is appropriated as a liberating strategy to inscribe women's subjectivity, and to explore the female body and the self as they relate to writing and language. These writers' attempt to draw on female power and subvert male abuse of power through their writing is closely connected to theories of l'écriture féminine developed by Hélène Cixous and Luce Irigaray, who both espouse a feminist aesthetic outside the symbolic patriarchal order. Because of her concern with the exclusionary dynamics of institutionalized forms of power, Cixous suggests a strategy that implies the disruption of dominant institutions and forms of power. Such a strategy can be realized through the revolutionary practice of writing, which is embodied in the feminine text: "A feminine text cannot fail to be more than subversive. It is volcanic ... If she's a her-she, it's in order to smash everything, to shatter the framework of institutions, to blow up the law, to break up the 'truth' with laughter."[8] Such subversive feminine writing "is precisely the very possibility of change,"[9] because it dares to change conventions and norms. Moroccan Francophone women writers follow Cixous' dictum since they use their writing as a means to effect change within their community.

The writers' use of the female body as a site of knowledge is another strategy of resistance. While control of the female body is located within the private sphere, male dominance is also perpetuated in the public realm in a country that subjects its women to discrimination and legal subordination. Some novels have aspects of allegory in the sense that the female protagonist conceptualizes the public realm in terms of the projections of the schizophrenic self. Novels such as Siham Benchekroun's *Oser Vivre*, Touria Oulehri's *La Répudiée*, and Houria Boussejra's *Le Corps Derobé* emphasize the protagonists' journeys towards psychological growth, and expose the limitations patriarchal society imposes on their struggle for autonomy.

Oser Vivre (1999)

Benchekroun's novel *Oser Vivre* centers on Nadia, who marries her husband Ali out of love only to realize that her patriarchal marriage does not guarantee liberty and reciprocity. Her marriage also means adherence to societal conventions that often keep women from having an equal say. The novel begins with the protagonist shedding one identity and assuming another. Travelling by train, she describes how in the middle of the noisy train, "the memories of my very long life with A. flood my mind. My thoughts collide, and internalize the racket."[10] The train trip initiates a symbolic journey through memory. The transmutation of the protagonist from *je* (I) to *elle* (she) is indicative of her change of identity upon her marriage to Ali. The shift to *elle* (she) is also indicative of the juxtaposition between the narrator's construction of the self and the models of appropriate gendered behavior society provides for her. It is thus symptomatic of the juxtaposition between the feminine self and the outside world. Such connections between point of view and questions of identity allow us to read the protagonist's voyage into the past, told in a third person focalized narration, as indicative of the fragmentation and isolation experienced by the protagonist as well as her alienation in her community. The third-person narrative also carries a sense of disenchantment and crisis. The end of the novel, narrated in the first person, is indicative of a more unified subjectivity.

Nadia's identity is produced in different ways at different moments in the novel. She is aware of the extent to which her identity lies in the gaze of others: "Their gaze has since set to infuse in me, inexorably, duties and constraints. From that moment, I stopped growing."[11] Nadia is subject not only to patriarchal gaze but also to the gaze of other women, who carry from generation to generation the same values that degrade them. These women project onto her all the negative traits associated with female sexuality, submission, fear and acquiescence to male domination: "A little girl on the verge of becoming a suspect, I struggled under inquisitive and obscene gazes. In my nightmares, the verdict was threatening: watch out, pubic hair and incipient breasts. Imminent sex. Danger!"[12] The women set out to brainwash the protagonist with patriarchal values, thus contributing to her false consciousness: "The brainwashing process was about to begin ... Women are born to suffer ... Women are made to be submissive ... Women are at the service of men."[13] Nadia pins her hopes on her future husband, Ali, who promises her freedom from stifling social restrictions while maintaining the status quo. Her status, however, will change upon marriage to him. She has to give up her independence and become a wife, a daughter-in-law, and a sister-in-law in her new home. Nadia is full of dreams and ambition, but her husband and his family express unease at the prospect of her finishing her studies and pursuing a career. To protect her marriage, she is obliged to put aside her studies and aspirations, and to find justifications for her husband's control, angry outbursts, and withholding of affection.

Early in the narrative, Nadia describes her relationship with Ali as characterized by fear. Such fear substitutes itself for her fear of the mother, the first other: "My fear is an old skin ... stemming from my relationship with my mother ... And then it became more structured, even more institutionalized, since my husband."[14] The fact that the protagonist associates her fears with her mother shows that such fears reside in the unconscious and reflect her repressed desires. Luce Irigaray compares the unconscious and the female body with language, when she asserts: "Are women not, partly, the unconscious? ... is there not in what has been historically constituted as the 'unconscious,' some censored, repressed element of the feminine?"[15] The articulation of the unconscious and the female body clearly manifests in women's writing. In the novel, the desire underlying the protagonist's feminist commitment lies in the unconscious emerging of what is expressed in language. In articulating her fear, Nadia defines herself in relation to the other, especially the masculine other. Irigaray has pointed out elsewhere that "the matter for a woman is one of interposing between the other and herself, a negative that cannot be overcome."[16] Nadia feels like a stranger to herself. She realizes that she is only one among the women of her community who has insight into her predicament as a woman. Her narrative, therefore, becomes a means of articulating the truth she is discovering within the community: "Nadia wished she could have explained to her husband that she was not seeking to denigrate anything, that the most important thing to her was to be able to choose her own truths, whether they belong to the Orient, to the Occident or whatever civilization."[17]

Nadia refuses to submit to the idea that a stifling patriarchy should determine the course of her life. As she follows a path of increasing estrangement from patriarchal society, she blames conventional women, who uphold the rules of patriarchy, for their own unhappiness. Ultimately a feminist notion of truth gains power over a patriarchal one. She reflects on traditional motherhood as the source of women's oppression and concludes that having children is a means of enslaving women: "Sometimes one wonders if we can serve humanity in other better ways than to expand, so stupidly, in small family cells, reproducing to infinity."[18] The protagonist's idea of motherhood resonates with some feminists' view that women's reproductive role is the cornerstone of their oppression. American radical feminist Shulameth Firestone advocates a biological revolution in which women seize control of the means of reproduction to achieve liberation.[19] For the narrator-protagonist in *Oser Vivre*, it is patriarchy which forces women to be mothers. Reproduction is therefore characterized by compulsion. Seeking to empower herself, Nadia decides to leave her marriage, even if it means losing custody of her children. She is now "free to leave home without an alibi or permission ... Free to come back at a time that is suitable for her. Or not to come back. Free to go off on a journey ... to an infinite number of forbidden, illegal places. To leave without being accompanied, surveilled or protected."[20] Even though the reader knows that a free femininity cannot ever find full social expression, there is the sense of a vague utopia in the background. Thus, the shift back in point of view to *je* (I) signifies the beginning of a new truth, as well as the birth of a new subjectivity.

Le Corps Derobé (1999)

Like Siham Benchekroun, Houria Boussejra tackles head-on the problems women face in patriarchal Morocco. Her first novel, *Le Corps Derobé* (1999), is based on the real life story of the author's tumultuous relationship with her mother, which led to her struggle with depression and eventual suicide in 2001. In the novel, the extreme physical and verbal abuse of the protagonist is not an isolated event, but rather symptomatic of a society that determines individual behavior and condones the use of violence against women. In her essay "Les écrits des femmes du Nouveau Maroc: Les Romans de Houria Boussejra," Valerie Orlando argues that Bousserja's style of writing is reminiscent of canonical authors such as Marguerite Duras and Marguerite Yourcenar, who ceaselessly "cherche à approfondir, connaître et déterminer le rôle et la place de la femme dans le monde" [seek to deepen, know and determine the role and status of women in the world].[21] According to Orlando, Bousserja's novels are works of existential philosophy that feature concepts associated with existentialism such as desire, knowledge, self-realization and alienation.[22]

In *Le Corps Derobé*, the protagonist describes her experience of abuse as including alienation from her own body. Thus, her anonymity signifies the loss of her identity. Jacques Lacan has argued that alienation is associated with the mother's absence in language. Alienation also becomes a means for the child to distance himself from the pain and from the experience of the self.[23] Leila is born into a set of societal expectations that decreases her true experience of self. According to Andreas Hussein, "It is male vision which puts together and disassembles a woman's body, thus denying woman her identity and making her into an object of projection and manipulation."[24] As a woman, Leila does not learn how to express an authentic self because she has to adhere to the cultural values and norms of her society. She is defined as an object not only by the biological fact of the female body but also by patriarchal society:

> She has understood, for a very long time, that as a woman she could claim no life, no will. The path was all traced by time perennially. She was only recognizable by her body-object which had to be used for a while until the community decrees its death at the moment where it reaches sainthood by the divine power of motherhood or when years will have left their wake. It is the lot of every woman. Even in the great illusion of modernity, she remains a slave to her master.[25]

The novel shows the many ways in which women uphold patriarchal values and participate in their own subordination. Women are perpetrators of violence and aggressors in abusive situations. By depicting women as violent, the novel calls into question our conception of femininity and masculinity, reveals the limits of feminist ideology, and overturns the ideological structures involving gender that govern the Moroccan experience. In one instance, the narrator tells of her rape by a woman who threatens to kill her to coerce her into submission and silence:

> The woman took her by the hand and walked to the door. They crossed the corridor. Leila found herself in a small, dark room. She did not know what was happening. The other lowered her pants, the culotte, to the knees ... put her finger in her private parts and moved it back and forth ... She felt terrible pain; It was dark. As she was standing, a hot liquid flowed between her legs. She could not scream.

While in the emergency room, Leila feels dissociated from her body: "An unbearable view. Leila was elsewhere, detached from her body; she did not feel it anymore. From now on it was not part of her anymore."[26] Through the rape scene, the author writes the history of the subjected and violated body. Despite the violence and brutality that Leila experiences, she is able to resist her oppressors through a politics of the body. She is also aware of the distinction between her body and the cultural meanings assigned to it by her oppressors. By leaving her body behind, Leila manages to survive, since her bodyless femininity becomes her resistance to violence. Even though Leila's body is marked by rape, she is able, through her bodyless self-identification, to embark on a journey of critical self-consciousness: "It has been a long time since she no longer existed. Only her shadow dragged her along the different spaces from incomprehensible times that moved before her."[27]

Leila feels dissociated not only from her own body, but also from the community of women, because of the absence of female role models who do not adhere to traditional or acceptable "feminine" behavior. The absence of female role models in the home and in the community promotes her feeling of self-alienation. Thus, the novel shows the author's vacillation about and distrust of feminism as an effective strategy for challenging patriarchy and Morocco's dictatorial political system. It hints at feminism's failure to recognize female violence and calls for the need to "challenge notions of homogenous aggressive masculinity and passive femininity."[28] The author also hints at the double standards in the Moroccan feminist liberation movement, where women espouse modernism when it suits their ideals and endorse tradition when it suits them: "Leila could not be friends with women, because, for her, despite their feminist struggle, they all end up selling themselves in one way or another. They continue to impose traditions when it suits them and to demand liberty and equality when the circumstances are favorable."[29]

Leila also sees through the hypocrisy of her mother's modern life. Despite the fact that her mother typifies the modern, liberated, career woman who dresses in Western-style clothes, she is stuck in a backward, anti-modern, and paralyzed mode of thinking with regard to sexuality: "Her husband had to pay her each time he took pleasure from her body." The mother's choice to commodify her sexuality is attributed to the fact that under patriarchy she is taught that sex is what she is for. Women choose to sexualize their own subordination, since they have been brainwashed to believe that they are worthy only when their rate of exchange is high. Leila's mother may wear modern clothes, but what is important is that her mentality has not changed; when even educated women like Leila's mother are stuck in outdated mentality, any hope for gender equality is but an illusion. Here, Houria Boussejra points to the failure of Moroccan women to fulfill feminist and liberatory ideals of the feminist movement. The author not only advocates overturning decades of patriarchal institutions that discriminate against women, but also seeks to change the actual mentality of an entire generation of Moroccan women.

La Répudiée (2001)

Like Benchekroun's *Oser Vivre* and Boussejra's *Le Corps Derobé*, Touria Oulehri's novel *La Répudiée*[30] denounces patriarchy and advocates its subversion. The novel centers on Niran, an educated middle-class woman who grew up in Fez and has been married for 15 years only to find herself repudiated because of her sterility. Oulehri published her novel in 2001, before the 2004 Moudawana took effect and before repudiation and polygamy were restricted.[31] From the very outset, the female protagonist gives the reader an insight into the complexity of "schizophrenic" Morocco. Through the characterization of Niran's mother and sister-in-law, who live in Al Hajeb, a rural Berber area, the author represents the dichotomy between rural and urban women. The mother and sister-in-law are introduced as traditional women who incite Niran's husband to divorce his wife for the sole reason that she is sterile. Less than half of Moroccan women can be characterized as rural now as the result of rapid urbanization. The official statistic is 35%, but many areas are semi-urban (i.e. on the outskirts of the major cities), and most of these areas are traditional. Yet, not all women residing in urban areas can be called modern. According to Moroccan scholar Fatima Sadiqi, "Rural and urban women relate differently to language, space, traditions, household economy, and education and, hence, develop different ways of resisting patriarchy."[32] Sadiqi argues that in terms of space, rural women do not use the private/public space dichotomy in the same way urban women do. The novel addresses this public/private division during Niran's trip to Fes El Jedid, a commercial district in Fes. Within the traditional, male-dominated space of Fes El Jedid, the protagonist felt uncomfortable: "I felt fragile in my femininity; my lips, full of make-up, seemed to me indecent before these men and especially women, most of whom dressed in jellabas, their hair covered with a scarf."[33] The narrator describes moments when she and her female friends transgressed male dominated spaces: "We find ourselves, from time to time, in this noisy district that is full of life, but mainly occupied by men. We were happy to invade their formerly reserved spaces."[34] Within Moroccan feminist discourses, the idea of gendered space has been very influential. Fatima Sadiqi refers to public space as men's space where social norms are dictated.[35] For Fatima Mernissi, this dichotomy is in accordance with the Arab-Muslim tradition, which explains the entrenchment of patriarchal power and "social institutions designed to restrain [women's] power: namely segregation and legal subordination in the family."[36]

Niran's life story is a tantalizing example of such legal subordination. Confident that he has rights which give him alternative choices, Niran's husband proposes to her that she find him another wife: "No matter what uterus ... provided that we have a child; the baby will be yours"[37] His characterization of woman as a uterus is a verbally explicit representation of old-entrenched attitudes that degrade the role and status of women as mere sexual objects and reproductive machines. Niran's repudiation papers arrived as soon as she refused to consent to her husband's right to polygamy: "The same day I received the official notice of repudiation. A traitor and a coward. He understood that I would never accept the injustice of polygamy."[38] The protagonist experiences intense pain at her husband's betrayal. Her internal psychological conflict following repudiation stems from the meshing of her self-identity and the broader image of herself as a married woman. She considers her role as wife an important part of her self-identity, but once her relationship with her husband ends, she experiences a crisis in her public image. Thus, she refuses to reveal her inner distress to her family, and keeps her private life from the public realm in order to avoid the public circulation of gossip or scandal:

> I live by myself since the separation because of the shame brought by the public image of abandonment. Even my parents do not know about what happened. I rarely see them, invoking, as an excuse, work and writing projects. My mind is pained by these questions that continue to haunt me: 'Why?' Why did he so brutally leave me? Why did society and the law give him the right to repudiate me with impunity, by simply invoking my sterility, while they forbid me to do the same?[39]

Even worse, the repudiation caused a deterioration in her body. The novel associates the body with forces in nature, since it implicitly draws parallels between the repudiation that destroyed her body and mind and the earthquake that resulted in the total destruction of the Moroccan city of Agadir in 1961. The narrative is punctuated by real-time reports of the natural disaster unfolding in Agadir and by eye-witness accounts of the event. Just as she cannot do anything about her situation, the inhabitants of Agadir could do nothing about the earthquake. There is no going back to the way things were before it happened. Niran's repudiation is as destructive as an earthquake since it shook her whole being. Yet, just as after an earthquake things are built back stronger and better than they were before, the narrator is going to emerge stronger from her experience:

> I knew that, for the moment, fragile and abandoned, I could perceive the world only through the eyes of a victim; yet I had the desire to reconstruct myself stone by stone, to reformulate my conscience, my being, to create new markers, new values, new methods for a different existence.[40]

An abrupt rhetorical shift in the narrative turns repudiation into an opportunity for regaining a feminist consciousness, self-knowledge and a mature identity: "For the first time in my life I will be 'adult.'"[41] While repudiation has shattered her world and identity, it also offers the potential for personal growth alongside the opportunity to build a stronger feminine and social identity that challenges the patriarchal conception of womanhood as married and reproductive. She feels determined to resist the stereotypes of a society that stigmatizes sterile women as deficient and a threat to the patriarchal order. In defiance of societal norms, the protagonist feels comfortable with her body, celebrating her sterility rather than hiding it: "My body, not having succumbed to any pregnancy and having maintained its slimness, gives me great pleasure to adorn it and live in it."[42] Niran's celebration of her body symbolizes her independence. She wonders why women need men to acknowledge their essence and their intelligence. She refuses to be reduced to a sexual object, resists assimilation into the male order and remains immune from feeling desire for the male other: "I refuse to be viewed as merely a reproductive body that brings pleasure to a male."[43] The protagonist's emerging subjectivity and voice threatens to remake patriarchy.

The novel mediates the protagonist's reconstruction of her female identity not only at the level of identity reconstruction but also at the level of space. The traditional *hammam* (Moroccan public bath) offers an opportunity for Niran to appropriate space, and thus becomes a means for self-discovery, self-healing and introspection in a simple setting:

> It is the only place where I become reconciled with my body as well as with my femininity because women there, being removed from the male gaze and social pressures, move with a kind of natural ease, even when fat or old. There is no sense of shame because women exhibit their nude bodies with decency. At times odors from sweat and vapors pollute the air, forcing the newcomers to wash with water.[44]

The visit to the *hammam* is a time of pleasure where the protagonist can reconcile with her own body. Her journey to Casablanca, later in the novel, is also a journey of self-discovery, where she realizes that she can achieve a sense of self and autonomy only on her own.

Documenting Human Rights Abuses

In addition to their fierce denunciation of patriarchy, Francophone Moroccan women writers have also either used fiction to relate past human rights violations (Houria Boussejra) or relied on their own experience with imprisonment and torture to write more autobiographical accounts (Malika Oufkir). These texts are situated within the context of the period known as "Sanawat Arasas," "*Les Années de Plomb*" (the Lead Years)–a time of coups, political trials, torture, rebellion and severe repression lasting from 1963 to 1999.

"Poème de prison" (1978)

Saida Menebhi was a member of the national students' union "Union Nationale des Etudiants du Maroc" (L'UNEM) and the Marxist-Leninist organization "Ila Al Amam." She was arrested in 1976 and sentenced to seven years' imprisonment for her political activities. She died in December 1977 at the age of 25 during a collective hunger strike to demand the release of political prisoners. During the first two years of her imprisonment, Menebhi composed a series of poems and wrote several letters that were first published in Paris in 1978. In the following poem, Menebhi describes the ugly reality of the prison where she was being held. Images of torment and punishment run througout the poem:

> La prison, c'est laid
> Tu la dessines, mon enfant
> Avec des traits noirs
> Des barreaux et des grilles
> Tu imagines que c'est un lieu sans lumière
> Qui fait peur aux petits
> Aussi pour l'indiquer
> Tu dis que c'est là-bas
> Et tu montres avec ton petit doigt
> Un point, un coin perdu
> Que tu ne vois pas
> Peut être la maîtresse t'a parlé
> De prison hideuse
> De maison de correction
> Où l'on met les méchants
> Qui volent les enfants
> Dans ta petite tête
> S'est alors posé une question
> Comment et pourquoi
> Moi qui suis pleine d'amour pour toi
> Et tous les autres enfants
> Suis-je là-bas?
> Parce que je veux que demain
> La prison ne soit plus là.[45]

[Prison is ugly
You draw it, my child
With black lines
Its bars and gates
You can imagine that this is a place without light
That scares children
Also, to indicate it
You say that over there
And you show it with your little finger
There is a spot, a lost corner
That you do not see
Perhaps the woman has told you
About the hideous prison
About the house of correction
Where we put the wicked
In your little head
You then wonder
How and why
Me who is full of love for you
And for all children
Why am I here?
Because I want in the future
That prison is longer here]

La Prisonnière (1999)

In addition to poetry, political prisoners used memoirs and other genres of fiction to explore pain in equal detail and with comparable effectiveness. Malika Ouflir's autobiography *La Prisonnière* (Stolen Lives)[46] evolved with co-author Michelle Fitoussi and has been translated from French into nineteen languages. The author, the eldest daughter of General Mohammed Oufkir, was adopted during her parents' lifetime as companion to the royal princess Lala Amina. She was thus well-placed to know the privileges of an absolutist king and the punishments for incurring the monarch's displeasure. When her father was executed for treason by order of the king, and she along with her mother and siblings were imprisoned and made to suffer for twenty years, she had an insider's knowledge not only of imprisonment but also of who had ordered the punishment of herself, her mother, and her siblings.

The author's view is somewhat limited by gender in a male-dominated power structure. The narrative brings out gendered themes dealing with mother and father figures. Hassan II is depicted as an absolute and patriarchal tyrant, whom the author comes to resent, but she never reproaches her father General Oufkir for his coup d'état against the King. Against the backdrop of the palace, the author foregrounds her mother Fatima as an all-powerful and influential figure in her life. The narrative foregrounds the mother-figure as a speaking subject who refuses to submit to patriarchal constraints rather than a passive sufferer. In laying claim to her own voice, the author, for her part, refuses the role of marginal other and proclaims her authority as a speaking subject. She acknowledges that she is a good storyteller and uses this gift to distract her mother and siblings during their long imprisonment. Writing with a collaborator in France, once she was in happier circumstances, she used the same gift for other purposes in her memoir. The author's desperate need, as victim/survivor, to keep the reader fixed on her story of imprisonment and pain makes for disruptions in the narrative and avoidance of facts about her father's past. Oufkir provides testimony to the story of her torture and imprisonment within collective human rights discourse and against the patriarchal, collective tradition which would silence her. She admits her loss of words whenever she wants to describe the horrifying prison Bir El Jdid, where she and her family spent ten years: "In this death camp ... we had been pariahs, cast out by the world, waiting for the end that was so slow in coming."[47] The author, who not only suffered the death of her father, but also permanent removal from her community through imprisonment, metaphorically tells the story of her death: "I had mourned the death of my father. Now I was mourning my own life."[48] She later realizes that death is being forced upon her against her will: "All the time we were being pushed back down towards the dead, when we so desperately wanted to stay among the living."[49]

Read more than a decade after its publication in French and English, the book deepens understanding of absolute monarchy and the current rejection of dictators in an ongoing "Arab Spring." The book has contributed to the rise of political consciousness in Morocco and to the curbing of royal despotic powers. It has had a great impact on a present monarchy different from the one that preceded it. The book is also part of more general testimony for a Truth-and-Reconciliation process (similar to such processes in other nations, notably South Africa) that portends greater democratization in Morocco. Morocco's present king, Mohammed VI, has learned from his father's intransigence and has tried to balance maintaining stability with the process of democratizing and having Morocco emerge as a modern multi-ethnic state, with equal rights of citizenship for women and men, and women's representation in government. He must please both the impatient and the traditionalist, while retaining support from the privileged (even if that category includes the "corrupt").

Les impunis, ou les obsessions interdites (2004)

Houria Boussejra's novel *Les impunis, ou les obsessions interdites* (2004) shows, however, that not much has changed in society and politics in the last decade since King Mohammed VI ascended the throne in 1999. The novel was published posthumously after Boussejra's suicide in 2001. The events are narrated from the viewpoints of different characters. The novel oscillates between the "Lead Years" era and the present, when corruption and abuse of power are still rampant. Multiple viewpoints give the author much more flexibility in narrating instances of abuse of power in both past and present situations. The author introduces two male characters who abused political power during the era of Hassan II, and who are still engaged in abuse in the present era, which shows that Morocco's Equity and Reconciliation Commission has not really addressed the human rights abuses of the past. Anouar Azzedine is an official who engaged in the torture of Bouchra, while mocking her involvement in politics: "Tu veux faire de la politique, dis? ... Tu es faites pour ... donner des enfant!" [You want to do politics, right? ... You are made for ... bearing children.][50] Azzedine Anouar's torture of Bouchra gives him erotic pleasure: "Azzedine sentait son sexe dourcir sous les coups de laquelle le lanières qui lacèraient le dos de Bouchra le long du corps de laquelle du sang dégoulinait."[51] [Azzedine felt his penis harden from the blows inflicted on Bouchra's lacerated back, and on the body from which blood gushed forth.] The torture of prisoners like Bouchra was carried out in the erotic register of rape, bondage, and control of female prisoners' bodies. Youssef, a friend of Azzedine, was himself a witness to such monstrous torture. He is shown in a different narrative thread offering bribes to seek out and kill his enemy, and to win elections. Despite the fact that political figures like Azzedine Anouar and Youssef were involved in corruption cases and criminal acts during the "Lead Years" era, the extent of their corruption continues unabated under the new regime: "Youssef, avec l'appui de son ami Azzedine Anouar, ne ratait plus aucune occasion pour s'enrichir. Il délogeait les paysans endettées et achetait de nombreuses terres. Devenu entrepreneur, il construisait des immeubles d'une laideur étonnante qu'il revendait aux prix fort, profitant de la crise du logement." [With the support of his friend Azzedine Anouar, Youssef missed no opportunity to enrich himself. He evicted indebted farmers and bought more land. Being a contractor, he built astonishingly ugly apartment buildings which he sold at high prices, taking advantage of the housing crisis.][52]

By depicting characters who are involved in violence, either as perpetrators or as victims, the novel shows that violent and abusive personal relationships are symptomatic of the political violence and corruption pervading Moroccan society. The author places male violence against women and children and the mechanisms society develops to push it out of sight within the context of the human rights abuses of Morocco's past, thus burying these violent acts in the collective unconscious – the realm of the unknowable. And if these violent acts are thus buried there, then do they really exist? Similarly, women and children, as fully sovereign beings with individual and collective agency in their own right, do not exist. They are instead mere objects to be used and abused at will – precluding any need or necessity for remorse or reform.

At the outset, the author represents the dark side of Morocco, where a large percentage of children are homeless: "Abandonnés, ils travaillaient le matin dans l'enceinte de marché, se faisaient mendiants l'aprés-midi et erraient le soir à la recherche d'ivrognes assez affaiblis pour être délestés des quelques dirhams oubliés au fond de leurs poches."[53] [Abandoned, they worked in the morning inside markets, as beggars in the afternoon, and roamed the streets at night looking for drunkards weakened enough to be robbed of the few remaining dirhams at the bottom of their pockets.] Khalid is one example of such children. He is repeatedly raped by Fadel, who offers him shelter only to sexually abuse him. Children, however, are not the only victims of violence, for women suffer from the effects of abuse as well. While the novel describes women as victims of rape within the institution of marriage, it also depicts them as survivors and resistors who defy the marriage institution and break away from their abusive husbands to seek self-fulfillment. The author's critique of marriage as legalized prostitution attests to her feminism and her belief in women's right to control their own bodies. To exact revenge against a husband who rapes her as a means of exercising his marital control, Rahma stabs him, and puts his body in a bag. After placing the bag in the car trunk, she disappears into the night, and drops the body into the sea. She later puts her children into an orphanage and resorts to prostitution to support herself. Ilham, another female character in the novel, is also subjected to marital rape by her husband Farid, a modern intellectual who publishes articles on "les droits de la femme au Maroc" [women's rights in Morocco],[54] and who once organized a conference on "modernisme dans le monde Arabe" [Modernism in the Arab World.][55] Ilham discovers that her husband's modern life-style is but a façade: "J'avais cru trouver en Farid un homme different de tous les archetypes de la société. N'avait-il pas fait des études en sciences politiques? J'avais été séduite par ses discours qui me paraissaient extraordinaires." [I thought I had found in Farid a man different from all the archetypes of males in society. Has he not studied Political Science? I was seduced by his speeches that appeared to me to be extraordinary.][56] Out of a desire for vengeance, Ilham began taking new lovers: "It was then that I realized that I never knew what it was like to enjoy my body, to experience sexual pleasure, and to experience the ecstasy of self-oblivion."[57] The novel depicts abusive marriages as part of the violent past of Moroccan society. Not much has changed in Morocco politically. What has changed is women's response to marital abuse. The author mentions Aicha Chenna, a Moroccan writer and women's rights activist, who founded the self-help organization "Solidarité Féminine" to offer support to single mothers and their children. The novel, however, does not discuss Chenna's work.

In conclusion, this study attempts to link Francophone Moroccan women writers' demand for change to their use of different genres to inscribe the gender notions of hierarchy that they contest. These are the notions that deny women free agency by defining them only in relation to their social location within the private sphere. While Moroccan women have achieved a lot on the socio-economic and cultural levels, the limitations on their agency often lie in forces that are beyond their control. Despite these hurdles, women writers are changing the context of how Morocco is read and viewed in the twenty-first century. In the coming decades, it will be fascinating to see to what extent future generations of women will benefit socio-culturally and politically from the writings this generation of female writers has left them.

Notes

1   Najib Redouane, *Écriture Feminines au Maroc: Continuité et évolution* (Paris: L'Harmattan, 2006), 12.

2   Valerie Orlando, *Francophone Voices of the "New" Morocco in Film and Print: (Re)presenting A Society in Transition* (New York: Palgrave Macmillan, 2009), xii.

3   Some of the reasons she cites are the following: 1) Loudly and clearly, the women state their dissatisfaction with the lowered status of women who go against the demands of modern life, 2) They break the taboo by revealing their inner selves, a new way of expression after always remaining quiet, 3) They are exposed mercilessly to hostile and contemptuous judgements, dictated by preconceived notions and unmitigated by

discernment, and strengthened by a heritage whose earlier, more lenient, times have been forgotten. See also Farida Bouhssoune, "La Littérature marocaine féminine de langue Française: la quête de Nouvelles Valeurs (Moroccan women writing in French: The quest for new values)," in *Litteratures Frontalières, Edizioni Universita di Trieste 20, Anno X* (July–December, 2000), 50.

4 Ibid., 22.

5 Siham Benchekroun, "ÊTRE Une Femme, ÊTRE Marocaine, Ecrire [Being a woman, being a Moroccan, a writer]," in *Le récit Feminine au Maroc*, ed. Marc Gontard (Paris: Presses Universitaires de Rennes, 2005), 19.

6 Ibid.

7 Ibid.

8 Hélène Cixous, "The Laugh of the Medusa," trans. Keith Cohen and Paula Cohen, *Signs* 1 (1976): 888.

9 Ibid., 879.

10 Siham Benchekroun, *Oser Vivre* (Casablanca: Empreintes Edition, 2008), 5.

11 Ibid., 10.

12 Ibid., 70.

13 Ibid., 70.

14 Ibid., 6.

15 Luce Irigaray, "Women's Exile," trans. Couze Venn, *Ideology and Consciousness* 1 (1977):70.

16 Luce Irigaray, ed. *Teaching* (London: Continuum International Publishing Group, 2008), 228.

17 Siham Benchekroun, *Oser Vivre*, 82.

18 Ibid., 127

19 Shulameth Firestone, *The Dialectic of Sex: The Case for Feminist Revolution* (New York: Farrar Straus Giroux, 2003).

20 Siham Benchekroun, *Oser Vivre*, 206.

21 21. Valerie Orlando, "Les écrits des femmes du Nouveau Maroc: Les Romans de Houria Boussejra." Expressions Maghrébines, 8(1), 2009: 95.

22 Ibid., 95.

23 Jacques Lacan, *The Language of the Self: The Function of Language in Psychoanalysis* (Baltimore: The Johns Hopkins University Press, 1968).

24 Andreas Husseyn, *After the Great divide: Modernism, Mass Culture, Postmodernism.* (Bloomington: Indiana University Press, 1986). 75.

25 Houria Boussejra, *Le Corps derobé*, 78.

26 Ibid., 73.

27 Ibid., 74.

28   Lee Fitzroy, *Mother/rapist: women's experience of child sexual assault perpetrated by their biological or adoptive mother* (Clayton, Victoria, Canada: Centre for Women's Studies, Monash University, 1997), 44–45.

29   Ibid., 83–84.

30   Touria Oulehri. *La Répudiée.* Casablanca: Éditions Afrique-Orient, 2001.

31   In 2004, three years after Touria Oulehri published her novel, the current king, his majesty Mohammed VI, appointed a commission of jurists with the aim of reforming the Moudawana. The reforms, which were instituted in 2004, were groundbreaking in terms of the new rights they have granted Moroccan women

32   Fatima Sadiqi, *Women, Gender and Language in Morocco* (Leiden; Boston: Brill, 2003), 165.

33   Ibid., 63.

34   Ibid., 44.

35   Fatima Sadiqi, "Feminization of Public Space: Women's Activism, the Family Law and Social Change in Morocco," *Journal of Middle East Women's Studies*, no. 2 (2006): 25.

36   Fatima Mernissi, *The Veil and the Male Elite: a Feminist Interpretation of Women's Rights in Islam*, First published in 1975, trans. Mary Jo Lakeland (Bloomington: Indiana University Press, 1987), 19.

37   Touria Oulehri, *La répudiée* (Casablanca: Afrique Orient, 2001), 27.

38   Ibid., 38.

39   Ibid., 12.

40   Ibid., 67

41   Ibid., 55

42   Ibid., 18.

43   Ibid., 80.

44   Ibid., 76.

45   Saida Menebhi. *Poèmes, lettres, écrits de prison.* Paris: *Comité de lutte contre la répression au Maroc,* 1978.

46   Malika Oufkir and Michele Fitoussi, *Stolen Lives: Twenty Years in a Desert Jail*, trans. Ros Schwartz (New York: Hyperion, 2001).

47   Ibid., 197.

48   Ibid.

49   Ibid., 150.

50   Houria Boussejra, *Les impunis, ou les obsessions interdites* (Rabat: Editions Marsam, 2004), 64.

51   Ibid., 65.

52   Ibid., 72–73.

53   Ibid., 23.

54 Ibid., 37.
55 Ibid., 40.
56 Ibid., 35.
57 Ibid., 40.

CHAPTER 5

Tactile Labyrinths and Sacred Interiors: Spatial Practices and Political Choices in Abdelmajid Ben Jalloun's *Fí al-Tufúla* and Ahmed Sefrioui's *La boîte à merveilles*

Ian Campbell

Twenty-first-century CE editions of travel guides to Morocco include maps of the city of Fez that differ in an important respect from maps in twentieth-century CE editions. The new guides contain detailed maps of the old city of Fez, founded in the eighth century CE and long one of the cultural capitals of the Maghreb. In 1912, the French formally colonized Morocco,[1] and with their typical enthusiasm for *The Civilizing Mission*, they began to rationalize lands that had nominally been under one Muslim dynasty or another for over twelve centuries. In other parts of the Arab World, such as Cairo, old city walls through labyrinthine towns were demolished and replaced with Hausmannian boulevards. However, in Morocco, the French typically built a new city alongside the old, as in the case of Fez: a new French city, mappable, designed from a plan, just across a narrow valley from the labyrinth of the old Moroccan city.

The travel guides used to advise visitors that there was no sense in providing a detailed map of the old city in Fez. Such maps as existed generally showed the two main routes through it, several notable plazas and culs-de-sac, the Qarawiyyín mosque-university, and the gateways to the mappable city outside the old city's walls. The rest of the old city was filled in on the maps with grey halftone. With the advent of satellite photography, however, mapping the old city has become commonplace, and newer travel guides contain detailed maps.[2]

This represents a last step in a long process of dominion over the Maghreb by the Western gaze of legibility and mappability; there is no longer even one place, even at the center of the high culture that once sustained Fez, that cannot be brought under the gaze of the Western reader. In another way, this represents a small triumph of the old city's resistance to the Western gaze; after all, it's the center of a booming tourism industry that has helped to develop the region's moribund economy. Mapping the old city did, however, put many of the local, human guides out of business.

This study examines two semi-autobiographical novels whose child protagonists experience the labyrinth of old Fez directly: for each of them, learning to map the labyrinth is an important part of his coming of age. Abdelmajid, the narrator of Abdelmajid Ben Jalloun's *Fí al-Tufúla (In [My] Childhood)*,[3] comes to Fez in late childhood, having grown up in Britain, where a very different organization of urban space holds sway. He finds the labyrinth bewildering and alien, and he ultimately adapts by learning to map the strange culture of his "homeland." In Ahmed Sefrioui's *La boîte à merveilles (The Box of Wonders)*,[4] the narrator Mehdi grows up in Fez and thus finds the labyrinth less troubling. Yet as Mehdi grows up, he learns that his family are strangers to Fez: they are Amazigh or "Berber" people who have come from the mountains to the city to make a better life.

Both novels were published in the period when Morocco, after years of increasingly violent struggle, succeeded in wresting independence from France.[5] Both novels are set in the 1930s, before the struggle had begun in earnest; neither undertakes any significant discussion of colonization or its effects. Both novels make a number of political choices in their portrayal of colonial Fez and its spatial practices: both show a tension between Western notions of legibility and mappability and the organization of space in traditional Moroccan culture. Both come out firmly on the side of modernity and Western spatial organization, though *Fí al-Tufúla* is significantly more open about this than *La boîte à merveilles*. If these novels represent an embryonic "national literature,"[6] rather than atomistic works of personal remembrance, the nation they portray looks to the West, though it is grounded in traditional culture. It should be noted that narratives of childhood are common in Moroccan literature: Ben Jalloun and Sefrioui inaugurate a long tradition. Author, editor and political prisoner Abdellatif Laâbi and essayist and academic Fatima Mernissi have both published accounts of their childhood in Fez, for example.

Labryinthine Space in Fí al-Tufúla[7]

Fí al-Tufúla describes in great detail first Ben Jalloun's childhood in Britain, then the difficulties he had adjusting to his "native" Morocco, then his gradual embrace of that culture through his secondary studies at the Qarawiyyin. Much of the significance of the text stems from the autobiographer's status as an outsider. This enables him to provide a critical ethnography of traditional culture in colonial Morocco.

Subsequent critics have pointed out the elitism inherent in his critique. Hamid Lahmidáni, writing in 1985,[8] argues that the use of Ben Jalloun's childhood persona is at best disingenuous.[9] Young Abdelmajid finds the ordinary practices of traditional culture and its material poverty alien and troubling: *Fí al-Tufúla* thus represents the point of view of a narrow, Westernized elite. Muhammad Berada, whose 1987 novel *Lu 'bat al-Nisyán (The Game of Forgetting)*[10] is one of the finest achievements of Arabic-language Moroccan literature, writes in his Arabic translation of Abdelkébir Khatibi's *Le roman maghrébin (The Maghrebian novel)*[11] that: "The dominant perspective, the interpretations and the commentaries that the writer's adult awareness presents are a romantic, nationalistic point of view ..."[12]

Young Abdelmajid's perspective on urban spatial organization echoes the work of the French cultural geographer Henri Lefebvre on abstract space. Lefebvre's primary interest in his writings on space lies in the relationship of spatial practices, which "structure lived reality, include routes and networks, patterns and interactions that connect places and people, images with reality, work with leisure,"[13] to the social practices of (sub)cultures. Lefebvre argues that in Western Europe spatial practices underwent a transformation from space structured by monuments to abstract space, wherein natural features and human interactions were subordinated to an abstract grid. The dominant feature of abstract space is *legibility*: the city is open to the gaze of anyone who is able to read it. For Lefebvre, this transformation and all spatial practices serve the needs of political power: the transition to abstract space went hand-in-hand with the increasing domination of capitalist modes of production.[14] In Manchester, Abdelmajid experiences abstract space first-hand:

> When we rode the streetcar, I took to staring out the window, contemplating the city whose energy and animation grew and grew as we advanced through the commercial and industrial avenues. It could really give one the idea that the city itself had also awakened with its inhabitants, for my eye could not rest anywhere except on tireless, ever-increasing activity that really tempted me to get up and move around, to work; but I didn't know what I might devote myself to.[15]

The gridlines of the city are open and readable to Abdelmajid: he "reads" these avenues and is inspired to get up and work. Manchester's spatial practices transform him into an abstract worker on an abstract grid. This abstraction is further echoed in the language of the passage: when he writes "It could really give someone the idea," the Arabic text uses the word *al-mar ʾ*, not a personal pronoun like "me" or "you," but an impersonal noun used where an English speaker might say "one."[16] But later, once Abdelmajid "returns" to Morocco, his tendency toward abstraction is challenged by the significantly different urban practices of colonial Fez:

> We quickly entered the city to pass through its narrow streets ... Is this the city that my uncle had been saying from the first day that it exemplified the truth of the country? The people must not be able to walk in the street without bumping shoulders. We entered at night, and saw the pale, sad streetlamps as if they were lamps left in place after a funeral.[17]

Abdelmajid cannot "read" Fez; the streets are too labyrinthine and narrow, the buildings present neither façade nor windows, and the light is too weak. People are forced to bump shoulders personally rather than become abstract workers. Traditional Moroccan cities are organized according to the principles of what I call *labyrinthine space*:

- A resistance to legibility and mapping, arising from the lack of central urban planning or a bird's-eye viewpoint
- The need for cultural or linguistic competency rather than literacy: in order to find one's destination, a guide rather than a map is needed
- Reliance on the tactile and on a more direct link to the human body, rather than on the visual and an abstract link to a mathematical grid
- The presence within the labyrinth, hidden from view except to those who have earned the right to guidance, of a sacred interior space subject to the gaze of all who can enter

In *Fí al-Tufúla*, the sacred interior space is the Qarawiyyin, the only place in the whole city that impresses Abdelmajid.[18] He matriculates at the university, but he does not stay long as a student of the traditional curriculum. Rather, he becomes tangentially involved with a group of nationalists, and from there with a group of nationalist poets and writers. He creates within his family's home a sacred interior of his own; this in turn enables him to create a "map" of the Moroccan writers of his day, which he publishes as an article in an Egyptian journal. Applying the principles of abstract space to writers raised within the labyrinthine gives Abdelmajid discursive and even political authority among his peers: he becomes the man one needs to impress in order to become a notable writer. I argue that this is in effect an act of colonization: by rendering the space of Moroccan writers legible and mappable, Abdelmajid is applying abstract space to his "native" land and thus gaining power for himself. At the same time, however, he creates from a group of individual writers an embryonic Moroccan national literature, and thus indirectly serves the cause of unifying Moroccan resistance to European colonialism.

The Sacred Interior in Fí al-Tufúla

The sacred interior is a space where the gaze prevails: in the family home, everyone can see the garden or fountain within from their balcony, and anyone on a balcony is visible to everyone else. The sacred interior is *legible* space, especially when compared to its labyrinthine exterior. It is possible to view and read people in such a space because they have already passed the test of belonging to the tactile labyrinth. While the prevailing logic of the sacred interior is visual, there are also other senses, such as hearing, smell, and touch, involved in the sacred interior; the gaze is less one of reading than one of mutual recognition, and often of family relations.

The twin spaces of the tactile labyrinth and sacred interior are not without precedent in the study of Moroccan literature. The critic Abdelkebir Khatibi, in his influential 1967 work *Le roman maghrébin*,[19] proposes the labyrinth and the grotto as two of the spaces that define Moroccan literature in the post-independence period. Writing on the work of Algerian novelist Kateb Yacine, Khatibi argues:

> Kateb makes use of two spaces that mythology makes use of: the grotto and the labyrinth, and one sociological space: the street. Against the rigid compartmentalization of the colonial city, Kateb reacts by a powerful theatricalization of the Arab street. A tragic space par excellence, it is the spectacle of violence, the foyer of revolution. If the familial space consitutes a refuge of values, the street by contrast activates a series of explosive behaviors.[20]

For our purposes, however, two spaces serve quite adequately to mark off the social practices of the Moroccan city. In the autobiographical narratives of personal, urban, and national history examined in this study, the settings are entirely urban, so the grotto is too naturalistic a space to be entirely relevant. While the sacred interior within the Moroccan labyrinth has many naturalistic aspects, and informs and is created by social structure, it is an arranged naturalism that exists within an urban interior; furthermore, many of the sacred interiors encountered in Morocco have at best tenuous links to nature. As for the distinction Khatibi makes between the labyrinth and the street, the mythological and the sociological, upon close examination these will be seen to collapse into a single space. The street of the old city is itself the labyrinth.

Moreover, the tension between abstract space on the one hand and traditional spaces on the other is one that goes back to the very beginnings of Arabic literature and geography. The French scholar André Miquel, writing in 1967,[21] traces in great detail the changes in the understanding of geography and the impact of this understanding on human culture during the third and fourth Islamic centuries. An extremely reductive summary of Miquel's argument would state that in the third Islamic century, al-Jáhiz and other writers imported more or less uncritically the Greek concept of *klima* (*iqlím* in Arabic) directly into their writings on geography. The Greeks divided the Northern Hemisphere into seven "climes" based solely on latitude and claimed that the varying degrees of solar radiation in each clime were the determining factors in shaping the human cultures of that geographical area. As time passed, however, and the Islamic empire became increasingly Persianized, writers began to shift the meaning of *iqlím* until it came to have the same meaning as the Persian word *keshvar*, which denoted a city and its surrounding hinterlands. Human cultures became understood less as a result of insolation than as one of particular geographical circumstances: within the new *iqlím*, people shared linguistic and cultural unity. More than a thousand years ago, the imposition of an abstract grid from without was resisted by a more localized pattern of localities that required acquaintance with local conditions in order to understand them. It is no accident, argues Miquel, that geographical works increasingly incorporated travel narratives as time passed.[22] In the Modern Standard Arabic of *Fí al-Tufúla*, the word *iqlím* corresponds to the English "region," i.e., a locality rather than a cell in an abstract grid.

Labryinthine Space in *La boîte à merveilles*

Before analyzing the sacred interior space in both novels, let us first explore the tactile labyrinth of Fez as depicted in *La boîte à merveilles*.[23] In this quotation, young Mehdi, following his mother and her friend, momentarily loses them in a crowded, narrow street.

Unknown arms lifted me from the ground, made me pass above heads, and I finally found myself in a free space. I waited for a good time before I saw surging from the crowd the two immaculate *haïks*. The scene renewed itself several times during this trip. We crossed streets without names or particular aspects. I was attentive to the advice of my two guides; I applied myself to staying away from the donkeys, and inevitably bumped the knees of passersby. Each time I avoided an obstacle, another one presented itself.[24]

The extent to which the urban environment of Fez structures itself around illegibility and anonymity is evident in the language of the passage as well as in the events it describes. Instead of "people lifted me from the ground," Sefrioui has Mehdi say, "Unknown arms lifted me from the ground." This makes use of the French partitive article to describe an indeterminate number of arms, disconnecting these arms from the individuals who might have used them and transforming the arms into anonymous lifting machines, then further emphasizing this by describing the arms as *inconnus* (unknown). After passing over equally anonymous heads, Mehdi finds himself in "a free space," a bit of irony that only serves to underscore the crowded, tumultuous spectacle of the very narrow street. This free space is not a public square or a broad avenue, marked off by street signs and sidewalks, but rather a temporary zone where the density of people and donkeys is low enough for him to have a moment where he isn't about to be trampled underfoot.

When he looks back for his mother and her companion, he does not see the two women, or the two individuals, emerge from the crowd, but rather *les deux haïks immaculés* (The two immaculate haïks). The women have been replaced by their garments, the sort of all-concealing drapery familiar in Western images of the Muslim world, garments which are immaculate, devoid of signifiers that might differentiate one woman from another, which is of course precisely the point of such drapery. In Moroccan public space, the purpose of the spatial practice of full drapery for women is to implement the social practice that women aren't to be gazed at by anyone other than their intimates. The very word *haïk*, a French transliteration of the colloquial Arabic word *hayk*, provides an encapsulation of this trope of illegibility and anonymity, for the word is foreign to Sefrioui's French audience, marked off in italics, and wouldn't mean anything at all without the context that surrounds it. The word would be foreign and to a certain extent unsignifying to even a reader familiar with both colloquial Arabic and Moroccan social and spatial practices – the plural of *hayk* in Arabic is *huyúk*[25] – and Sefrioui's pluralizing of the word in the French manner by adding an *s* only serves to illustrate the unreadability of this passage.

Similar scenes are repeated several times, varying iterations of the same unreadable conclusion. The streets have neither names nor architectural characteristics that make them stand out as readable. Whereas the streets of a Western city operate according to a logic of visibility, with clear lanes marked off for pedestrian and vehicular traffic, the streets of Fez are narrow, winding, and filled with all manner of traffic; they are a shared, crowded space in which the inhabitants are largely unreadable to one another. Instead of a clear gaze out through broad avenues, Mehdi is confronted with one anonymous obstacle after another.

What allows Mehdi to make it to his destination in one piece is the presence of a guide, here in the person of his mother and her friend. Even from underneath their anonymizing *haïks*, the women are able to navigate the streets because the way is familiar to them; their knowledge allows Mehdi to get to the tomb, whose location is on no map. In the Moroccan city, to find the true path a stranger must consult with one of the locals, who will in turn guide the stranger to a destination, as in this scene, where Mehdi, his mother, and her friend go to visit Si El Arafi, a *fqih* or religious scholar, in an unfamiliar quarter of their own city:

> We had hardly any trouble finding the house of Si El Arafi. The people of the Seffah quarter, proud to be the neighbors of such an illustrious man, pressed forward to give us information. A child of my age was offered to accompany us. He guided us through a labyrinth (un dédale) of streets increasingly narrow, increasingly dark, increasingly burdened with piles of trash and stray cats. We finally ended up in a small plaza drenched in sunlight. The child who accompanied us pointed his right index finger toward the central door, stuck the left index finger into his nostril and went away without saying anything.[26]

At first glance, it might not seem that foreign to a Westerner simply to find the right neighborhood and ask for directions; indeed, such a scene plays itself out in Western cities many times every day. But there's a fundamental difference between the spatial practices and social structures that sustain the Moroccan city and the spatial and social practices of the Western city. In Fez, there is no map: whereas a visitor to a Western city could use a good map, a telephone directory, and literacy skills to find a spiritual advisor at a particular number on a particular street without needing to ask anyone, the visitor to Si El Arafi must ask the residents of the Seffah quarter to guide him.[27] And just as the Western system implies a host of spatial and cultural practices – from literacy in a standard dialect, to the use of an abstract, bird's-eye view to represent the city, to the set of cultural practices that make it seem advantageous to register one's self or business in the directory – the system used by Mehdi's mother to find her way also entails a set of cultural practices that find resonance in the spatial practice of the city. The visitor needs to speak the local dialect of Arabic, something that requires assimilation to the urban culture of Fez; Mehdi's mother is a montagnarde and thus most likely a Berber and not a native Arabic speaker at all. The visitor needs to be someone who can approach the locals without antagonizing them; without their guidance, the visitor would be lost in the maze of streets (*dédale de rues*). The visitor needs to be someone whom the locals consider worthy of meeting the *fqih*; if it were French soldiers, or bureaucrats, or Catholic priests, the locals might simply pretend not to know where the man who is the pride of their neighborhood resides – or pretend not to understand the question.

We can see the anonymity and illegibility of the urban streetscape of the Maghreb not only in the cultural practice of guiding that is derived from it, but in the language of the passage, as well. Sefrioui describes the neighborhood as a labyrinth, yet even in doing that he has to use a Western word, derived from Dædalus, the mythical inventor of the labyrinth – a man who was able to build himself wings to give himself a bird's eye view of Crete and a clear line of flight away from the island. This need serves to emphasize how foreign even the act of verbally mapping out the twisting pathways of the quarter of the Moroccan city can be. This is underscored further by the repetitive vagueness of the passage; the streets become narrower and narrower, more and more shadowed, more and more full of obstacles that block or threaten the anonymous path for the decidedly ailurophobic Mehdi. Though Si El Arafi's house itself is well-lit, the path to it can only be drawn by the guide, who can only engage in a bit of silent sign language before he departs.

The Moroccan city, like any city, requires literacy to find one's way, but in a Moroccan city, a *cultural* literacy is required, based not so much on absorbing the right signs but rather on presenting them correctly. The tactile nature of the labyrinth and its connection to the body is further emphasized by the mute actions of the child pressed into service as a guide; rather than tell the visitors where to go, the child uses one finger to point and sticks another one up his nose, using not words but gestures to indicate the path. The body, not the abstract gaze, is what traverses the tactile labyrinth.

The Sacred Interior in *La boîte à merveilles*

The Fez in which Mehdi grows up contains not only tactile labyrinths but also sacred interiors. Throughout the narrative, Mehdi describes a number of sacred interiors that help to shape his social development. He already has the cultural competency to gain access to some sacred interiors, such as his family home, by virtue of his birth. He gains access to others, such as the tomb of a local saint, through the guidance of his parents. Yet other spaces, such as the schoolroom, provide him with the cultural competency to go further, and one space – the titular box of wonders – he creates for himself to ease the stress of adaptation to his social and spatial environment.

Moroccan spatial and social practices pervade young Mehdi's life. His family becomes "more Fassi," more urbanized, by purchasing a newfangled kerosene lamp to light the house: "All the 'best' people see by the light of oil,"[28] his mother says. The resulting brilliant light sustains the household by drawing mother, father, and son together over the dinner table:

> The seer who was called 'Auntie Kanza' came up to admire our new acquisition, and wished us all sorts of prosperities. My mother glowed with happiness. She must have found the life worth living and the world peopled with beings of infinite goodness. She crooned, fed with tenderness a stray cat foreign to the house, laughed about nothing.[29]

His mother's social transformation from a rural immigrant to a proper Fassi woman is complete with the spatial transformation of the family's dark apartment into a sacred interior. Sefrioui's text further emphasizes this transition by having Mehdi's mother shine with happiness, mirroring the new lamp that has brought her such status that the seer comes to grace them with her presence. Mehdi's home, an interior to which he has access because of his status as a family member, is now a sacred interior, providing him with that much more comfort with respect to his status as an inhabitant of Fez.

As a young boy, and an only child at that, Mehdi demands a great deal of his mother's attention. His mother, however, has a number of pressing emotional needs of her own, not least of which is the anxiety produced by being a foreigner among the ladies of Fez. When the pressures of daily life get too much for her, she goes with her Fassi friend Lalla Aïcha to the tomb of the local saint, Ali Boughaleb,[30] in order to pray. Since Mehdi's mother has nobody else to watch him while she is out with her friend, she somewhat reluctantly brings Mehdi along; he follows them through the labyrinthine streets of the city until they arrive at the tomb and pass through its gates:

> We soon found ourselves in a courtyard that seemed immense to me. At the center sat in state four clay urns filled with water. Beyond this courtyard the zaouia opened up. On each side was a square room that led to the bier of the saint, two doors leading to the pilgrims' rooms ... Arriving in front of the bier, Lalla Aïcha and my mother began to call with great cries for the saint to come to their aid. Each was unaware of the other's words, each exposed to him her little miseries, struck the wood of the bier, whined, pleaded, wished ill upon her enemies. The voices rose, the hands struck the wood of the bier with more energy and passion. A sacred delirium took over the two women. They counted all their ills, exposed their weaknesses, asked for protection, claimed vengeance, admitted their impurities, proclaimed the compassion of god and the power of Sidi Ali Boughaleb, in calling for his pity.[31]

It is evident in this quotation that the function of the sacred interior is to perpetuate a societal consensus through a gathering of those qualified to enter the space. Moroccan cities such as Fez have few large, open, publicly-accessible spaces, which makes the courtyard seem so large to Mehdi. By its very nature as a saint's tomb, the space serves as a holy site and links the mundane to the transcendental; the intercession by the saint on behalf of the petitioner serves to contain death and provide continuity between the lost Golden Age and the present. The process of praying to the saint unbinds the individuality of each woman. Each is taken over by *a sacred delirium*, brought out of herself and into an eternal consensus by her spatial relationship to the tomb of Ali Boughaleb.

When Mehdi begins to go to the *msid*, or Qurʾanic school, the entire educational paradigm is centered around the shining light of the instructor and the undifferentiated murmurings of the students who are rote-memorizing the verse of scripture the master has given them. This educational paradigm, the *halqa* or circle of learning, has many of the attributes of the sacred interior. The master appears to be dozing, yet he reaches out and whacks a few students more or less at random when he hears a voice in the chorus mispronounce one of the words of the sacred text; this arbitrary discipline reinforces the students' cultural credibility by picking out – at least in theory – the voice of the stranger and singling it out for punishment. Only when reciting their verses correctly do the students belong within the sacred interior of the school.

Later, the master tells the students that as part of the celebration of the lunar New Year, "Our *msid* must be lit at midnight."[32] The students work hard over several days to whitewash the walls of the schoolroom and to place small oil lamps around the walls and ceiling. On the night of the New Year, the students and their parents, all in their best clothes, gather in the illuminated schoolroom to celebrate:

> I was no longer the unique prince in the vest; I was becoming a member of a congregation of young lords, all richly dressed, singing under the direction of a king of legend ... This morning, the most ordinary objects, the most deprived beings, mixed their voices with ours, demonstrating the same fervor, abandoning themselves to the same ecstasy, claiming with the same gravity as us, the grandeur and the compassion of God, creator of all living things ... After the recitation of the Qur'an, we sang hymns. The parents of certain students sang with us. They had come to accompany their children. They perhaps didn't have the same task as we: they were celebrating the Achoura at the *msid* like they did in their own childhoods.[33]

This ritual not only forms the children into a group within the now even more sacred interior of the schoolroom but also brings the generations together in a consensus of tradition and worship. Because the children have passed their oral examinations by successfully reciting the Qur'an without standing out from their peers, they are allowed the fine clothes and parental admiration that transforms them into a congregation of young lords instead of a diverse group of children of tradesmen and immigrants. The social boundaries between them are erased by the bright light of the many lamps; the resemblance to the newly-illuminated apartment after the purchase of the kerosene lamp is no coincidence.

Further extending the status of the schoolroom as sacred interior is the collective effort that has been undertaken to transform it for the holiday. The oil for the lamps, a considerable expense for any of these poor families, was brought in bowls and bottles by the students from their parents' kitchens. The chalk for the whitewashing was brought by one of the parents, who was a whitewasher by trade, and the students had taken a collection to put new straw mats on the floor for the occasion. Gaining the cultural competency and credibility represented by the memorization of the Qur'an, then, is not the only factor involved in gaining access to the sacred interior; the very process of creating the sacred interior involves the sort of consensus and cultural competency that structures it.

Mehdi is a rather nervous child whose mother is too busy to assuage all his anxieties. In her absence,[34] Mehdi hits upon a rather novel solution that makes use of Moroccan space and spatial practices. He accumulates a number of shiny objects –

buttons, beads, a glass bottle-stopper – and stores them within a small box that he keeps in his bedroom. This is the titular box of wonders: whenever Mehdi feels anxiety and can't get his mother to pay attention to him, he retreats to his room, opens the box and holds the objects therein up to the light. He has created a sacred interior for himself, one that serves as a kind of fetish that takes him away from the anxiety of being a child in a world of adults.

> At night, the house fell back into silence. I took out my Box, emptied it on a corner of the mattress, looked at my objects one by one. This evening, they did not speak to me; they lay inert, sulky, a little hostile. They had lost their magic power and had become cagey, secretive. I put them back in their box. Once the cover was back on, they woke up in the darkness to give themselves over to fastidious and delicate games. They did not know in their ignorance that the insides of my Box of Wonders could not resist my contemplation. My innocent glass stopper grew, enlarged, attained the proportions of a palace of dream, ornamented with light and precious drapery. The nails, the porcelain buttons, the pins and the beads were changed into princesses, slaves, young men; they went into this palace, played sweet melodies, fed upon fine treats, had a go at the swings, flew into the trees to snack on the fruit, disappeared into the sky on the wing of the wind in quest of adventures.[35]

Mehdi's experience in this rather furtive and erotic exploration of his box of wonders subtends a hybrid space whose attributes come from both the sacred interior and the space of fairytales that interests Mehdi. Before his gaze illuminates them, the objects in Mehdi's box lay, or in French, *gisaient*, the word used for a corpse lying in a tomb, relating back to what he has seen of the saints' tombs and how his mother and her friend invoke the saint as a guide. Mehdi has absorbed the storytelling conventions of his culture well enough that he's able to people a sort of story with the dreamed-of elements of his box of shiny wonders.

The Façade in *La boîte à merveilles*

A fundamental transition toward the role of storyteller takes place when Mehdi and his mother pass the façade of the French colonial office:

> To our left stood a monumental gateway decorated with nails and hammered bronze of very fine work.

> – Wow! Tell me whom that house belongs to?
> – It's not a house; it's an office for Christians.[36]
> – I see Muslims going in.
> – They work with the Christians. The Christians, my son, are rich and pay well those who know their language.
> – Will I speak the Christians' language when I'm bigger?
> – God preserve you, my son, from all contact with these people whom we don't know.[37]

The gleam of the façade attracts Mehdi, who wants to know more about whoever might exhibit such a wonderful spatial practice – in a traditional Moroccan city, buildings typically turn inward, presenting blank walls, usually entirely without windows, to the street – but his mother turns him away from this. For Mehdi's mother, the façade, like the French, is something to be avoided; for Lefebvre, it is the Western means of organizing space in a nutshell:

> A façade admits certain acts to the realm of what is visible, whether they occur on the façade itself (on balconies, window ledges, etc.) or are to be seen from the façade (processions in the street, for example). Many other acts, by contrast, it condemns to obscenity: these occur behind the façade.[38]

This is the only mention of the French in *La boîte à merveilles*, but we can see the effects of the French and of Western spatial practice on Sefrioui himself, who in this autobiographical narrative describes his own origins as a montagnard child in Fez in the late colonial period. While there's nothing overtly nationalistic at all in Sefrioui's narrative, the effect of Western culture is most evident in the fact that *La boîte à merveilles* is written in French rather than in Arabic, and Sefrioui was indeed paid well by French patrons, if not necessarily by the French government. To further understand the extent to which Sefrioui's identity was influenced by Western, abstract spatiality, just look at his conception of his childhood subjectivity: "My memory was a blank slate (une cire fraîche, "a fresh wax") and the smallest events were there engraved in unerasable images. I still have this album to brighten up my solitude, to prove to myself that I haven't yet died."[39] The spatial relationship of author/narrator to subject is here the Western trope of legibility; once the events of his childhood engraved themselves upon the fresh tablet of his memory, this tablet would then be readable – and it would also replace the tomb as a symbol of the absent presence of death. He can map himself out from a bird's-eye perspective, something which is not at all native to Moroccan culture and which allows him to view his life from a perspective that makes him a narrator in the Western sense.

The Sacred Interior in Fí al-Tufúla, Again

Abdelmajid's young life is not entirely structured by the abstract urban grid. His family is Moroccan and Muslim, and while his father has molded himself into a Western businessman, he remains fundamentally Moroccan, especially in structuring his family life. This manifests itself in his spatial practices and the social practices they engender. Early in the narrative, Abdelmajid's mother grows ill and dies, yet despite his son's obvious pain, his father refuses to let him see his mother's body. The Petronous family, their neighbors and Abdelmajid's caretakers throughout much of his mother's illness, cause a conflict when they insist that five-year-old Abdelmajid be taken in to see his mother's corpse lying in state, even though it goes against traditional Moroccan sociospatial practices. That he has been allowed to enter into a forbidden spatial relationship renders his father and nursemaid tá'ih,[40] a word that means "lost," or "distracted," with the more poetic implication that they have become lost in a tíh, or labyrinth. His transgression of normative spatial relationships has caused his Moroccan family to react in a manner he expresses spatially, in terms of blockage. Because his family is so confused, Millie Petronous takes him outside to the park, under the light of the full moon, and tries to console him:

> Its light filtered along the branches and lit up the lawn. The lofty shadows of the trees spread out underneath them on the ground. The scene seized me with its glory and tranquility, but Millie turned me away from it with her speech. I heard her say: 'Don't be sad, little one. This is life; your mother hasn't gone away, and won't go away, because she was a good woman. So she'll remain with us in spirit, and God will reward her for her goodness and she'll live in the Blessed Gardens. Don't fear for her, and try not to be sad. Look at the sky; heaven is there, behind the moon and behind the stars. If you want to see her, just wait for the full moon, then look at it. Don't you see her there, looking down at you, smiling, happy? Look; don't you see her?'[41]

Essentially, Millie adapts Abdelmajid's spatiality to a Western context by moving his perspective from the particular and tactile to the abstract and visual. In the first movement of the scene, Abdelmajid leaves the house in order to experience his grief in a naturalistic setting. He has essentially inverted the sacred interior of Moroccan space by moving out to the English lawn, creating something closer to Khatibi's grotto in the circle of trees. He has performed a kind of hybridity between Western and Moroccan space by creating a space where the tactile bodies of the trees and their capacity to block the light of the moon generate a labyrinth on the lawn. Millie's repetition of the verbs *rá'á*, "to see," and *nazara*, "to look/gaze," underscore the extent to which the mother in the moon as a source of solace depends on a clear line of sight to the moon above. Abdelmajid's full moon takes the place of the reader of the map of the city, looking down from a bird's-eye view to help him decode what is a confusing text for a child of any nationality: the culture of adulthood.

Before Abdelmajid can step into a soothing place, however, he meets the influence of Millie, who instead imposes Western spatial practices upon him. She has him concentrate on the abstract gaze of the moon rather than the tactile trees, using language to turn him away from the space he has created. She emphasizes the link between the moonlight and his mother's gaze, no less abstract since his mother is dead, and continues to emphasize the lines of sight and the visual, mapping aspects of this manifestation of grief. Thus, Millie's speech to a certain extent replicates the violence of Western colonization of the Maghreb; though of course she is only trying to help a young boy for whom she cares assuage the grief brought on by the death of his mother, it is undeniable that she imposes her own, Western spatiality upon the hybrid coping mechanism into which he has transformed the grove of trees.

Political Spaces in Moroccan Literature

As noted above, for Lefebvre, sociospatial practices are essentially political in nature; a close reading of Miquel's argument would demonstrate that this was true in the Abbasid era as well. The spatial organization Abdelmajid imposes on the confusing streets of Fez and on the writers he has become acquainted with is essentially an act of colonization, imposing Western abstract space on the labyrinth of colonial Morocco.

An analogous argument for *La boîte à merveilles* is a little less direct: perhaps the text concerns itself only with Mehdi's boyhood since there are no colonists or politicians in the novel. *La boîte à merveilles* is nevertheless a deeply political text, not only in its use of space but in its very presentation. When Mehdi sees the façade of the colonial bureau, he's deeply impressed – and this is even before he learns that the French pay well those who know their language. We know nothing of what happens to Mehdi the character after the text of *La boîte à merveilles* comes to a close, but

Sefrioui the author gained fame and fortune by publishing his semiautobiographical novel in French. His main audience was not Moroccan at all, but rather readers in metropolitan France: *La boîte à merveilles* was published in Paris, not Morocco. Sefrioui is therefore mapping the old city: he exposes old Fez to French readers who are curious about what life might be like in these distant, soon to be independent colonies. This is evident from the first page of the text:

> I saw, at the bottom of an impasse that the sun never visited, a little boy of six years, setting a trap for catching a sparrow, but the sparrow never came. He so desired this little sparrow! He wouldn't eat it, nor martyr it. He wanted to make it his friend … We lived in Dar Chouafa, the house of the seer. On the ground floor lived a seer of great reputation. From faraway neighborhoods, women of all conditions came to consult her.[42]

From the start, Sefrioui is an object of his own storytelling. He views himself not only from the sort of elevated perspective characteristic of abstract space but also as a benevolent colonist: he wants to cage the sparrow only to make it his companion. Moreover, his family lives in the traditional Fassi style, a group of apartments centering in a courtyard, in a house named for the seer, *al-shawwáfa*, derived from Arabic *sháfa*, "to see/look," the colloquial counterpart to the formal verbs *rá'á* and *nazara*, those used in the citation from *Fí al-Tufúla* when Abdelmajid looks at the moon. From its very beginning, the text of *La boîte à merveilles* is entirely wrapped up in the abstract gaze, even if it never leaves Fez nor discusses politics. As such, it presents us with a map, in a Western language, of a labyrinthine space from an abstract perspective, and it is, like *Fí al-Tufúla*, a colonial text.

Notes

1   C.R. Pennell, *Morocco Since 1830: A History* (New York: New York University Press, 2000), 151–160.

2   See, e.g., the difference between the 1995 edition of the Lonely Planet guidebook and its most recent iteration in 2012.

3   Casablanca: Matbaat al ʿAndalús, 1956. Citations in this chapter are taken from the second edition (Casablanca: Dár Nashr al-Ma3rifa, 2006), as this is the edition studied in secondary schools and is thus much more widely available to interested readers.

4   Paris: Seuil, 1954.

5 And Spain, though Spanish colonial authority was never more than nominal. See Pennell, 166–167.

6 Fí al-Tufúla is part of the secondary-school literature curriculum in Moroccan schools, so it, at least, is viewed as a foundational text.

7 In 2008, I published an article in the *Journal of Arabic Literature* that examined in detail the use of urban space in Fí al-Tufúla; readers who wish further detail are advised to seek it in that article.

8 Hamid Lahmidáni, al-Riwáya al-maghribiya wa-ru'yat al-wáqi' al 'ijtimá'i: dirása binyawiya takwíniya. (Cairo: Dár al-Thaqáfa, 1985) 253–255.

9 Reliance on the perspective of a narrow, educated, Westernized elite is the standard trope for Arabic-language Moroccan novels throughout the 1960s and well into the 1970s. It is only with the novels of Muhammad Zafzáf, the first of which was *al-Mar'a wa-l-Warda* (*The Woman and the Rose*) (Beirut: Manshúrát Gallery Wáhid, 1972), that we begin to see protagonists more representative of the vast majority of Moroccans.

10 Rabat: Dár al 'Amán. An excellent English translation by Issa J. Boulatta is available as *The Game of Forgetting* (Austin: The Center for Middle Eastern Studies, 1996).

11 Abdelkebir Khatibi, *Le Roman Maghrébin* (Paris: Maspero, 1967).

12 Berrada (tr), "al-Riwáya al-maghribiya," from *al-mulhaq al-wathá'iqiy* (Casablanca: manshúrát al-bahth al-jámi'í, 1971), 142.

13 Andy Merrifield, *Henri Lefebvre: A Critical Introduction* (New York: Routledge, 2006), 112.

14 Henri Lefebvre, *The Production of Space* (Oxford: Blackwell, 1991), 268–269.

15 Ben Jalloun, 39.

16 A.-L. de Premare, *Dictionnaire Arabe-Français*, 12 vols. (Paris: Editione L'Harmattan, 1994), 3: 293–294.

17 Ben Jalloun, 83.

18 Ibid., 39.

19 Abdelkebir Khatibi, *Le Roman Maghrébin* (Paris: Maspero, 1967).

20 Ibid., 104.

21 *La géographie humaine du monde musulman jusqu'au milieu du 11e siècle* (Human geography of the Islamic world until the mid-eleventh century) (Paris: Mouton, 1967).

22 Though it must be mentioned here that for Miquel, travel narratives have another purpose: to make foreign lands seem more alien and therefore make the Islamic empire seem less fragmented than it was. See Miquel, 69.

23 Ahmed Sefrioui, *La boîte à merveilles* (The Box of Wonders) (Paris: LeSeuil, 1954).

24 Ibid., 42.

25 A.-L. de Premare, *Dictionnaire Arabe-Français*, 12 vols. (Paris: Editione L'Harmattan, 1994), 3: 293–294.

26 Sefrioui, 149.

27 Si El Arafi is blind and makes his living from dispensing advice and blessings.

28 Ibid., 36.

29 Ibid., 36.

30 Ali Boughaleb, a twelfth-century CE saint of Chalab.

31 Sefrioui, 22–24.

32 Ibid., 61.

33 Ibid., 108–109.

34 One of the major plot points of the novel is Mehdi's father losing his job and having to go to the countryside to do agricultural work; this transforms Mehdi's mother, already a stranger in town, into the head of household.

35 Sefrioui, 43.

36 Ibid., 21.

37 Ibid., 146.

38 Lefebvre, 99.

39 Sefrioui, 9.

40 Ben Jalloun, 17.

41 Ibid., 17.

42 Sefrioui, 7.

CHAPTER 6

Monstrous Offspring: Disturbing Bodies in Feminine Moroccan Francophone Literature

Naima Hachad

Mythical Silence and Audible Words

Because of their attachment to the historical and social realities of Moroccan women,[1] Francophone Moroccan literary works by women, since their first appearances in the early 1980s,[2] have habitually been underscored by critics for their testimonial function. For example, Jean Dejeux identifies the use of the autobiographical "I" as a reflection of the authors' desire to put an end to the social marginalization of women and to communicate the experiences of women to the reader.[3] Even if Dejeux recognizes that the use of first person narration does not represent a compilation of raw documents, but is rather constituted byf "re-arranged" memories,[4] he nonetheless suggests that women's narratives heavily rely on autobiography, something also emphasized by Marc Gontard in his various studies on this literary corpus.[5] While these studies emphasize different ways in which the autobiographical genre has been appropriated by the authors, they also tend to discuss these works as testimony by native informants. Indeed, Rachida Saigh Bousta also describes a "deep desire to bear witness"[6] and equates the female author's text to a work of sociology, alluding to the fact that writing is a secondary activity for the majority of these women, many of whom work primarily as sociologists, anthropologists, journalists, or psychiatrists.[7] Emphasis on the autobiographical dimension is thus imposed, whether it is recognized or denied by each author.[8] This aspect is directly linked to what is often read as the desire to give voice to the experiences of women and to inscribe these voices in a national history traditionally dominated by men.[9]

Exposing women's silence and silencing is thus central to female Francophone Moroccan narratives and their criticism; the more women write, the more the theme of silence is emphasized, leading to what Suellen Diaconoff calls "the myth of the silent woman." To challenge this myth, both Diaconoff and Redouane insist on the important involvement and visibility of women throughout the history of Morocco. For Redouane, women's literary and intellectual production in the last three decades has even given new directions to research.[10] Furthermore, Diaconoff regards the persistence of "the myth of silence" as a paradox, saying:

> So, we have to ask, silent women? Passive women? Repressed women? ... Indeed, regardless of various laments, Moroccan women have neither been silenced, nor are they totally silent about their 'I.' It is important to declare this, because so many contemporary Moroccan women repeat the mantra that, given the kind of instruction of the non-'I' they receive as girls, women either cannot speak, or that if they do, they can only tell stories of their own subjugation. The result of such lamentation about women's lack of voice, or lack of effective voice, despite the evidence of the contrary, is 'the myth of the silent woman.'[11]

Diaconoff cites the works of Rita El Khayat, Fatema Mernissi, and Abdallah Mdarhri Alaoui in order to reaffirm a long tradition of women's expressing themselves either through the written text or orally.[12] She adds that the image of the silent woman "is misleading and ultimately both treacherous and collusive in the insidious effects that it produces."[13] To her, such an image, even though propagated by women themselves, fails to account for women's acts of speaking.

This essay proposes to look at the very dynamics of the contradiction that lie behind this paradox, as well as the intricate demarcations between the autobiographical (here, defined as the report of events witnessed in the surrounding society) and the fictional (which may include the way in which these events or facts are rearranged), from a larger perspective that exceeds the authors' respective histories or women's history. It ultimately seeks to move past gender differentiation and bring out the testimonial beyond autobiography. For Moroccan authors there exists a complex relationship between silence and speech corresponding to the distinct periods of Hassan II's reign, which began with a repressive period referred to as the "Years of Lead"[14] and moved toward a relatively free period in the final years of his reign. The three novels analyzed – *L'Arganier des femmes égarées* (*The argan of the lost women*) by Damia Oumassine,[15] *Le Corps dérobé* (*The stolen body*) by Houria Boussejra,[16] and *Cérémonie* (*Ceremony*) by Yasmine Chami-Kettani[17] – epitomize some of the complexities of the last years of Hassan's II reign, a pivotal period marked by gradual liberalization and returning ghosts from a traumatic past. In these novels, experiences of women from various ethnic and social backgrounds are related within a larger perspective that translates movements and struggles of a transforming society.

Each of these novels can be seen as a distinct example of the dynamics that perpetuate "The myth of the silent woman." This essay will explore precisely what motivates and what lurks behind this repeated lament. Repetition is indeed important here since, notwithstanding their originality, the three novels display thematic and formal continuities[18] with prior literary Francophone production by women. The essay will also look at whether repetition is a sign of limited resonance, due to the inability to be heard, which is tantamount to silence in many respects, or whether, through repetition, the lament's referent could have slightly shifted to emphasize the dialectic between change and resistance, thus demonstrating characteristics of a society in transition. Indeed, in *Francophone Voices of the "New" Morocco in Film and in Print: (Re)presenting a Society in Transition*, Valérie Orlando[19] summarizes Morocco's dilemma as reflected in contemporary cultural productions in the question, "Is there a future for Morocco?"[20] Orlando describes a country "caught between its past and its future," displaying "the disparity between rich and poor"[21] and the trauma of "voices that have been effaced by violence."[22] She then concludes, "Transition has created a schizophrenic state that is continuously contradicting on a variety of subjects, from matters of human rights and freedom of the press to economic reform."[23] As Orlando notes, the word *schizophrenia* is frequently used by journalists writing for the Francophone newspaper *TelQuel* and their readers in published comments[24] to describe all aspects of Moroccan society. The three novels analyzed in this essay may in fact be described as schizophrenic explorations of the deep contradictions of a society that holds its individuals hostage. In spite of slightly different foci, the various narratives present individuals struggling to realize their desire for freedom, emancipation, and happiness, while violently clashing with mutilating social attitudes. This confrontation produces a society of bullies and victims and a cycle of repetition and inevitability that sometimes blurs the distinction between the two categories. Often death and renunciation prevail, yet the lament is also a cry of revolt and a transformative subversion of the power dynamics and attitudes that sustain such a society.

Space and Confinement

L'arganier, *Le corps*, and *Cérémonie* each communicate a powerful sense of imprisonment, largely conveyed through inescapability from sociocultural and familial ties. This bind, instead of constituting a supportive network that helps the individual attain self-realization, works as a constraint for the protagonists in their struggle to achieve social, economic, and emotional fulfillment. A significant symbol of such a bind is the return to the family home, village, or country, as is the case in *Cérémonie* for Khadija,[25] who seems to have no other choice but to return to her childhood home after her divorce. The affirmation "For her, it is the only house possible,"[26] which opens the novel, soon becomes a mark of confinement, as it turns out to be that which prevents the protagonist from creating alternative spaces of happiness. Instead of being a refuge for the rejected and wounded Khadija, the family home is slowly exposed as a cursed site for the female members. The serenity of the past that Khadija is trying to invoke in order to ground herself and her family after their traumatic experience (their departure in the middle of the night from an indifferent husband and father who goes so far as to renounce his rights to his children) is brutally interrupted by her cousin Malika's assessment: "While you are calmly walking along, the familiar ground collapses beneath you, and you are faced with emptiness. And there you are, honey, hanging above the abyss, where the slightest movement could be fatal."[27] Malika's reference to an abyss, symbolizing her cousin's vulnerable condition, primarily refers to Khadija's loss of identity. Paradoxically, the family home becomes a prison for Khadija because it strips her of her adulthood and independence. In spite of being an accomplished architect, thirty-seven-year old Khadija is unable to live independently with her children; most of all, she has to become a young girl again[28] and is forced to conceal her femininity. Khadija's cousin, Malika, is a sympathetic observer of the scene:

> Lalla Rita [Khadija's mother] ceremoniously opens the tissue paper. Malika first sees the three caftans for the children on top ... Malika gasps with real pleasure, but underneath the three caftans now spread on the bed, she discovers the one meant for her cousin, made of pink lace, the tender pink usually associated with very young girls. The pale shimmer of the pearls on the edge emphasizes its fragility. 'It is a young girl's caftan!' She protests. Lalla Rita lets a smile appear, unable to conceal her feelings of both humiliation and anger.[29]

Khadija's mother further explains that "it is unnecessary for the moment [for Khadija] to attract attention."[30] Khadija has literally to disguise herself to assuage her mother's feelings of humiliation and guilt.[31] Not only is Khadija forced to deal with the brutality of her marriage and the failure of her love life, she is also dispossessed of her own story, wounds, and body. She is pressured into renouncing any signs of her identity as a woman and is encouraged to contract her body in order to fit the image of "a flower bud, slender and small; a queen's hips confined in virginal lace."[32] Khadija is deprived of her experience and her feelings as she is "summoned to take sides within her own story, her tears are a tribute to the enemy camp."[33] She must hold them back like so many drops of lead, hollowing out within her the trenches of her future loneliness. The young woman is thus silenced, and as her livable space literally and symbolically shrinks, so do her chances to heal. For the first half of the novel, Khadija is slowly expelled from the narrative and functions as an object of reflection for other women of the family, primarily Malika and, to a lesser extent, her mother Lalla Rita. Even when she accesses discourse in a first-person narration halfway through the novel, Khadija can only ruminate on her failure in a long monologue, a failure that thins down as it is slowly absorbed by the many failures that haunt the family history, turning the family house into a prison and cemetery that has witnessed, among other real or symbolic deaths, Aunt Aïcha's confinement and agony.[34]

This sense of inescapability is also conveyed in Maïlouda's story in *L'Arganier*. To protest "the torture [that her husband] planned to impose upon her body and soul,"[35] that is his refusal to let her participate in the village's celebrations through dancing and singing, Maïlouda deserts the family home and her children to begin a journey of wandering in search for independence and pleasure. She first becomes a *cheikha*,[36] thus satisfying what is often assumed to be a secret desire of women. Indeed, the *cheikha*, a symbol of nomadism, rootlessness, freedom, excessive and licentious pleasure, is at once scorned and envied by other women:

> The faces looked up at the stranger and stared at her shamelessly. The stranger, who surely was a *cheikha*, was wearing a green caftan, and her hands and neck were loaded with gold jewelry. After a moment of surprise, the housewives assailed her with inquisitive questions ... Maïlouda was watching her with curiosity. She was facing an actual *cheikha*! Don't they say that *cheikhates* are the only free women in a Muslim country? No strings, no obstacles, and a life of continuous pleasure.[37]

Although Maïlouda discovers soon after her escape with the *raïss*[38] that there is no real freedom for a woman who is not under the protection of a man, her impulsive behavior testifies to a deep desire to rebel against prohibitions on women's pleasure. The very contradictions that guide Maïlouda's experience and emotions while away from her husband and children provide ironic commentary regarding the impossibility for women to experience both freedom and pleasure. The narration of her adventures also confirms a similar dynamic. Indeed, it is as if a woman's decision to abandon family life for the sake of freedom is inconceivable. The reader is faced with making sense of the inconsistencies that Maïlouda is facing: her desire "to live like a leaf in the wind, light and free"[39] and her remorse and guilt upon leaving her children and humiliating her parents. The narration of her adventures after her escape starts with the following observation: "Fifteen years after that cursed day, Maïlouda is still unable to understand how she was able to let herself be taken in so easily."[40] This statement not only erases the bold, rebellious impulse that originally leads Maïlouda to protest against injustices of marital life, it also turns her into a passive object in the hands of the malefic *raïss*, thus precipitating her next departure. These contradictions continue to unsettle the narration of Maïlouda's journey. Every break of social restraints and every experience of pleasure is mitigated by a sense of passivity and guilt:

> [The *raïss*' hand] sensually caressed her legs and slowly moved upward. Around them, everything was silent. The room with its closed windows seemed to invite them to surrender to pleasure ... Her senses were violently stimulated; she abandoned herself to his trained hands, moaning like a trapped animal. What she was afraid of had just happened. It was real; she had become his mistress. The hashish helped her forget for a while, but she was never able to fully embrace her new life.[41]

Similar to the description of the critical moment of her escape, Maïlouda's agency and rebelliousness are moderated with allusions to her regret or her sense of helplessness. As if notions of freedom and pleasure for women are unacceptable, even their fictional narration, like Maïlouda herself, must remain veiled by remorse, "a moral prisoner of the past."[42] This movement back and forth between poignant affirmations of the desire for freedom and painful expressions of regret continue to tear up the rhythm of the narration until the final and surprising outcome of Maïlouda's journey. In an unexpected turn of events, she returns to her husband, who takes her back after fifteen years of wandering.

Maïlouda returns tired, weakened, and damaged, and this bears witness not only to inescapability from the socio-cultural and familial milieu but also to the agonizing renunciations women must undergo regardless of the paths they choose. Their dilemma is powerfully conveyed throughout the contradictions that work from within the narration and that can be summed up in Maïlouda's address to the street she had momentarily inhabited in Casablanca:

> You never stopped accusing me! And you were right! I admit that I am an unworthy wife and a bad mother. But everything is not so simple. I nonetheless concede that, somewhere in my mind, I am happy that I no longer have obstacles to my freedom.[43]

From this statement, one can easily imagine that Maïlouda's life after her return to the family home will be filled with regret and remorse.

If the return to the family home serves to contain any chance of rebellion and change for Khadija and Maïlouda, the sense of confinement and loss, as well as its relation to the "tribe," is even sharper in *Le corps*. The main characters of the novel, Leila, and her father, Mohammed, are both unable to leave their house of torments. Paradoxically, the two characters, often described as orphans or as desiring to be orphans, are unable to break free from family ties that are abusive and mutilating. As an adult, Leila keeps returning to the home where her mother physically abused her daily and where she, at the age of five, was raped by another woman, a traumatic experience aggravated by her mother's indifference:

> Leila got up to leave. Each time she visited the house, she felt like she was losing herself; she no longer knew how a life could be made. The overwhelming hostility shut down the hope that rose in her each time she decided to visit her. She thought to herself that she must be insane to keep going back toward her torturer. But she didn't know what else to do.[44]

The return to the scene of trauma and its narration in the form of flashbacks alludes to the protagonist's unconscious and impulsive reenactment of traumatic experiences. It could be read as a process of healing in which, as Van der Kolk and Van der Hart have explained, the narration of traumatic events brings relief.[45] However, in Boussejra's novel, the accent is clearly put on an oppressive society, symbolized by the mother. The suppression of the individual is inscribed in the novel through Leila's extreme physical pain and the psychological violence Mohammed undergoes, both inflicted by mothers who become epitomes of the patriarchal figure. Their malaise and suffering come from their confinement in families where, as Leila realizes, "the 'I's' don't exist."[46]

The poignancy of the two characters' physical and mental struggles is amplified by the multiplication of the "tribe." For example, after the remarriage of his mother when he is thirteen or fourteen, Mohammed leaves the house and is adopted by a Frenchman who lives a few miles away. The narrator adds, by way of explanation for Mohammed's decision to recreate a family environment with the Frenchman, "Everyone needs to be recognized, identified, and classified because no punishment can be greater than being ignored by the tribe."[47] The characters' itineraries are thus partly determined by a dialectic that consists of their desire to break free from family ties and the desire to create new ones, failing again and again. After the Frenchman tries to abuse him sexually, Mohammed immediately joins the army, another family substitute. Unable to overcome the feeling of melancholy that continues to inhabit him in spite of his professional success, Mohammed tries to find relief in his relationships with prostitutes. When he meets Leila's mother, he thinks, "With her, I will be fulfilled; nothing will be missing, she will complete me."[48] However, he soon realizes that the family life he builds is only "a sunny hell"[49] that he can no longer bear and that puts him right back in the cycle of melancholy and wandering:

> Each evening, he went to the neighborhood bars. The Mandarin was his favorite. He never spoke about his mother or his father. Everyone was his family, and he liked being in this atmosphere. He neither recognized any value he could embrace nor any fixed system that would enslave him through interdicts imposed by others. He ignored these interdicts. There, he was unaware of the meaning of the words 'society' and 'tribe.'[50]

Mohammed finally leaves the family home. Despite his love for his children, he decides to flee the fatherly responsibilities he finds overwhelming, as well as the violent environment created by his wife, who feels neglected and fails to understand his thirst for freedom and independence. However, Mohammed's attempt to escape is cut short when he decides to move in with yet another prostitute and thus finds himself caught again in the cycle of repetition. Furthermore, like Leila, who can't seem to stay away from her "torturer," Mohammed becomes tired of his wandering and futile quest for freedom, and he decides to respond positively to his sons' requests that he return to the family home. The inevitable failure of this gesture underscores his personal failings: Mohammed dies on his way home. Lying on the ground, he is described as "a man fighting darkness ... His last battle's foam appeared on the corner of his mouth."[51] Mohammed's death, then, emerges as his greatest and most successful act of resistance.

Mother Society, My Torturer?

The parallel between Mohammed and Leila, father and daughter, is both thematic and formal. Their stories are interwoven, and their suffering and suffocation within the tribe are contrasted, often with the use of quasi-identical words or expressions. They both identify themselves as orphans or express their wish to be orphans; they both express their aversion for the tribe and formal attachments that are not chosen by the individual; mostly, they both suffer from solitude and alienation. Beyond these similarities, the emphasis is also put on a liberating alliance between Mohammed and Leila, which is visible in the dialogue the protagonist creates with her father after his death. Indeed, Mohammed's death triggers the narrative and allows Leila to overcome the wall of silence she has surrounded herself with since childhood. Adult Leila not only succeeds in expressing the brutality and incomprehensibility of the acts of mutilation she has undergone since childhood but also remembers her father, the lessons he taught her, and, in saving him from oblivion, initiates a possible process of healing.

Thus, rather than following in her mother's footsteps, Leila follows, or is made to follow, in those of her father. Boussejra depicts a complex situation where it is no longer simple or comfortable to talk about "a condition of women," or even a "feminine writing," at least not within a discourse that feeds on a radical separation between the masculine and the feminine. Indeed, Rachida Saigh Bousta not only indicates elements of continuity between literary texts written by women and those written by male authors,[52] but also, with reason, warns against a firm distinction between "masculine" and "feminine" writing.[53] What Bousta refers to as a form of imitation[54] is linked to a woman's desire to conquer a space traditionally occupied by men.[55] However, the commonalities between female and male authors could also be explained by social evolutions and the relationship between the figure of the writer (whether female or male) and these evolutions. Like Bousta, Diaconoff notices possible differences between men and women even when they are writing about the same themes.[56] She also notices that the possibility for women to invest in themes that challenge the status quo is related to "the liberalization of the 1980's and especially the mid-1990's onward."[57] The connection between recent changes in society and the figure of the writer in general is also emphasized by Valérie Orlando:

> Since 1999, with their pens, women have more vocally challenged the traditional masculine privilege and patriarchal traditionalism that impede women's sociocultural and political enfranchisement in society. Their works also underscore the fact that women's literary production is as much rooted and invested in historical and revolutionary events and contemporary social issues as that of men.[58]

Although all three novels are subtle illustrations of this statement, in *Le corps*, Boussejra clearly adopts a narrative form and themes that very clearly assert such a posture.[59] The patriarchal society she exposes victimizes both men and women, fathers and daughters; furthermore, women participate in its perpetuation. The alliance that Boussejra creates between Leila and her father signals not only victimizing attitudes that aggravate gender differentiations, but also the desire to create a dialogue between men and women to challenge these attitudes. Najib Redouane recognizes this feature in the work of other female writers:

> The implication of women and their ability to speak can only happen in a plural world: to be truly oneself is to be no longer in confrontation, in conflict, or in opposition to men, but in dialogue with them and with society. Most female Moroccan writers 'declare that their work is meant to be a space of dialogue and exchange' and affirm the necessity for them to renew their style and keep it in constant movement in order to create and recreate another writing, one that is true and current.[60]

Boussejra, too, implicitly states that dialogue between men and women is a necessary component of any narrative of liberation. Indeed, the father's story emerges at a moment of crisis in which Leila brutally hits a deadlock, faced with the hostility of a society she feels offers no prospect for liberation. Remembering the father is equivalent to her refusal to be defeated as he is the one who taught her to be free in thoughts and actions.[61]

The dialogue Leila creates with her father incriminates a society that crushes individuality. The woman, and more particularly the mother, becomes the symbol of a society that mutilates.[62] Reflecting on her alienation and inability to assimilate, the narrator concludes, "But women were her biggest enemies. Worshipped, our mothers exercise an absolute power over the life and death of quite a few generations."[63] Leila's excessive condemnation of women certainly calls for new understandings and attitudes to challenge patriarchal domination in contemporary Moroccan society. The mother is used both as a symbol (of a murderous society, not only unable to protect its members, but also literally and symbolically killing them) and also as a literal referent marking women's responsibility in the perpetuation of such a society. This latter point is also crucial in the other novels, especially in *Cérémonie*, where Aïcha's mother is clearly designated as partly responsible for her confinement and her resulting death[64] or with the exploitation of child-maids by Lalla Najia.[65] In *Le corps dérobé*, the mother and society are amalgamated and denounced with the same violence to expose a complex dynamic that is often disregarded in traditional radical separations of the masculine and the feminine: "Who dared to say that men are women's enemies? When we throw ourselves at this immense object of desire once our mother society has banished us."[66] The analogy between the father and the daughter and the dismissal of women as hyper-victims is a provocative strategy, calling attention to a stagnant society that produces victims, both male and female. This idea is confirmed by the last chapter, in which the mother directly enters the discursive space and testifies to her own suffering and victimization. Here she describes herself as a woman who has been forced to lose her humanity, caught between the appearance of a liberated woman and the constraints imposed upon her as a woman existing in a society in transition. Despite her education, her marriage to a man she has chosen, and her prestigious job, she is reduced to a monster under the sacrifices required by her situation as the oldest daughter of a poor family and as a working mother.

Mutilation, Death and Mourning

These three novels expose a violent and a merciless society in which victims seem to multiply endlessly and where it isn't always easy to distinguish clearly between victim and victimizer. The exposition of a paramount violence does not claim to erase power dynamics or to put everyone at the same level, ignoring that some categories are more vulnerable than others. Rather, it signals a society that produces violence at all levels. This violence is expressed through the multiplication of wounded, mutilated, and ill bodies. Physical abuse, especially rape, is overwhelmingly present in the narratives, further exposing a victimizing society. Indeed, rape is encountered everywhere and remains the most powerful symbol of patriarchal domination and the fragility of women. Both *L'arganier* and *Le corps* contain explicit scenes of rape, two of which are committed against children: five-year-old Leila and twelve-year-old Hafsa. The incommensurable pain that results from the violation of the child-body is conveyed through the notion of blackout:

> His greedy lips moved closer to her neck, then stopped at the nipple of one of her small breasts. Breathing noisily, he nervously removed her saroual. She fainted. When she woke up, the feeble light had disappeared ... Even more than the pain she felt in her under-belly, her tainted clothes made her realize what had happened.[67]

This somewhat elliptical description of Hafsa's rape reveals both the extreme violence and the society's trivialization of the act. Its partial erasure from the narrative reflects its future erasure by social and familial authorities. It also indicates the violence that consists in the accusation of the victim, who, in the eyes of society, becomes as responsible for the act as the perpetrator. Finally, it indicates the perversity that diverts attention from the violation of the body to its depreciation in a society that considers a raped body a tainted one. The stigma turns the body of the victim into a corrupted, sometimes even criminal, entity that requires punishment. Hafsa's silence, her subsequent relationship with her rapist, her humiliation and condemnation by the rapist's wife and by her aunt, and finally her marriage to an old man bear witness to this dynamic. Even at twelve, Hafsa realizes this, and her attention to her tainted clothes, her silence, and the resurgence of her grandmother's advice about the value of virginity indicate her conditioning, as well as her programmed defeat.

Leila's rape is also first conveyed through the notion of blackout and is narrated as a non-event, partly lost in a confused memory:

> Women from her neighborhood quickly gathered around the blood that was pouring from her legs. Leila no longer felt anything, no longer saw anything. She felt she was elsewhere. She felt as if she were watching a film that was showing her own fate. ... The mother never believed her. She told her that it was only an invention, a hallucination, it could never be true. ... She forgot. For many long years she felt almost normal, equal to herself, but something was there, she felt it deep inside.[68]

This description constitutes the first fragment of the memory of Leila's rape and emerges as an explanation for the character's alienation. It also inaugurates a long and painful process of self-exploration and rebellion through which the protagonist seeks recognition of her open injury. The double trauma – the rape and its omission by the mother – is inscribed in the very structure of the narration of the event, through the distance between this first appearance of the rape and the second, some sixty pages later.[69] This physical distance expresses the mental and temporal discrepancy caused by the lack of recognition, thus precluding the possibility for the initiation of a healing process.

The narrations of both rapes stress the lack of validity of the violated body, leading to the alienation of each character and her subsequent removal from society. For Hafsa, the healing process never begins, as she is forced into the events of her life without ever fully accepting them, until her final fall and suicide. Leila becomes an "orphan" who finds herself caught in a meaningless quest – the search for the loving and protective mother – all the while knowing the futility of her endeavor. When these injuries go unrecognized, the victims are condemned to a fall, announced progressively in each of the narrations through allusions to madness. Hafsa hears voices and is unable to sleep. Leila's extreme distress could also be equated to a form of madness.

Violations of the body and the resulting malaise are corroborated by other accounts and allusions to rape. Besides Hafsa's, other examples in Oumassine's novel include the secretary who is sexually and otherwise abused by her boss, a situation that drives her to quasi-madness;[70] Fatima's repeated rape by a husband she hadn't chosen, which leads her to attempt suicide;[71] the girl raped by Fatima's cousin, Mahfoud, and their forced marriage to each other to avoid a prison sentence for the rapist.[72] In *Cérémonie*, the author also alludes to the rape of a child-maid by a man in the family she works for.[73] In *Le Corps*, Leila's rape is narrated side by side with allusions to Mohammed's possible rape. Even though Mohammed's rape is never clearly stated, the confusion around what happened between Mohammed and the Frenchman, and the ambiguous statements referring to the incident that seem to trigger Mohammed's departure, as well as the description of his physical and mental state after the incident allude to rape.[74] Allusions to incomprehension, pain, betrayal, loss of innocence, violence, aversion, destitution, and defeat echo emotions and feelings encountered in explicit descriptions of rape. This incident's interpretation as the fact that men and, more particularly, young boys are also victims of rape is doubtless a valid reading, corroborated by other narratives by Boussejra.[75] However, the ambiguity of the narration of this incident, as well as Mohammed's subsequent abuse by his wife, suggests other possible readings, which, without neutralizing the tangible pain of rape, amplify its signification as a transgression of the integrity of the individual in a society that devours its individuals. Indeed, the exposition of the journeys of victims of rape underscores the interruptive aspect of this deeply violent act. Rapes, especially perhaps those that are also acts of pedophilia, constitute losses from which victims never recover, making rape comparable to infanticide. Furthermore, whether they literally die or become socially and mentally secluded, the isolation of victims of rape points to a progressively collapsing society.

The idea of a disintegrating society is corroborated by the novels' secondary narratives, also populated with cases of victimization that lead to the individual's isolation and disconnection from the social and familial networks. The novels' main narratives around the victimization of women are mirrored by minor narratives that inscribe women's treatment in the social and cultural fabric, overwhelmingly dominated by distrust, violence, abuse, and injustice. In *Cérémonie*, Lalla Fatèma's pain and helplessness highlight this environment, as she witnesses her son's taking refuge in religious fundamentalism as a response to social failure. At a family gathering, she explains to the audience that her son's absence is due to what he considers his religious duty, since he now refuses to have any physical contact with women, including his mother. Lalla Fatéma further explains the reason she has lost her son: "My son is not fulfilled with his life, I know that. He is now nearly forty, alone, without a companion or children. His job, that he left to help his father at the shop, brought him little satisfaction."[76]

Moulay's isolation is a response to another isolation. His mother describes him as someone who has lived in the prison of his flesh,[77] who now flees for another prison, "like a man who has fallen to the bottom of a well and only desires to live in the darkness."[78] Just as Mohammed's experience parallels that of Leila, Moulay's story echoes that of Khadija, who "quivers as she hears her aunt's words. She, too, has lived that way for years, as a woman who has fallen to the bottom of a well and who only desires to live in the darkness."[79] Duplication of corresponding journeys is the main narrative technique of *Cérémonie*, and Khadija is also associated with uprooted peasants who are forced to leave their homes and live in unfamiliar cities;[80] her sense of destitution and ennui is reflected in the mass of unemployed young men who spend their days aimlessly smoking cigarettes or hashish.[81] These parallels that punctuate women's narratives underscore the idea of generalized malaise and suffocation. Characters are described as "hallucinating puppets performing gestures that have been emptied of their meaning,"[82] or held in abeyance above an abyss, transfixed, "as if any gesture could provoke a collapse."[83] These descriptions illustrate the violence resulting from what both Diaconoff[84] and Orlando[85] describe as a society torn between the past and the present, and facing an uncertain future. Khadija's destiny exposes the clash between modernity and a certain idea of tradition made of gestures that have become obsolete, thus creating estrangement and isolation. Chami-Kattani's description of the unemployed and unoccupied youth and Oumassine's depiction of extreme poverty in remote villages also allude to the consuming violence that works from within a polarized society. Indeed, as recently reported by NPR analyst Deborah Amos, "the gap between rich and poor in Morocco is one of the widest in the Arab world."[86]

Agony and (As) Revolt

Death is preferable. Pushed by an uncontrollable feeling of panic, she ran towards the slope leading to the souk. She didn't see the plastic bottle in her way and tripped, collapsing on the rocky ground of the cemetery. The man desperately stared at the red puddle forming around his wife's small body ... Hafsa died without ever waking up. The child, a light-skinned little girl, did not survive her mother's death.[87]

Pregnant Hafsa's gesture epitomizes both the ideas of an infanticidal society and individual acts of revolts. Her gesture cannot be read without thinking of the acts of Mohamed Bouazizi[88] or Amina El-Filali,[89] who have become figures of revolt and revolution in North Africa. While El-Filali and other women protesting the violence of the status quo in the Arab world have been described as "Bouazizis" and revolutionary forces by Mona Eltahawy,[90] characters in these novels are their fictional counterparts. Beyond the authors' involvement in civil society, the creation of such characters transform female authors in Morocco into agents who anticipate and provide the catalyst for social change, from the reform of the Moroccan family code in 2004[91] to other social protests in Morocco in recent years. As for working through Morocco's traumatic past, in their repeated lament against silence, these authors, and many others since the mid-1990s, helped instigate Morocco's Justice and Reconciliation Commission.[92] Indeed, Orlando's study of new voices of Morocco shows that the line between literature and activism is blurred, as many authors are also social and political activists, and many contribute to innovations in the country's social and political domains. Thus, Hafsa, Mohammed, and Aïcha could also be read as fictional "Bouazizis" who prefigure in literature the extreme gestures of revolt that eventually lead to real social activism.

If death and renunciation overshadow the narratives of the three novels, revolt emerges as a strong counterpart, working from within the narratives of mutilation and silencing. In *Cérémonie*, Aïcha's death leads to emotional and psychological turmoil that prompts Malika to reevaluate her cultural heritage and the familial and social values that have been transmitted to her. She literally puts these values to the test by confronting them with Aïcha's personal agony. To make sense of Khadija's situation and save her from death, she recalls the agony of their aunt, Aïcha, who, deprived of the pleasure of married life and motherhood, succumbed to cancer, described as "a *djinn* [that] entered her left breast, then moved to her right one, a glutton, it devoured her from the inside."[93] In her curative reconstruction of Aïcha's story, Malika links her agony to dysfunctional familial attitudes. She describes Aïcha's father's unusual passion for Aïcha as something that transformed her into an eternal bride, covered with presents and suffocating attention that covered her death rattle: "Aïcha was like a queen in the heart of her family. Each one of her arrivals was anticipated like a special event ...; but it was something else, her flesh was birthing death, and no one wanted to imagine her despair."[94] The father's anomalous love and the silence that sustained it not only killed Aïcha but also turned her into a murderer. She gave birth to her own death. Moreover, her maternal breast, deprived of its function, turned into a sinister entity that not only devoured her body through a generalized cancer, but also caused her to devour her children inside her.[95]

Aïcha thus becomes the epitome of a society that suffocates its individuals. However, the memories attached to her produce a chaotic rattling that gives the text its rhythm. This undetermined subterranean voice emerges as an unpredictable force that can cause the narrative to disintegrate at any moment, thus interrupting the cycle of repetition and the transmission of mutilation and suffering symbolized by the legends that run through the family from generation to generation, testament to incomplete and failed revolts. The inscription of storytelling and the appropriation and interpretation of the stories being transmitted creates a polyphony of voices that destabilizes the narration and results in delirious monologues that threaten its coherence. These narrative strategies emerge as eruptions of words meant to defeat silence and cause transformation. In *L'arganier* and *Le corps*, these strategies are echoed by the inscription of impetuous, even mad gestures, which also interrupt the state of stagnation and apathy, thus prescribing changes to come. Even though these gestures, especially those of suicide, indicate the limits of a suffocating society that is on the verge of imploding and disintegrating, they are also transformative in their ambiguity as both acts of renunciation and of revolt.

Notes

1   Suellen Diaconoff, *The Myth of the Silent Woman: Moroccan Women Writers* (Toronto: University of Toronto Press, 2009). In her study of Female Moroccan authors, Suellen Diaconoff mentions "Sexuality and the body, violence, unhappy relationships, and new formulation of female identity in the political community" as some of the recurrent themes, 24; Najib Redouane, *Ecritures féminines au Maroc: continuité et evolution (Female writers of Morocco: continuity and evolution)* (Paris: L'Harmattan, 2006). In his analysis of fourteen female Moroccan authors, Najib Redouane underlines a plurality of themes that highlights Moroccan women's condition as it has been shaped by traditions and practices of Moroccan society, 13.

2   Halima Ben Haddou, *Aïcha la rebelle (Aïcha the rebel)* (Paris: Jeune Afrique, 1982). Considered to be the first Francophone novel written by a Moroccan woman.

3   Jean Dejeux, *Littérature féminine de la langue française au Maghreb (Moroccan women's literature in French)* (Paris: Editions Karthala, 1994), 116.

4   Ibid., 118.

5   Marc Gontard, "L'Etre-femme au Maroc: Marocaines de l'intérieur et de l'extérieur:

Leïla Houari, Noufissa Sbaï (Being female and Moroccan: Moroccans from within and without: Leïla Houari, Noufissa Sbaï)," *Le Moi étrange: littérature marocaine de langue française (Strange words: Moroccan literature in French)* (Paris: L'Harmattan, 1993), 179–200; Marc Gontard, "L'autofiction féminine au Maroc (Women's autobiographical fiction from Morocco)," *Voix de la Francophonie (Belgique Canada Maghreb)*, Dir., Lydia Anoll and Marta Segara (Barcelone: Publicacions de la Universitat de Barcelona, 1999), 337–347.

6   Rachida Saïgh Bousta, *Romancières marocaines: épreuves d'écriture (Moroccan novelists: The hardships of writing)* (Paris: L'Harmathan, 2005). Translation from French to English are the author's.

7   Ibid., 25.

8   Ibid., 19–20.

9   On the relationship between the literary texts by Maghrebi female Francophone authors and the historical milieu as well as theoretical approaches related to this issue, see also Valérie Orlando, "To Be Singularly Nomadic or a Territorialized National: At the Crossroads of Francophone Women's Writing of the Maghreb," *Meridians* 6.2 (2006): 33–53.

10   Redouane, 11.

11   Diaconoff, 61.

12   Ibid., 62.

13   Ibid., 60–62.

14   The "Years of Lead" are generally considered to be the period from the accession of Hassan II in 1961 until the late 1980s and early 1990s. In 1990, the king instituted the National Consultative Council on Human Rights. At this time, he released many political prisoners and granted the most prominent ones a voice in government. His reign continued until 1999.

15   Damia Oumassine, *L'Arganier des femmes égarées* (Casablanca: Editions Le Fennec, 1998).

16   Houria Boussejra, *Le Corps dérobé* (Casablanca: Afrique-Orient, 1999).

17   Yasmine Chami-Kettani, *Cérémonie* (Arles: Actes Sud, 1999). Citation from the three novels are translated into English by the author.

18   For example, though he declares in the introduction that there is no unifying theme, Redouane nonetheless mentions the re-appropriation of the self in a society where women are reduced to silence as the common ground that drives the narration, 12.

19   New York: Palgrave Macmillan, 2009.

20   Ibid., 1.

21   Ibid., 2.

22   Ibid., 3.

23   Ibid., 3.

24 See for example Omar Radi, "Internet. Je clique donc je suis," *TelQuel* 518 (April 2011), in which the author describes the relationship between sex and religion as an illustration of Moroccan schizophrenia. See also the article by Ali Amar, former co-founder and editor of the Casablanca weekly *Le Journal hebdomadaire*, "Le Maroc: grand producteur de schizophrénie," *SlateAfrique*, November 2011.

25 Chami-Kettani.

26 Ibid., 7.

27 Ibid., 11.

28 Ibid., 42.

29 Ibid., 42–43.

30 Ibid., 42.

31 Ibid., 43.

32 Ibid., 43.

33 Ibid., 14–15.

34 For an analysis of the inscription of Death in *Cérémonie*, see Isabelle Larrivée, "La crypte et la vie, étude de *Cérémonie*, de Yasmine Chami-Kettani (The tomb and the life, a study of *Ceremony*, by Yasmine Chami-Kettani)," *Frontières* 14.2 (Spring 2002): 29–33.

35 Oumassine, 32.

36 A female performer who sings and dances in celebrations, traditionally for a male public. The *cheikha* is also often associated with prostitution.

37 Oumassine, 36.

38 The male lead musician in a folklore band that is usually composed of a *raïss* and several *cheikhates*.

39 Oumassine, 39.

40 Ibid., 42.

41 Ibid., 43–44.

42 Ibid., 59.

43 Ibid., 59.

44 Boussejra, 96.

45 Bessel A. Van der Kolk and Onno Van der Hart, "The Intrusive Past: The flexibility of memory and the engraving of trauma," in *Trauma: Explorations in Memory*, ed. Cathy Caruth (Baltimore: The Johns Hopkins University Press, 1995), 158–182.

46 Boussejra, 28.

47 Ibid., 37.

48 Ibid., 60.

49 Ibid., 87.

50 Ibid., 67.

51   Ibid., 100–101.

52   Saigh Bousta, 14–15.

53   Ibid., 11.

54   Ibid., 14.

55   Ibid., 25.

56   Diaconoff, 20.

57   Ibid., 24.

58   Valérie Orlando, *Francophone voices of the 'new' Morocco in film and print: (re)presenting a society in transition* (New York: Macmillan, 2009), 71. In this sense, Boussejra, Chami-Kettani, and Oumassine are part of a Moroccan literary tradition and could be considered as the followers of the creators of *Souffles*, the revolutionary review, founded 1966 and banned in 1972, when its founder Abdellatif Laâbi was imprisoned. Claiming the invention of a "littérature portant le poids de [leur] réalités actuelles, des problématiques toutes nouvelles en face desquelles un désarroi et une sauvage révolte [les] poignent (literature bearing the burden of [their] contemporary realities, of new problems [they] are gripped by)." *Souffles* and the texts of its contributors – Tahar Ben Jelloun, Abdelkébir Khatibi, Mostapha Nissaboury, and Mohammaed Khaïr-Eddine, among others – caused a fundamental break with traditional conceptions of literature to allow for the expression of a different, bilingual, and bi-cultural self. See Abdellatif Laâbi, "Prologue," *Souffles* 1 (1966): 3–6, http://clicnet.swarthmore.edu/souffles/s1/1.html.

59   On the inscription of the country's memory as way to bring about change in the works of Houria Boussejra, see Valérie Orlando, "Les (E)cri(t)s des femmes du 'Nouveau Maroc': les romans de Houria Boussejra (Women's writing(s) of the 'New Morocco': the novels of Houria Boussejra)," *Expressions Maghrébines* 8.1 (Summer 2009): 85–104.

60   Redouane, 13–14. Translation from French to English is the author's.

61   Boussejra, 29.

62   The association between the mother and society is also an element of continuity between Boussejra's work and other Maghrebi Francophone literary texts, especially those written by men. Indeed, since its appearance, Maghrebi Francophone literature has largely displayed the figure of the mother as a source of memory and as a symbol of the castrating patriarchal society. For the theme of women and motherhood in Maghrebi Francophone literature, see Hédi Abdel-Jouad, "'Too Much in the Sun': Sons, Mothers, and Impossible Alliances in Francophone Maghrebian Writing," *Research in African literatures* 27.3 (Autumn 1996): 15–33, and Naïma Hachad, "Mère, mémoire, mort: célébration et sacrifice du corps maternel dans *La Mémoire tatouée*, *Le Livre du sang* et *Amour bilingue* d'Abdelkebir Khatibi (Motherhood, memory, death: Cele-

bration and sacrifice of the maternal body in *The tattooed memory, The book of blood, and Love in two languages* by Abdelkebir Khatibi)," *CELAAN Review* 9.2–3 (Fall 2011): 103–119.

63   Boussejra, 9.

64   On the relationship between mother and daughter and maternal violence in *Cérémonie*, see Marie-Bétrice Samzun, "*Cérémonie* de Yasmine Chami-Kettani, ou l'emergence d'une parole solennelle (*Ceremony*, by Chami-Kettani, or the emergence of a solemn word)," *Expressions Maghrébines* 8.1 (Summer 2009): 39–49.

65   Chami-Kettani, 59.

66   Boussejra, 29.

67   Oumassine, 17.

68   Boussejra, 12–13.

69   Ibid., 74.

70   Oumassine, 97; 102.

71   Ibid., 100.

72   Ibid., 72.

73   Chami-Kettani, 60.

74   Boussejra, 45–47.

75   For example, *Les impunis, ou les obsessions interdites* (Rabat: Editions Marsam, 2004).

76   Chami-Kettani, 68.

77   Ibid., 68.

78   Ibid., 71.

79   Ibid., 71.

80   Ibid., 9.

81   Ibid., 12.

82   Ibid., 13.

83   Ibid., 12.

84   Diaconoff, 19.

85   Orlanddo, 30.

86   Deborah Amos, "In Morocco, The Arab Spring's mixed Bounty," *National Public Radio* (February 2012), http://www.npr.org/2012/02/07/146526685/in-morocco-the-arab-springs-mixed-bounty.

87   Oumassine, 144.

88   This 26-year-old Tunisian man set himself on fire on December 17, 2010, to protest the confiscation of his wares and official brutality. His act is considered to be the catalyst of the Tunisian Revolution that led to the fall of president Ben Ali and the wider Arab Spring.

89   A 16-year-old Moroccan girl who committed suicide in March 2012 after a judge, in agreement with her parents, ordered her to marry her rapist.

90   Mona Eltahawy, "Why Do They Hate Us?" *Foreign Policy* (May–June 2012).

91   King Mohammed VI reformed the Moroccan Family Law in 2004. The new code establishes more equality between sexes in matters of marriage and divorce, restricts polygamy, and provides protection for single mothers. For an unofficial translation of the document in English online, see the website of the international non-governmental organization Human Rights Education Associates, http://www.hrea.org/moudawana.html.

92   On January 7, 2004, King Mohammed VI appointed Driss Benzekri, a former political prisoner (1974–1991), to head the newly formed Justice and Reconciliation Commission. Like the 1999 Indemnity Commission, the Justice and Reconciliation Commission accords blanket immunity from criminal prosecution to perpetrators and victims alike. It concentrates on identifying, verifying, and reporting the process of uncovering the truth about detention and secret torture sites during the Lead Years from the 1970's to 1990's.

93   Chami-Kettani, 23.

94   Ibid., 84.

95   Ibid., 84.

CHAPTER 7

Hegemonic Discourse in Orientalists' Translations of Moroccan Culture

Naima El Maghnougi

From the 1980s onwards, cultural as well as postcolonial turns in translation studies have had a considerable influence on literary translation and have marked a turning point in the field. The theory of translation has expanded from normative to descriptive studies, from dealing with translation as a purely linguistic transfer to viewing it as a metonymic transfer which involves cultural perspectives. According to Lefevere and Bassnett,[1] the study of translation has moved from a formalist approach toward larger issues of context, history, and convention. Literary translation, as they explain, has to be established in a certain context; this contextualization brings culture, politics, ideology, and power into view. In fact, the cultural model in translation studies has demonstrated that translation is not merely a matter of a linguistic transfer or a substitution of a source text by another target text, but rather a more complex cultural transposition of the translated text. Catford has described literary translation as a complex negotiation between two cultures.[2] Subsequently, all translation theories developed within the cultural paradigm have emphasized both the textual and extra-textual dimensions of translation; some of these theories have even highlighted the priority of extra-textual effects on the translator's strategies and decision-making in the process of translation. This approach enables translation theorists to relate translation to the historical, social, and cultural systems within which it occurs.[3] Translation, traditionally considered a secondary activity, turns out to have important functions in both the source and target cultures; translators are seen as powerful agents in the process of translation. The roles of the translator in cultural mediation, including questions regarding intervention and impartiality, are more recognized than before. Most importantly, the cultural turn introduces concepts such as patronage and ideology as major factors that may interfere, not only with the production and distribution of literary texts, but also with their rewriting and interpretation via translation. The cultural approach opens, then, new perspectives in understanding and analyzing literary translation by showing how:

> Complex manipulative textual processes take place: how a text is selected for translation, for example, what role the translator plays in the selection, what role an editor, publisher or patron plays, what criteria determine the strategies that will be employed by the translator, how a text might be received in the target system. For a translation never takes place in a vacuum, never in a void, and there are all kinds of textual and extra-textual constraints upon the translator.[4]

On another level, the postcolonial paradigm has widely shaped translation studies in the last decade and has given birth to a new trend in the field of translation: postcolonial translation studies. The postcolonial approach suggests that intercultural translations are to a great extent constrained by the manipulation of power relations between dominated and dominating cultures. Within this paradigm, the focus is more on the representations this discipline produces, the powers it serves, the cultural hierarchies it constructs, and the inequalities it consolidates. Accordingly, literary translation is seen as an important discursive means of maintaining and disseminating the imperial powers. In *Sitting Translations: Post-structuralism and the Colonial Context*, the prominent postcolonial critic Tisajwini Niranjana explains how asymmetry and inequality of relations between people, races, and languages have been widely maintained via Western literary translation and interpretation:

> The rethinking of translation becomes an important task in a context where it has been used since the European enlightment to underwrite practices of subjectification, especially for the colonized peoples. Such a rethinking – a task of great urgency for a postcolonial theory attempting to make sense of 'subjects' already living in 'translation,' imaged and re-imaged by colonial ways of seeing – seeks to reclaim the notion of translation by deconstructing it and re-inscribing its potential as a strategy of resistance.[5]

In 1978, Edward Said's ground-breaking work *Orientalism* promoted challenging views about the Western cultural encounter with the Orient, and Said powerfully redirected literary criticism and cultural studies.[6] Edward Said highlights the relationship between literary translation and representation of the Other: he explains that Western knowledge of the Orient relies primarily on the traveler's and Orientalist's textual construct of the native culture, and he argues that the hegemonic discourses that feed such accounts are also reflected in the Orientalist's textual translations of local culture.

It is almost impossible to study literary translations without considering the culture of translation and its politics, since they ultimately inform and shape both the production and reception of literary translation. Moreover, translation is not only a process of intercultural exchange and understanding between distant cultures but also a process of manipulation and submission to the hegemonic power of images and images of power created and nurtured by the Western culture during the colonial era as the only authentic representation of the Other. Drawing on Talal Asad's metaphor of "cultural translation," we can begin to see how Orientalists' and travelers' cultural and textual translations of Morocco are inscribed in a system of homogenizing and domesticating Moroccan culture so as to fit the discursive parameters of the dominant power and its poetics.[7] The foreignizing strategy Paul Bowles applies in his translation of Mrabet's tales, by emphasizing their exotic nature, does not preserve the foreign characteristics of these stories, but rather domesticates them according to his romantic representation of Moroccan culture. Analysis of Paul Bowles' translation shows that the selection of material that he chose to translate into English from Moroccan culture is highly manipulated to respond to his Orientalist and ethnographic conception of Morocco and its culture. His translation of Mrabet's oral stories *The Lemon*[8] and *Love with a Few Hairs*[9] demonstrates a hegemonic depiction of Tangiers and its natives and reflects the same romanticized and exoticized images of the barbarously primitive and decadent Morocco which Bowles invests in his own fiction and travelogues.

The Interaction of "Self" and "Other" in Cross-cultural Translations

Translating from culture to culture means, first and foremost, bringing to the receptors of translated texts from the target culture new facts and ideas inherent in the source culture. Accordingly, the receptor's cultural knowledge of the Other is significantly enriched, and the ability to comprehend and understand its cultural difference increases considerably. On another level, Abdessalam Ben Abdel Ali in his book في الترجمة (*On Translation*) explains that translation not only guarantees survival and continuity to the translated text, but also assures the survival and the growth of both language and thought.[10] This may also explain why translation increases substantially during the most flourishing eras of thought and literature, something evident in both Western and Arab cultural histories. During the eighth century CE, translations increased considerably during the rule of the Abbasid's Caliph of Baghdad, Al Mamoun, who built the famous Bayt al-Hikma or House of Wisdom where philosophers and scientists translated from Greek and Persian. A similar experience took place in Europe in the Renaissance Era; George Steiner explains the importance of translation in a time that was marked by significant political and social upheavals:

> At a time of explosive innovation ... translation absorbed, shaped, and oriented the necessary raw material. It was ... the matière premiere of the imagination. Moreover, it established a logic of relation between past and present, and between different tongues and traditions which were splitting apart under stress, nationalism, and religious conflict.[11]

Similarly, Anuradha Dingwaney's article "Translating 'Third World' Cultures"[12] highlights the importance of translation in cross-cultural exchanges and considers translation as the primary means "by which cultures travel": translation can open broader horizons for intercultural exchange and avoid us being confined "within the bounds of our own culture."[13] Anuradha recommends that translation enables alien cultures and languages to "interrogate" and allow the "Self" to be affected by the "Other" and thus "to be transformed and rendered more open to the claims of other languages and cultures."[14] Translation is then a fertile space where the "Self" culture encounters and interacts with the "Other" culture. Anuradha conceives of this reciprocal exchange as a necessary foundation for a successful translation between and across cultures.[15]

However, the cultural turn in translation studies has demonstrated that translation is a constraint-driven process in which different factors interfere at both the micro and macro levels. In addition to the difficulties encountered by translators in the linguistic transposition of a source text into a target text, because of the phonological, morphological, lexical, syntactical, pragmatic, and rhetorical differences that exist between languages, the cultural transposition of the source text can never be impartial or objective; rather, it is influenced by the cultural, ideological, and political affiliations of the translator and his/her subjectivity. What is more, it is believed that cross-cultural translation is never innocent and can, indeed, be manipulated to reinforce hegemonic discourses about cultures, especially in colonial and postcolonial conditions.

Viewed in this way, literary translation yields enormous power in constructing representations of foreign cultures. The intercultural encounter taking place through cross cultural translations between the West and its former colonies is conceived as the prime domain whereby the tensions of differing groups are manifested through the different modes of representation and different discourses. It shows how culturally defined discourses affect translation and how hegemonic discourses, especially in their discursive forms, become violent means of demarcating the Self from the Other. Accordingly, cross-cultural translation must be studied in connection with the target system and its poetics, with the cultural, ideological, and political discourses that feed it and have an important impact on the selection of the texts to be translated. Such a study may raise legitimate questions like: why are certain texts selected for translation at a given time and others ignored? Why was *The Thousand and One Nights* translated by Orientalists such as Antoine Galland, Richard Burton, and Edward Lane? Why did Fitzgerald choose to translate *Rubaiyat of Omar al-Khayyam* instead of any other Persian poetry? Why does Paul Bowles translate the oral tales of marginalized Moroccan story tellers? Edwin Gentzler tries to provide an answer to these inquiries as he points out:

> Subjects of a given culture communicate in translated messages primarily determined by local culture constraints. Inescapable infidelity is presumed as a condition of the process; translators do not work in ideal abstract situations or desire to be innocent, but have vested literary and cultural interests of their own, and want their work to be accepted within another culture. Thus they manipulate the source text to inform as well as to conform to existing cultural constraints.[16]

Edwin Gentzler mentions an inherent characteristic in literary translations, that the translated texts are strongly embedded in the cultural environment of the target culture and that the translator necessarily abides by prevailing aesthetics and ideologies, attempting to domesticate his translations to the needs of the receiving environment. Instead of domesticating foreign texts, some translators choose a foreignizing strategy in their translation; their alibi is preserving the foreign characteristics of the text, whether they are linguistic or cultural. The eighteenth-century German translator and philosopher Friedrich Schleiermacher, as André Lefevere explains in *Translation, History, Culture*, defends this strategy of foreignization because, according to him, if the translator "Moves the reader towards him ... his translation should therefore sound 'foreign' enough to its reader for that the reader to discern the workings of the original language ... the culture of which the original was a part."[17] However, the issue of domestication and foreignization in literary translations gains further prominence in Laurence Venuti's book *The Invisibility of the Translator: a History of Translation*.[18] According to Venuti, the translator's invisibility is the result of a domesticating strategy which the Anglo-American translators apply in order to "[a]chieve the linguistic and cultural adaptation of the source text in the target language, and hence produce a fluent and transparent text which will be easily read by the target public."[19] This domesticating strategy then dissolves the foreign characteristics of the translated text and makes it read coherently as if it were not really a translation. Venuti adds that any foreign text, before it crosses the cultural frontiers of the greeting system, has to submit to a "domestication revision"; this domestication also means that the selection of any source text has to conform to the domestic cultural values and aesthetics of the target culture, which usually entails a process of exclusion or admission of certain texts. Venuti argues that the domestication of literary translations is "[s]ymptomatic of a complacency in British and American relations with cultural others," a complacency which he describes as "imperialistic abroad and xenophobic at home."[20] Most importantly, Venuti believes that such translations are powerful enough to "[re]constitute and cheapen foreign texts, to trivialize and exclude foreign cultures, and thus potentially to figure in racial discrimination and ethnic violence, international political confrontation, terrorism, and war."[21]

Venuti's negative attitude towards Anglo-American tendencies in domesticating translations, and his preference for a foreignizing strategy instead, are contradicted, however, when we read him in a more recent publication, *Translation As Cultural Politics*, where he explains his stand clearly:

> What I am advocating is not an indiscriminate valorisation of every foreign culture or a metaphysical concept of foreignness as an essential value; indeed, the foreign text is privileged in a foreignizing translation only insofar as it enables a disruption of target-language cultural values, so that its values is always strategic, depending on the cultural formation into which it is translated.[22]

Venuti's focus is on the target culture, therefore, and his foreignized translation does not aim at preserving the foreign text as such, but his ultimate objective is to unsettle and subvert dominant values and patterns in the target context. Moreover, Venuti's foreignizing ethics in translating the Other can be achieved only in "domestic terms" and "domestic discourses and styles"; and "the linguistic and cultural differences of the foreign text can only be signaled through domestic difference into the values and institutions at home."[23]

Actually, the idea of affecting cultural change by means of translating foreign texts is also highlighted in Edwin Gentzler's article, "Translation, Counter-Culture, and the Fifties in the USA."[24] Gentzler explains that Bly's creative modern poetry, which he nourishes with "The trauma of the unconscious" and "The daring, the sensuousness, and savagery characteristics" of his images, is inspired by his translation of foreign poetry, and his innovative style in poetry enables him to disrupt the North-American verse which he finds "Rational and sterile."[25] Most importantly, Gentzler inscribes "The counter-cultural movement in the Sixties" led by Bly in the new tradition some American poets, writers, and translators adopted widely in translating foreign cultures and wonders:

> Why does Langston Hughes translate Lorca before most white Americans have heard of him? Why is Bly reading Spanish poets in the library at Oslo? What is Merwin doing in the mountains of Spain and Portugal, translating oral tales told by medieval *juglares* and passed on in ballad/oral form for centuries?[26]

Gentzler notices that the period of the sixties in the United States was marked by the American translators' interest in foreign oral cultures, fables, ballads, and tales which are "[t]empered by a folk tradition."[27] As a matter of fact, it is not a mere coincidence that Paul Bowles' translation of Moroccan oral stories happened in the same period to which Gentzler refers in this article, as well as in his book *Contemporary Translation Studies*, in which he argues that the new American tradition of translating foreign cultures is vividly encouraged by publishers in the United States, who prefer to publish "[a] Mayan/Guatemalan or North African/Berber text." Because, as Gentzler explains, "'It is open to interference' and contains 'foreignizing' elements."[28]

Cross-cultural Translations in Colonial/postcolonial Conditions

Edward Fitzerald, The English poet and translator of *Rubaiyat Al Khayam*, wrote to his friend E.B. Cowell in 1857: "It is an amusement to me to take what liberties I like with these Persians, who, as I think are not poets enough to frighten one from such excursions, and who really do want a little art to shape them."[29] André Lefevere relates this boastful declaration of Fitzerald to the Western treatment of texts originating from cultures which they conceive of as peripheral. Susan Bassnett, for her part, considers Fitzgerald's statement within the "master-servant relationship" existing between the source text and the translator; this hierarchical relationship, she argues, enables the translator to take total liberty in rewriting and shaping the translated text, simply because it originates from an "inferior" culture.[30] In fact, the asymmetry in power relations in the translational encounter between imperial cultures and the colonies' culture constitutes the core of the postcolonial approach to translation studies. Because, as Bassnnet and Trivedi assert in *Postcolonial Translation: Theory and Practice*, the postcolonial approach to literary translation perceives Western translation as a "one-way process" which targets the translation of native texts for "European consumption, rather than as a part of a reciprocal process of exchange."[31] Most importantly, Bassnett and Trivedi recognize that colonialism and translation go hand in hand and that they are "[t]he central act of European colonization and imperialism in America."[32] As a matter of fact, the emergence of a postcolonial theory in translation is quite justified:

> In the postcolonial period, when the empire writes back it is not surprising to find radical concepts of translation emerging from India, from Latin America, from Canada, from former colonies around the world that challenge established European norms about translation.[33]

The reconsideration of literary translation in colonial and postcolonial conditions is, in fact, unavoidable since these translations constitute an interesting component of the Western literary canon that is highly exploited to produce and maintain the hegemonic colonial discourses of the West vis-à-vis the natives. Moreover, translation, as demonstrated by postcolonial translation studies, is manipulated to reinforce colonial rule. In this respect, Edward Said argues that translation serves colonizing policies in two ways: On the one hand, it makes strategic knowledge about the colonies and their inhabitants available to officers and militaries, and on the other hand, the West relies on translation to legitimate its power and enhance the hegemonic cultural representation of the natives as a means to contain them and subjugate them under colonial rule.[34] Said argues that translation has widely misinterpreted and misrepresented Oriental cultures, especially Islamic culture, and has caused what he calls "cultural antipathy." Accordingly, Said inscribes Orientalists' literary translation in the Western project of domesticating the Orient to "[t]hereby turn it into province of European learning."[35] Translation, according to Edward Said, helps Western Orientalists to "gather in" and "rope off" the Orient.[36]

Talal Asad draws the same relationship between British ethnographers' cultural translation and their textual translations. Asad considers these translations through the unequal relations of power existing between "[t]he anthropologist, who typically belongs to a powerful culture, and the natives he or she writes about and 'translates,' who are typically illiterate or at least belonging to less powerful cultures than the anthropologist's."[37] Asad argues that the ethnographer in such conditions of power is "accorded authority to uncover the implicit meanings of subordinate societies" in the process of his cultural translation.[38] What is more, Asad believes that "[t]he representation/translation that the ethnographer as a 'cultural translator' produces of a particular culture is inevitably a textual construct."[39] He adds that this textual construct, usually presented as scientific text, gains privilege and may be retranslated in a third world language "and influence the mechanism of self-representation within that language/culture."[40] This intricate relationship between translation and ethnography and its power in constructing the image of the Other also underpins Niranjana's analysis of literary translation within the colonial project. Niranjana suggests that translation both shapes and takes shape "within the asymmetrical relations of power that operate under colonialism";[41] and argues that in the postcolonial context, translation has become a significant site for raising questions of representation, power, and historicity. Niranjana explains that the asymmetry and inequality in relations between people, races, and languages has been widely maintained not only in Western translation and interpretation but also in other disciplines such as history and anthropology: "The practice of subjection / subjectification implicit in the colonial enterprise operate not merely through the coercive machinery of the imperial state but also through the discourses of philosophy, history, anthropology, philology, linguistics, and literary interpretation."[42]

To admit that the politics of stressing the hegemonic image about the Arabs in the Orientalists' translations belong to the past is, indeed, a big illusion because, as Edward Said points out in *Culture and Imperialism,*

> Appeals to the past are among the commonest of strategies in interpretations of the present. What animates such appeals is not only disagreement about what happened in the past and what the past was, but uncertainty about whether the past is really past, over and concluded, or whether it continues, albeit in different forms, perhaps.[43]

Translation is a process of manipulation and submission to the hegemonic power of images created and nurtured by the target culture as the authentic representation of the Other. Unfortunately, what Orientalists started in the nineteenth century CE and continued through the twentieth century CE and even now in the twenty-first; Paul Bowles' translation of Moroccan oral tales provides strong evidence for this reality.

Inhabiting the Exotic in Paul Bowles' Translations of Moroccan Culture

Tangiers played a major role in Paul Bowles' actual birth as a writer. However, he was by no means the first traveler to Tangiers, and no doubt the experiences of the writers and artists of different nationalities who visited Morocco affected him. Contextualizing the experiences of Bowles alongside those of other travelers suggests that he did not arrive innocently upon the scene. Rather, he was attracted by the mysticism and exoticism in the portrayals of the city by other foreign travelers, ethnographers, writers, and artists. Actually, what demarcates Tangiers from the rest of the Moroccan cities is its history as an international and cosmopolitan city, colonized by several nations at once. It was known to fascinate Western visitors. Speaking about what attracted the majority of Westerners to this beautiful city, Mohammed Laamiri says:

> Tangier is the place where dreams of exotic pleasures are realized and fulfilled ... Tangier is a place for the gratification of the senses, ranging from wandering in tortuous narrow streets, to drinking mint-tea and smoking illegal substances in old cafes, to visiting exotic spaces and lingering along its beach.[44]

Laamiri argues that Tangiers' image has been widely affected by the generations of tourists, especially artists of various media, who have "[c]ulturally transformed the city into an exotic space." According to him, "Tangier made Paul Bowles, but Paul Bowles contributed to the making of international cultural fame of the city."[45] Laamiri points out that what is interesting about Paul Bowles' choice of spaces in his narratives is their distinctive, exotic attraction.[46] Likewise, Allen Hibbard asserts in *Paul Bowles, Magic & Morocco* that Tangiers for Bowles was a place of novelty, surprise, and magic, and that he was somehow "under the spell of Tangier."[47] Hence, Bowles' curiosity was triggered by the charm of this Moroccan city and its inhabitants; Allen explains that Bowles was like an anthropologist who enjoyed watching the behavior of the Moroccan natives because he considered them like "[a]ctors performing a theatrical play; Each Moroccan gave the impression of playing a part in a huge drama."[48] Moreover, Bowles' awareness of the exotic and his desire to inhabit it are clearly expressed in his autobiography *Without Stopping*: "My curiosity about alien cultures was avid and obsessive. I had a placid belief that it was good for me to live in the midst of people whose motives I did not understand."[49] Bowles' statement echoes what his compatriot, Mark Twain, had written on his first visit to Morocco. Sixty years before Bowles' first visit, Mark Twain wrote this: "Tangier is the spot we have been longing for all the time ... we wanted something thoroughly and uncompromisingly foreign ... and lo! In Tangier we have found it."[50]

Talking to Daniel Halpern about his interest in Tangiers, Bowles says, "I'm merely trying to call people's attention to something they don't seem to be sufficiently aware of"[51] and to make them question their basic assumptions. The aim is to "[a]ffect the reader's dislocation," as Bowles states. The dislocation of the reader is realized, then, by the tropes of kif, magic, spells, and trance dances which are recurrent elements in Paul Bowles' short stories and novels. All of these defamiliarizing tools are, in fact, what enable the romantic writer to free his mind from the interference of reason and to journey far away into the magic of Tangiers. As a matter of fact, it is almost impossible to consider Bowles' artistic experience in Tangiers without invoking his Orientalism. Indeed, Bowles' attempt to "disclose" the secrets of Tangiers boosted his literary talents and inspired most of his abundant literary productions during his stay in that city. *The Delicate Prey, A Distant Episode*, and his first novel, *The Sheltering Sky*, which hit the bestseller list, are all organized around the experience of living in Tangiers. Bowles' narratives take readers to places and experiences beyond the ordinary. He presents Tangiers as "an Arabian poem." It is, indeed, an "Orientalist fantastic dream." Bowles' romantic and orientalist attitude towards Tangiers is further consolidated by his desire to retain the primitive natural beauty of Moroccan cities and keep them undamaged by Western modernization.

Bowles, in his preface to his novel *Spider House*, implicitly objects to the government interest in the modernization of Fez. He fears that the Moroccan cultural forms he admires will be eradicated by the nationalists' desire to be European and modern.

> I wanted to write a novel using as backdrop the traditional daily life of Fez, because it was a medieval city functioning in the twentieth century. If I had started it only a year sooner, it would have been an entirely different book. I intended to describe Fez as it existed at the moment of writing about it ... I soon saw that I was going to have to write, not about the traditional pattern of life in Fez, but about its dissolution.[52]

Bowles' obsession with the traditional and primitive features of Moroccan cities is no doubt a romantic obsession with everything that is raw and not transformed by modernity. This may lead one to think that if Bowles translates the oral stories from recordings of oral performances in Moroccan dialect and not from written sources, it is because he believes that the illiteracy of the storytellers with whom he collaborated protects the primitive and exotic ambiance of the oral stories and keeps them as if they had been handed down from past memories of popular culture in Morocco.

Bowles collaborated with a number of illiterate Moroccan storytellers and writers such as Larbi Layachi, Mohamed Mrabet, and Mohamed Choukri. The relationship Bowles had with these Moroccans was not only based on friendship and cooperation; these cultural contacts were on some level also sexually charged and connected to their collective enjoyment of kif and hashish. Layachi, Mrabet, and Choukri were raised in desperate poverty and deprivation and survived the drudgery of miserable jobs before they began to earn their living as writers. All of their narratives relate to their experiences of surviving at the periphery of Tangiers' economic and intellectual life. They all speak from the margins of Moroccan society, sites of interest for Bowles. According to the works of these authors, kif, magic, and trances are alienating and powerful agents that produce lonely and criminal subjects. The presence of kif reinforces altered states of consciousness, a trip outside time and space to free their minds from the interference of reason; kif is used as a means to move outside the ties of the real world. Abdeslam, one of Mrabet's protagonists in *The Lemon*, is depicted under the effect of kif:

> The kif was making him feel very heavy, and he heard a roar like the sea in the back of his head. He wanted to stretch out on his bed ... As he lay there looking upwards with his hands folded over his chest like a dead man, he lost track of time as it went by, and he forgot where he was.[53]

Why does Bowles direct his interest to translating the oral stories of an unknown Moroccan story teller such as Mohamed Mrabet? Of course, no one can deny that this collaboration might satisfy the egocentrism of Bowles vis-à-vis the marginalized storyteller and the economic power he has over him, but in reality this is not the only thing that attracts Bowles' attention to the oral narratives. Rather, it is the image they reflect about Moroccan culture and its people. These oral stories depict Moroccan society as a place of magic, sorcery, prostitution, hashish, sexual deviation, and violence. Most of Mrabet's protagonists are attracted to kif-smoking, drinking, and sex. They meet women, residents of brothels, and European men with whom they live as lovers. In many of the stories, prostitutes attempt to poison the protagonists, who use violence to take revenge. In *The Lemon*, Abdeslam meets a dockworker named Bachir who takes Abdeslam to his house. Later, however, Bachir becomes an adversary when, in a drunken frenzy, Bachir tries to force Abdeslam into his bed. Abdeslam tries to get away, and he slashes Bachir's face open with razors embedded in a lemon in his hand.[54] Perhaps not coincidentally, Mohamed Mrabet's voice matches that of Bowles in his own fiction: Mrabet confirms the strange, violent, and erotic aspects of Paul Bowles' Tangiers, and seems to justify Bowles' own characters' preoccupation with kif-smoking, sexuality, indolence, witchcraft, and spells.

Paul Bowles' literary collaboration with Moroccan storytellers was greeted with strong criticism among Moroccan intellectuals. His translation of Laarbi Layachi's autobiography *A Life Full of Holes* was strongly criticized by Moroccan intellectuals. Abdellah Laaroui writes that "Bowles may have thought he had grasped Moroccan life at its most authentic, but what has he grasped other than his own fantasies?"[55] Tahar Ben Jelloun published an attack on Bowles'collaboration with Mrabet in the French daily *Le Monde* and described it as a violation: Ben Jelloun suggests that the translations are Bowles' "own writing in disguise," and that everything is wrong in this enterprise.[56] In this regard, Brian T. Edwards points out:

> Bowles' interest in and devoted representation of folk culture, Berber musical forms, and the underbelly of Moroccan society troubled many Moroccan intellectuals. The very themes that drew many American readers to Bowles's work – especially magic, danger, and the primitive – were the themes that frustrated Moroccans, who apparently saw in Bowles's attention a devaluing of the Moroccan nationalist project.[57]

Edwards confirms the idea that these stories are aimed at the Anglo-American audience, yet at the same time the stories suggest that Moroccan storytellers are also aware of the audience, whether Bowles himself or the wider audience in the United States, and that this awareness has shaped their stories significantly. However, we cannot be certain about stories delivered orally to the translator: we have lost the original story-telling situation and cannot reconstruct it from the traces in the text. Actually, much suspicion has been triggered by the literary collaboration of Mrabet and Bowles not only because of Mrabet's illiteracy, which affects communication between him and Bowles, but also because of the power relations between them. The illiteracy of Mrabet gives Bowles more power in interpreting, reconstructing, and rewriting his stories, and thus gives him more control over the translated texts. Moreover, Bowles' ambivalent attitude towards his role as a translator and editor of the stories gives rise to yet more doubt about their authorial authenticity: in *Love with a Few Hairs*, Mrabet's first collaboration with Bowles is listed as being translated and edited by Paul Bowles. Their second novel, *The Lemon*, is described as having been translated from the Moroccan dialect Arabic and edited by Paul Bowles in collaboration with Mohammed Mrabet. Similarly, the title pages in all these books ignore Bowles' efforts to tape and then transcribe oral tales into written language.[58]

Issues of authority and communication in Bowles' literary collaboration with Mrabet are indeed controversial. Bowles translates Mrabet's stories from tapes recorded in Moroccan dialectal Arabic, Riffian, and Spanish which Mrabebt usually used while recounting his stories; this means that Bowles would have had to do much work to produce the final translated written version of Mrabet's oral stories. Bowles' translation then evolves through a process of recording, transcribing, and translating. In this case, the act of transferring the oral text to a written one is strongly mediated by the translator, and Mrabet's stories had certainly undergone many modifications, omissions, and additions before Bowles could edit them.[59] This aspect shows the authority Bowles had over Mrabet's stories and enhances the inequalities in the power relations between an American translator and a Moroccan storyteller. The incommunicability of the literary collaboration of Mrabet and Bowles is further reinforced by the untranslatability of certain Moroccan Arabic words which Bowles retains in their original form, including "mahal," "jotia," "Mejdoub," "Fqih," "haik," "mandoubia," "Oukil eddoula," "taifor," "fasoukh," "djaoui," and "tsouk." The same terms also figure in Bowles' own stories. This suggests either that their cultural meaning cannot be rendered adequately in English or that Bowles, by allowing the Moroccan colloquial word to figure in the standardized American text, wants to challenge the mainstream language by introducing foreign vocabulary. In sum, Bowles' translation of Mrabet's stories does not guarantee the communicability of their literary collaboration, on the one hand because it operates within unequal cultural power relations and on the other hand because the intercultural exchange between Bowles and Mrabet is obstructed by their disparate linguistic backgrounds.

Love With a Few Hairs / *The Lemon:*
A Site for Hegemonic Representations of Moroccan Natives

Love with a Few Hairs is the first product of Bowles' collaboration with Mrabet, published in 1967. The protagonist of this short novel, a young Moroccan named Mohammed, develops an interest in a young woman named Amina with whom he falls in love at first sight. Unfortunately, after he behaves unacceptably towards Amina at the cinema, she rebukes him and ceases to trust him. Mohamed then goes to a witch in Bni Makada for a magic potion that will make Amina reciprocate his interest and affection. For the potion, the witch says, "You will have to bring me a piece of something she's worn or a few of her hairs. One or the other."[60] When Mohammed returns with a few of Amina's hairs, the witch pulls out a cloth sack and begins to search through it for things: packets of herbs and envelopes full of fingernails, teeth, and bits of dried skin. She shakes these things out onto a sheet of paper, along with Amina's hair. Mohamed, following the instructions of the witch, pours the powder in front of the door of Amina's house. The effect of the spell soon manifests itself, and Amina succumbs to Mohammed's advances; eventually they marry. Unfortunately, this plotted happiness soon transforms into an unpleasant drama. Amina's mother seeks help from a witch named Lalla Mariam who, to undo the spell, prepares a powder that Amina's mother sprinkles on the coals of the brazier in Mohammed and Amina's home. The spells are undone, and Mohammed separates from Amina. In revenge, Amina calls upon her women friends to aid her in a plot to poison Mohamed. On discovering Amina's plan, Mohammed enters a state of despair, but with the help of David, the English Nazarene with whom Mohammed lives and has a homosexual relationship, he decides to give up his love for Amina completely.

The Lemon is the story of a twelve-year-old Moroccan boy, Abdeslam, who wanders through his village after his father throws him out of the house. First, Abdeslam is invited by a welcoming Nazarene family, but after few days of living with them, he decides to lead his own life and goes to Tangiers. There he meets a drunkard longshoreman, Bachir. Still an innocent child, Abdesalam is not mindful of Bachir's homosexual advances. It is Aicha, the prostitute Bachir often brings home, who warns him of Bachir's intentions. Upon listening to the warnings of several women, Abdesalam becomes aware of Bachir's dangerous and aggressive tendencies; Abdesalam then leaves Bachir and gets a job in Si Moukhtar's café. When Bachir persistently pursues Abdesalam, the young boy takes a terrible revenge upon him. With a razor fixed in a lemon, he slashes the face of Bachir, who finally collapses under this determined attack.

The coexistence of Moroccans and Europeans in Tangiers is one inherent feature of this postcolonial city. However, the hierarchical organization of social relations between "Nazarenes" and the Moroccans in Mrabet's stories is highly informed by an hegemonic dichotomy: while the European citizens are associated with wealth, education, and rationality, Moroccan natives are on the contrary depicted as illiterate, irrational, poor, dirty, and dependent on the Europeans to earn their living. For some Moroccans, the Europeans are held up as exemplary models to follow, as in the example of *Love With a Few Hairs*, where Mohammed, the protagonist, works in the bar of an English settler, and his father ironically advises him: "You should be like the Englishman ... He doesn't go out in the street drunk."[61] Mohammed, in his state of despair, reflects this same attitude when he claims that without his European companion, David, he would have been lost. "He would say to himself, I'm lucky to have a friend who understands the world. He pulled me back when I was at the edge."[62]

The translated stories of Mrabet are exotic wares created for export and cultural artifacts for Bowles to exploit. The detailed descriptions of Moroccan cultural phenomena, the exaggerated sensuality of Moroccan figures, and the religious fanaticism of the characters are dominant aspects of the novels. In *The Lemon*, Bowles reports in detail a scene with the smell of incense, the sound of frenetic drumming, and the sight of a woman dancing for a crowd: an atmosphere of exotic behavior for Bowles' intended audience:

> The man had pulled off his Jellaba and shirt and was jumping up and down, naked to the waist. The other Aissaoua were busy bringing in armloads of cactus and thorn bush, pilling them in the centre of the courtyard. Soon there was a great mound. The man rushed over to the plants and began to trample them down, and then to dance on top of them. Then he lay down and rolled back and forth. In the end most of the needles were broken off in his flesh. Then he stood up, and they brought him fresh cactus to chew on. When his mouth was full of blood he began to growl and bellow like a camel, and froth ran down his chin. The leader stood up with a cudgel in his hand; he waved it at the man as if he were a camel, crying out the words a camel driver uses when he wants to keep a camel from walking into a crowd of people.[63]

A similarly exotic scene is depicted in Love With a Few Hairs during a ceremony for Driss, Mohammed and Amina's newborn baby. Mohammed is shown as an exorcist or a vampire who enjoys drinking animals' blood:

> The fqih seized one of the rams by its horns and Mohammed took hold of its body. Bismillah! Allah o akbar ala Driss! The fqih cried. He ran the knife across its neck, and the animal fell. Mohammed had set a glass nearby. Quickly he put it besides the sheep's neck and filled it with the blood that was coming out. While the ram was still living he drank it.[64]

Moreover, Paul Bowles' narratives show the beliefs of his characters in the supernatural, magic, and sorcery. In these stories, magic is used to interpret all of the behavior of Moroccan characters. It not only influences the course of events but also shapes their lives and destinies. To win Mina's love, Mohammed in *Love With a Few Hairs* seeks the help of a witch in Beni Makada whom his friend Mustapha introduces to him, an old woman wrapped in rags who prepares a love potion:

> She pulled out a cloth sack and began to search through it for things: packets of herbs and envelopes full of fingernails and teeth and bites of dried skin. She shook things out onto a sheet of paper, along with Mina's hair. Then over it all she poured a powder that looked like dirt. She folded everything inside the paper and put it into a tin. A long string of words kept coming out of her mouth. She threw benzoin onto the hot coals of the brazier and she put the tin in the center of the fire, stirring it for a long time until it all had become a black powder.[65]

Furthermore, both of the translated novels are overcharged with the sensuality of Mrabet's characters, including erotic heterosexual and homosexual scenes. In *Lemon*, Mohammed becomes a constant companion to Mr. David: "Mohammed had decided that during the next few days he would spend all his time with Mr. David, eating with him, drinking and sleeping with him, and going with him wherever he wanted him to go."[66] Whether or not Mrabet intended to provide a sexually-charged image of Morocco by portraying the sexual lives of his Moroccan characters remains debatable. However, Bowles' interest in translating Mohamed Mrabet's stories seems to be based primarily on an Orientalist perception of Moroccan culture and people.

Conclusion

Bowles' focus on Moroccan oral culture in these works reflects his essentialism towards Moroccan culture. The negative charge behind it is that it assumes a fixed and ahistorical essence of identity for the other. Such a fixed and ahistorical essence or identity of the other is pervasive in ethnographic writing. Even if Bowles has mastered Moroccan traditions, he is still a carrier of English language and American authority which is "[i]nscribed in the institutionalized forces of industrial capitalist society, which are constantly tending to push the meanings of various Third World societies in a single direction."[67] Bowles performs the role of mediator between the oral and the written, Arabic and English, but he does not contextualize the meaning of Mrabet's stories nor the alien culture in their Postcolonial environment. Instead, the heterogeneous aspect of Moroccan identities is jeopardized and homogenized by Paul Bowles' essentialism. The literary collaboration that Bowles engaged in by translating a Moroccan postcolonial storyteller's stories makes his work a rich source for a discussion of cross-cultural translation and asymmetry of power.

Notes

1   Susan Bassnett, *Translation Studies* (London & New York: Routledge, 1980); André Lefevere, *Translation, Culture, History* (London & New York: Routledge, 1992).

2   J.C. Catford. A Linguistic Theory of Translation: An Essay in Applied Linguistics (London: Oxford University Press, 1965).

3   Edwin Gentzler, *Contemporary Translation Theories* (Clevedon: Multilingual Matters, 2001), 119.

4   Susan Petrilli, *Translation, Translation* (Amsterdam: Rodopi, 2003), 433.

5   Tisajwini Niranjana, *Siting Translation: History, Post-Structualism, and the Colonial Context* (Berkeley: University of California Press, 1992), 4.

6   Edward Said, *Orientalism* (New York: Pantheon, 1978).

7   Talal Asad, "The Concept of Cultural Translation in British Social Anthropology," in *Critical Readings in Translation Studies*, ed. Mona Baker (London & New York: Routledge, 2010).

8   Mohamed Mrabet, *The Lemon*, trans. Paul Bowles (Fez: Moroccan Cultural Studies, 2006).

9   Mohamed Mrabet, *Love with a Few Hairs*, trans. Paul Bowles (Fez: Moroccan Cultural Studies, 2004).

10   Abdessalam Ben Abdel Ali, في الترجمة (Casablanca: Toubkal, 2006), 32.

11   Bassnett, 1980, 58.

12   Anuradha Dingwaney, "Translating 'Third World Cultures.'" *Between Languages and Cultures: Translation and Cross-Cultural Texts*. Eds. Dingwany Anuradha & Carol Maier. (Pittsburg: Pittsburg Press, 1995).

13   Ibid.

14   Ibid.

15   Ibid, 6–7.

16   Edwin Gentzler, *Contemporary Translation Theories*. (Clevedon: Multilingual Matters, 2001), 134.

17   André Lefevere, *Translation, Culture, History* (London & New York: Routledge, 1992).

18   Laurence Venuti, "Translation As Cultural Politics," in *Critical Readings In Translation Studies*, ed. Mona Baker (London & New York: Routledge, 2010).

19 Ibid.

20 Ibid, 13–14.

21 Ibid, 68.

22 Ibid., 78.

23 Ibid., 65.

24 Edwin Gentzler, "Translation, Counter Culture, and the Fifties in the USA," in *Translation, Power, Subversion*, eds. Roman Alvarez & Vidal Carmen-Africa (Clevedon: Multilingual Matters, 1996).

25 Ibid., 128.

26 Ibid.

27 Ibid., 132.

28 Edwin Gentzler, *Contemporary Translation Theories* (Clevedon: Multilingual Matters, 2001), 143.

29 Lefèvre, 1992, 3.

30 Susan Bassnett, *Translation Studies* (London & New York: Routledge, 1980), 3.

31 Susan Bassnett & Harish Trivedi, eds, *Post-Colonial Translation: Theory and Practice* (London: Routledge, 1999), 5.

32 Ibid.

33 Ibid., 3.

34 Said, 1978, 2.

35 Ibid.

36 Ibid., 78.

37 Asad, 27.

38 Ibid., 27.

39 Ibid., 7–8.

40 Ibid., 7–8.

41 Tisajwini Niranjana. *Sitting Translations: History, Post-structuralism, and the Colonial Context.* (Berkeley: University of California Press, 1992), 2.

42 Ibid., 1.

43 Edward, Said. *Culture and Imperialism.* (London: Random House, 1993), 1.

44 Mohammed Laamiri, "Tangier's Appeal and Western Voices: Between Geographical Nearness and Cultural Remoteness," in *Voices of Tangier*, eds. Khalid Amine, Andrew Hussy, & Barry Tharaud (Tangier: Abdelmalek Saidi and Wales Universities, 2006), 7.

45 Ibid., 8.

46 Ibid.

47 Allen Hibbard, *Paul Bowles: Magic & Morocco.* (California: Cadmus Editions, 2004), 1.

48 Ibid.

49 Bouchra Benlemlih. *Inhabiting the Exotic: Paul Bowles and Morocco*. A Doctorate Thesis. (London: Nottingham University, 2009), 60.

50 Ibid., 65.

51 Hibbard, 146.

52 Preface, 1.

53 Bowles, 95.

54 Ibid., 179–181.

55 Brian Edwards profile. Retrieved 3rd June 2010. www.english.northwestern.edu/people/Edwards%20article.pdf.

56 Bouchra Benlemlih, *Inhabiting the Exotic: Paul Bowles and Morocco*, Doctoral Thesis, Nottingham University, London, 2009.

57 Edwards, 20.

58 Ibid.

59 Ibid.

60 Mrabet, 7.

61 Mrabet, 2004, 1.

62 Ibid., 120.

63 Mrabet, 2006, 57.

64 Mrabet, 2004, 65.

65 Ibid., 9.

66 Ibid., 36.

67 Asad, 1986, 163.

CHAPTER 8

The Countercultural, Liberal Voice of Moroccan Mohamed Choukri and Its Affinities with the American Beats

Anouar El Younssi

Moroccan society throughout the twentieth century CE was fairly conservative and heavily influenced by Islamic tradition. A significant amount of literature – especially that penned in Arabic – published in Morocco in the last century manifested a tendency that avoided flouting, in any significant way, the social and religious norms prevalent in the country. A number of writers addressed issues of public concern, such as poverty; (illegal) immigration; corruption; the legacy of Franco-Spanish colonialism; Moroccan subjectivity, memory, and imaginary; and others. In particular, literature criticizing or responding to the former colonizers – especially the French – and the legacy of the colonial era abounded in Morocco post-1956. Moroccan writer Mohamed Choukri provides a curious case within this paradigm. His writing trajectory is characterized by rebellion, counterculture, and controversy. In his attempts to address the social ills within Moroccan society post-Independence, he produced a literature somehow different from that of his contemporaries, a literature that is audaciously non-conformist and highly controversial. Choukri's works broke many societal taboos within Morocco and beyond. In a very liberal way, his books – especially his autobiographies – explore in a rather crude way controversial issues pertaining to sex, masturbation, prostitution, drugs and alcohol, and religious critique. One is tempted to raise the following query: *How* and, more importantly, *why* does Choukri go about treating such controversial issues, given the conservative leanings of his Moroccan society? This essay attempts to answer this two-sided question. I want to underscore that any investigation of Choukri's works must be carried out through a profound and critical investigation of his life. One cannot fully understand and appreciate Choukri's works without a prior knowledge of the writer's personal life and the state of Morocco at the time he was writing. This essay thus follows a *historicist* approach.

I argue that Choukri's unusual upbringing in northern Morocco played a major role in shaping his philosophy of life and the world, in addition to shaping the way he portrays life in Morocco in his texts. From his early childhood, Choukri had to deal with hardships, including poverty, hunger, domestic abuse and violence, child labor, homelessness, addiction to drugs and alcohol, male prostitution, imprisonment, and so forth. It is important to stress that Choukri grew up in Tangiers at a time when the city was an international zone controlled by a panoply of Western powers, the US included. As an international zone, Tangiers housed a number of Western artists and literary figures, such as the writers of the Beat Generation, some of whom Choukri had the opportunity to meet and befriend. Even though Choukri developed his own writing style and produced literary works in his own way, we can still speculate about the compelling possibility of foreign influences on the Moroccan author's literary trajectory. Published in 1973, his first autobiographical novel *Al-Khubz Al-Hafi* – translated as *For Bread Alone* by Paul Bowles – could arguably be seen as belonging to an ongoing, international, countercultural movement, and hence its broader significance.[1] Choukri, through *Al-Khubz Al-Hafi* and other works, could be construed as venturing on a literary countercultural move in Morocco – and, by extension, in the Arab-Muslim world – a move that, in some ways, interestingly resonates with that initiated by Western figures associated with the Beat Generation in the United States and elsewhere. Generally, Beat literature was markedly non-conformist and countercultural; it questioned the status quo – notably the culture of normativity and capitalist consumerism – and most importantly modernist literature and art. In the Moroccan city of Tangiers, Choukri made contact with writers and artists associated with the Beat Generation such as Jack Kerouac, Allan Ginsberg, William Burroughs, Paul Bowles, Brion Gysin, and others. Also, Choukri was familiar with the works of some, if not all, of these writers and artists. An investigation of the countercultural aspects of Choukri's writings would bring forth interesting resonances and connections with the works of the above Western figures. I will discuss this point further later on in this essay. My critical intervention will attempt to account for the controversy surrounding Choukri by giving a detailed outline of the controversial subjects treated in his works, examining the author's upbringing in northern Morocco, and exploring the possibility of foreign influences on his works.

I will now proceed to provide a survey of subjects treated in Choukri's works that caused controversy inside and outside literary circles in Morocco. Choukri, as a writer, is a notorious taboo-breaker, at least within his home country. His writings in general incorporate the characteristics of a typical non-conformist and an iconoclast. He steps outside the mainstream literary milieu in his surprising, liberal treatment of issues deemed immoral by societal standards, especially at the time when he started publishing in the 1960s. Choukri condemns the suppression of topics like sexual exploitation and prostitution from public discourse, and dismisses Moroccan society's attitude as hypocritical; he believes that society in general is aware of the fact that "immoral" and unacceptable acts are perpetuated by people on a daily basis and yet censors an honest and open discussion of this reality. In his various writings, Choukri refuses to submit to cultural dictates; he chooses instead to defy society's constraints by opening up an honest discussion of sexuality, homosexuality, masturbation, prostitution, drug consumption, alcoholism, and other societal taboos. In his three autobiographical novels, *Al-Khubz Al-Hafi (For Bread Alone)*,[2] *Zaman Al-Akhtaa (Streetwise)*,[3] and *Wujuh (Faces)*[4] material pertaining to sexuality abounds. The author recounts in detail his own sexual experiences and those of his entourage. In particular, he relates his encounters and dealings with prostitutes in different cities in northern Morocco, especially Tangiers. Interestingly, most of his female characters are prostitutes, both Moroccan and foreign.

Choukri gives the reader a detailed – almost pornographic – account of his life of promiscuity and alcoholism. In *For Bread Alone*, for instance, he details his first visit to a brothel, a visit that marks his first experimentation with sex. The kind of language he uses to describe that experience is deliberately crude and shocking, at least to the Moroccan sensibility. He writes that the prostitute he was assigned to "began to take off her clothes … Then she turned her back … and I unbuttoned her brassiere, my eyes on the sparse hairs in the furrow between her buttocks."[5] He maintains this vivid, pornographic description of the scene as follows:

> With agitation I unbuttoned my fly. My heart was pounding … This one [the prostitute] will let me go into her the way a knife goes into living flesh. I am going to stab what is between her thighs … She lay back on the bed like a pair of scissors and opened her / blades. It was shaved … She seized my sex in her hand … She wet her fingers on her tongue and moved her hand down to the other mouth [the vagina]. Put it in now … Cautiously I entered her, sinking into her slippery mouth.[6]

Needless to say, the kind of language in the quotation is offensive to a Moroccan, Muslim sensibility, perhaps particularly in the early 1970s when *For Bread Alone* was published. In the quotation above, we note how Choukri curiously mixes crude sexual content with violent metaphors, thereby increasing the effect on the reader. He equates the act of love-making with that of stabbing "living flesh" with "a knife"; he imagines his penis as a knife cutting through the prostitute's vagina. He sees the prostitute's thighs as "a pair of scissors" and her vagina as consisting of two "blades." The various metaphors Choukri chooses all connote violence; both male and female sexual organs are portrayed as sharp, potentially harmful, tools. One could say that the shock effect generated in the quotation is two-dimensional: the Moroccan reader is initially shocked by the very nature of the subject matter (i.e. sexual intercourse), and is shocked a second time by the violent metaphors embellishing the sexual activity being described. The second dimension of the shock might extend to readers even outside Morocco and the Arab-Muslim world because of the pornographic description and the disturbing nature of the metaphors employed. The violent connotations in Choukri's language may reflect his violent, rough life – both at home and on the street. Young Choukri was constantly abused, emotionally and physically, by his father at home and by adults and other boys on the street after becoming homeless. Violence was a daily reality with which he had to cope, and so it may not be a surprise that he depicts a sexual experience in violent terms.

Choukri recounts how his promiscuity intensified after he left Tetouan for Tangiers. In Tangiers, he started to mingle with male and female prostitutes, pimps, drunks, thieves, alcoholics, drug dealers, drug addicts, and so on. This entourage was anything but pleasant. As noted above, Choukri lived an extremely rough life, especially before he gained recognition as a writer. He lived on the margin of society and had to deal with the underworld of Tangiers for several years. To return to the sexual taboos in *For Bread Alone*, in one instance the narrator recounts having sex with one of his female roommates, who, not surprisingly, takes prostitution as a profession. Choukri remains faithful to his writing trajectory by offering the reader a very crude, pornographic description of the sex scene that again incorporates different metaphors:

> I licked the hard nipples. Then with delight I began to suck on her right breast, filling my mouth with it ... Then with a smile she unbuttoned my fly. The blind dragon [the penis] rose up and stood rigid in her hand. She smoothed it briefly from its head to its roots, and set to work rubbing it against the lip between her legs. The hairs of the black triangle there are as rough as those on her scalp. The dragon feels the roughness as he scrapes his bald head on them.[7]

Despite the use of euphemisms, the language in the passage remains highly shocking to the Moroccan audience. The description of the sex scene is anything but romantic. Choukri seems to insist on incorporating crude sexual content in his works.

He does not feel inhibited in exploring topics his Moroccan society seems to insist on suppressing. In *For Bread Alone* still, Choukri even refers in passing to a scene of love-making between his parents; he writes that, on one occasion, he penetrated a prostitute and she, out of pain, cried "Ay, ay, ay! Not that way," and then remarks that he remembered once his "mother telling [his] father: Not like that! Like this!"[8] We should note in this regard that Choukri's reference to his parents' intercourse is provocative and offensive to a Muslim sensibility, a sensibility that holds parents' status to be quasi-sacred. Respect for and obedience to parents are pressing injunctions in Islamic scriptures, and are therefore taken very seriously by the Moroccan, Muslim community. Few writers in the Arab-Muslim World would dare make such a countercultural move. Choukri's allusion to his parents' sex life paints him as a notorious, "shameless" – even insane – writer.

Two other related taboos which surface in Choukri's texts are homosexuality and (male) prostitution. Even today, these two subjects are, to a large extent, not openly discussed by the Moroccan public. Choukri disrupts this paradigm. He reveals, for instance, that while young and desperate for money and food, he would prostitute himself. In *For Bread Alone*, we learn that, on one occasion, sixteen-year-old Choukri is being solicited for oral sex by an old Spaniard. This incident takes place when Choukri is a homeless vagabond, and, therefore, easy prey for sex predators. Choukri describes the incident with the Spaniard thus:

> From a car an old man was signaling to me ... He opened the door and said to me in Spanish: Get in. I got in and sat beside him ... He stopped the car in a dark section of the road ... With a caressing movement he runs his hand over my fly ... he unfastened the trousers, and my sex felt the warmth of his breath ... He began to lick it and touch it with his lips, and at the same time he tickled my crotch with his fingers ... / He took out his handkerchief and wiped his mouth ... He gave me fifty pesetas ...[9]

In addition to highlighting the homosexuality taboo, the scene offers an interesting case of postcolonial critique. The old Spaniard represents Spain/Europe/the West. His sexual exploitation of young Choukri could be read as a critique of Europe's colonial history and of colonial desire satiated through power. The scope and focus of this essay do not allow for pursuing this appealing subject of sexuality and postcolonial critique further, but it is worth mentioning in passing.

Though he draws on homosexuality and deals with homosexuals, Choukri's autobiographies also describe a number of sexual experiences with female prostitutes. In *For Bread Alone*, we read that he would regularly have sexual dreams about girls.[10]

When we look into his revelations and fantasies with regard to sex, we note that throughout his childhood and adult life, Choukri continued to long for and have sex with females. However, there is one scene in *For Bread Alone* where Choukri manifests a homosexual tendency. He speaks of his desire for an Algerian boy; he admits that he tries to have sex with the boy by force:

> The boy was handsome, and delicate as a girl. He wore shorts that came above his knees ... Then I persuaded him to smoke a cigarette and drink a little wine ... / We walked into a field of wheat. To be drunk is relaxing. His cheeks are pink, his lips bright red ... The wine ran through me, and I found myself trembling. My hand stroked his ... He made as if to rise. I seized his hand ... Before he could take his first step, I wrapped my arms around his legs ... I fell partially on top of him.[11]

This scene might paint Choukri not only as a homosexual but also as a rapist. Yet we have to caution the reader not to make any quick judgements. In other places in his writings, Choukri states explicitly that he was not a homosexual. For instance, in his biographies of Western authors who visited or lived in Tangiers, Choukri – the adult, mature writer – reflects on the homosexual tendencies of figures like Ginsberg, Kerouac, Burroughs, Bowles, and others. Interestingly, he clearly distances himself from their homosexual practices; he writes:

> They were writers and I still hadn't published my first story. I was immersed in reading the classics and Romantics, both Arabic and foreign. In the field of literature, I still had to sow my first seed, and I didn't share their tendency toward homosexuality. Later, I would realize that, in regard to his sexual orientation, Paul Bowles, like Jack Kerouac, is more discreet than the rest of them. But with Kerouac there was always the possibility that he would expose himself when drunk. Once, he stood up in a bar shouting, 'I fucked Gore Vidal.' In the forties and fifties, amongst writers and artists homosexuality was considered a kind of national sport, especially in the New York scene.[12]

While distancing himself from the homosexuality of the Beats, Choukri sought, sometimes with enthusiasm, their friendship and company. It is interesting how Choukri remarks that homosexuality was seen as a sort of "national sport" by the Beat writers. One might read this remark as offering some kind of justification for their homosexual leanings. Or it could be construed as an implicit critique. We're not quite sure how this remark is inflected.

A question must be asked: If Choukri so distances himself from those Westerners' homosexual tendencies, how are we then to account for his own desire for the Algerian boy in the previous quote? The scene described in that quote seems to complicate things because the passage hints at the boy's "feminine" posture: he is "delicate as a girl" and has pink cheeks and bright red lips. One might speculate that under the influence of wine and drugs, young Choukri might have imagined the boy an actual girl. By giving the boy attributes of femininity, Choukri seems to be implying that it wasn't his intention to have sex with the boy per se, and that the whole thing was a mistake. Greg Mullins affirms that a major task performed by Choukri's autobiography is "the consolidation of masculinity."[13] Mullins shows that, within Moroccan society, this "consolidation of masculinity" plays out through sexually dominating females and males alike. Mullins notes that Moroccan men raping other men doesn't paint them as "gays," but rather demonstrates their sexual advantage, which consolidates their virility.[14]

The same quote sheds light on another major taboo within Moroccan society, namely alcohol consumption. Alcohol is typically shunned in Muslim societies, at least formally. For instance, the mere mention of alcohol could cause embarrassment and discomfort at a typical family gathering. Yet in both *For Bread Alone* and *Streetwise*, there are multiple references to alcohol and alcoholics. Relating his first experience with wine, Choukri writes: "I drank wine for the first time, and was immediately ill ... I had no trouble the second time I tried wine."[15] Wine soon found its way into Choukri's daily life. Choukri and his friends would sit "around the table ... until five in the afternoon, mainly talking about the trouble in the streets as we drank our wine, smoked our kif ..."[16] By incorporating scenes of alcohol/wine consumption, Choukri breaks a major taboo and defies a Moroccan sensibility against the mention of alcohol. By no means does Choukri invent those scenes; they spring from his vivid recollections of a childhood marked by hardship and roughness.

Choukri, the writer, adopts a writing trajectory in line with the social realism trend in literature; he depicts what is happening in Moroccan society, focusing on its underworld, a marginalized group he knows only too well. Choukri presents the reader with his life of misery, promiscuity, and addiction unedited, not heeding society's reaction or censorship. Moroccan society, its ills, and "hypocrisy" post-Independence constitute his main points of critique. This proposition, in a way, answers the second part of the question posed earlier in the essay: Why does Choukri present a crude, harsh, dark portrayal of Moroccan society, and why do his writings find their *raison d'être* in breaking social taboos? Being an active social critic, at least indirectly through literature, Choukri observes his Moroccan–Tangieran, to be precise – society; sees how it harbors many wrongs; and decides to incorporate these wrongs in his works. In *Streetwise*, he avers in protest: "I wrote about everything that was wrong with the city [Tangiers]. I railed against it. The city's splendours that had once enchanted me were now drowned in hubbub and din."[17] The gloomy picture Choukri paints of Tangiers, as well as his own feelings of frustration and desperation in this quote, permeates his works. Choukri stresses that he does not include "the immoral" and "the crude" for their own sakes, but rather has a constructive goal. In an interview, he states that in his *Al-Khubz Al-Hafi*, he "present[s] immoral scenes in order to look for morality and ideals."[18] He adds that his major concern is why people "lose their human values."[19] Choukri was credited by some critics, notably for his unusual writing trajectory. Ferial Ghazoul, for one, notes in his essay "When the subaltern speaks":

> The Moroccan writer Mohamed Choukri is an exceptional figure: victim of the famine in the Rif where he was born in 1935, migrant to occupied Tangiers and Oran as a child and adolescent, he survived to tell a tale that many would rather not hear, because it represents the unspeakable horrors of cosmopolitan cities in the Third World.[20]

Drawing on cosmopolitan Tangiers, Choukri openly declares his crusade against the social ills he witnesses on a daily basis. He is utterly irritated by postcolonial Morocco and the state of Tangiers in particular. His accounts of the hardships of people, of prostitution, of alcoholics, of poverty, of inequality and social injustice, of hypocrisy, of politicians' double standards, and so on demonstrate his commitment to partake in the socio-politico-economic affairs of the country. His second autobiographical work, *Streetwise*, interestingly opens with the following sentence: "As I got off the bus I was accosted by a dirty, barefoot kid who couldn't have been more than ten years old."[21] Through this impoverished child Choukri gives the reader a glimpse of the troubles of postcolonial Morocco. It is a Morocco where ten-year-old children cannot afford shoes and clothes. The child in the passage looks dirty even to Choukri, the then twenty-year-old vagrant aspiring to start his schooling in the city of Larache and begging others for food and shelter. One might say that Choukri sees in this impoverished child a reflection of his own life of destitution.

The social ills in postcolonial Morocco would eventually alienate Choukri and push him to seek a life of isolation, seclusion, and bachelorhood. Reading Choukri's works, particularly *Streetwise*, one notices a *double* discourse of social bonding, on the one hand, and a quasi-rejection of society and relationships, on the other. Choukri's position towards love of women, for instance, is highly skeptical. After reading about the notion of love in the writings of such well-known Arab writers as Al-Manfalouti, Khalil Gebran, and Mai Ziadeh, he found out that "love was always tinged with death, or endless suffering, or obsession."[22] After drawing on these Arab writers, Choukri relates a scene with a prostitute to corroborate his pessimism and skepticism towards love, which speaks to his frustration with the state of his country. Choukri watches that prostitute sleeping; observes her body; and reflects deeply:

> I sat at her feet on the edge of the bed and lit a cigarette. I watched her as she lay there, her breath shallow, lost in an alcoholic haze. Now her beauty was that of a dead woman, the kind of beauty that appealed to the Babylonians and the ancient Greeks. I no longer found her in any sense attractive. The glory was gone ... Now she was free of all human artifice.[23]

The passage includes the rhetorical figure of oxymoron: The woman/prostitute being described has a kind of beauty that is already dead, and yet is still desired, at least by "the Babylonians and the ancient Greeks." To contradict this contradiction even further, Choukri asserts that she is hardly seductive. This rhetorical figure, in a way, shows Choukri's uncertainty, confusion, and doubt regarding love of women. Towards the end of *Streetwise*, Choukri states his views of love in clearer terms: "I'd never allowed any emotion to betray me. I'd always lived in a kind of state of emergency. I only loved what was fleeting. Love, in fact, didn't interest me unless it was big and fantastic, like in a book. I spoke about it without touching it or embracing it."[24] Choukri remains faithful to his double discourse on love. He is indeed charmed by "fantastic" love; yet this kind of love has no real, tangible existence for him. It exists only discursively, in poems, short stories, and novels; love remains elusive, beyond his embrace. In his autobiographies, Choukri seems convinced that his ideal woman is a mirage, a fiction, an imaginary notion he can indulge only in fantasies and fleeting poetic lines. It's important to point out that, throughout his life, Choukri remained determined to lead the life of a bachelor. He did not believe in marriage, and instead adamantly cherished and clung to his solitary life. In a biography of Choukri, Hassan Al'achaab – Choukri's life-long friend and former teacher – writes about Choukri's rejection of marriage. Al'achaab states that his own marriage alienated Choukri from him.[25] Choukri's distrust of marriage, women, and society at large influenced him to adopt a life of bachelorhood, isolation, and even despair. This is a consequence of his utter frustration with Moroccan society. His negative take on love speaks to the ills and troubles surrounding the domestic life of a large portion of the population. He makes a number of references to married men and women engaging in adulterous relations. From a historicist point of view, Choukri's bachelorhood and sexual experiences with various women/prostitutes help us better understand the sexual taboos that constantly surface in his works. His life of seclusion, on the one hand, and promiscuity, on the other, overshadow his oeuvre.

Nonetheless, Choukri's works have a social dimension, as noted earlier. In *Streetwise*, we learn that, while experimenting with literary writing, Choukri had the chance to meet with the well-established Moroccan writer Mohamed El-Sabbagh, who would read Choukri's writings and provide corrections and suggestions as to the kind of writing trajectory the novice Choukri was to adopt. Choukri, however, was aware of the fact that whatever writing he might produce would be markedly different from El-Sabbagh's, for the simple reason that the two men had lived different lives and came from different social backgrounds. Choukri documents his first visit to El-Sabbagh's house in these terms:

> I came out from his house wishing that I had a refuge like that. He went through my writings and corrected them, using words that were finely sculpted, transparent – but he was clay of one kind and I was clay of another. He didn't have to eat the garbage of the rich. He didn't have lice like me. His ankles weren't sore and bleeding. I wasn't capable of writing about the milk of small birds and touches of angelic beauty, and grapes of dew, and the paralysis of hunting dogs, and the songs of nightingales ...[26]

Choukri is by no means critiquing El-Sabbagh's literary trajectory or his choice of diction; he is only showing his divergence therefrom, albeit with a touch of humor. Choukri implies that his own literary diction has no place for "finely sculpted" and "transparent" words. His crude, blunt, offensive language mirrors the harsh reality surrounding him, his family, and his circle of friends and acquaintances. He would rather write about the poverty that haunts him and his family than about "the songs of nightingales." As stressed earlier, Choukri – the writer – is a social realist rather than an idealist or a romantic. Choukri is aware of his literary trajectory; he states: "When I said that my autobiographical *Al-Khubz Al-Hafi* [*For Bread Alone*] is more of a social document than a work of art I meant that I actually attempted a semi-documentary endeavor about a social group that included myself and my family."[27] In a study of Choukri's *Al-Khubz Al-Hafi* (*For Bread Alone*) and *Zaman Al-Akhtaa* (*Streetwise*), Ariel Sheetrit locates the two works within the modern Arabic autobiographical tradition.[28] She asserts that this tradition has two major characteristics. First, the center of focus is on a collective entity, rather than the individual – and in this it stands in stark contrast to the autobiographical tradition in the West. Second, the Arabic autobiographical tradition has "porous generic boundaries"; in other words, it has a tendency to blur genres, which contributes to its rich mode, bordering "on the novelistic, and often incorporat[ing] other genres, such as letters, journal entries, poetry, and the short story."[29] Sheetrit stresses that Choukri's two autobiographical novels are characterized by these two tendencies. Interestingly, Choukri chose to end *Zaman Al-Akhataa* with a poem dedicated to the city of Tangiers to show his profound love for the place despite its social and economic troubles. Needless to say, Choukri's writings draw on the Moroccan collective, not just on the author's individual life despite his personal leaning toward seclusion and bachelorhood.

Choukri's forays into the social ills of Morocco/Tangiers post-Independence unfold in his countless references to the taboo of drugs. His autobiographies detail his addiction to two narcotics: *kif* (a mixture of tobacco and chopped pieces of marijuana) and *majoun* (cannabis mixed with other ingredients). *Kif* and *majoun* are actually Moroccan-native drugs. In *For Bread Alone*, we learn that Choukri became addicted to *kif* and *majoun* when he was yet a teenager. When young Choukri started experimenting with drugs, he did so in secret: "I smoked in secret. The first time I ate a piece of *majoun* I fainted. Later I vomited what looked like moss. I went on being sick for several days, and life looked strangely different during that time."[30] Alongside *majoun*, Choukri also experimented with *kif*. He tells us that while working at a café he was encouraged by adult "men ... to smoke kif and eat majoun" and that at "[d]aytimes it was *kif* and work, but at night it was *majoun* and fun."[31] Choukri's everyday life revolved around the consumption of *kif* and *majoun*. It seems shocking and disturbing to see a twelve-year-old child become an addict of such strong drugs as *kif* and *majoun*. This explains why Choukri, the adult writer, finds it ludicrous to write about subjects like "the milk of small birds," "the touches of angelic beauty," "grapes of dew," and "the songs of nightingales."[32] Choukri has very little faith in themes pertaining to the realms of beauty and sublimity. The Arab poet and critic Muhyiddine Alladhiqani, in his introduction to Choukri's *Ghiwayat Al-Shahroure Al-Abyad* ("The Lures of the White Blackbird") states that "[t]he smoke of chimneys and the fume of cars and the dust of roofs where the homeless Choukri used to sleep painted him in black – and covered his face with ash and dust". And that's how he earned the title "the black sparrow."[33] In these unpleasant and harsh conditions, the innocence and beauty of childhood are irrevocably crushed.

Choukri's revelations with regard to his addiction to drugs at an early age are doubly shocking to a Moroccan sensibility influenced by religion. One might argue, as stated above, that Choukri's goal was to uncover the bitter reality that children in northern Morocco do become drug and alcohol addicts and lose their innocence. By writing about these disturbing issues, Choukri wanted to demonstrate that he was not the only child lost in the dirty circle of addiction; others had similar, or even worse experiences. In *Streetwise*, Choukri recounts how as an adult he continued to consume drugs and alcohol. Even after he became a teacher and started publishing, he continued to spend his nights in bars, consuming alcohol and drugs. Choukri relates that one night he got completely drunk and "made public [his] physical and spiritual bankruptcy."[34] This bankruptcy of Choukri's is compatible with the vicious cycle of addiction and promiscuity that marks the underworld of Tangiers, which our writer knows to the core.

It is not surprising that Choukri's first published book – *Al-Khubz Al-Hafi* (*For Bread Alone*) – was immediately banned after its publication in Morocco. The auto-biography was perceived as disrupting mainstream Arabic literature in addition to posing a challenge to religious clerics in Morocco and the larger Arab World. It was no surprise when Muslim clergy in Morocco petitioned the Secretary of the Interior at the time to ban its publication. The ban was imposed and remained intact for almost three decades. And its suspension was declared only shortly after King Mohamed VI succeeded his father, King Hassan II, to the throne. Despite the ban, a number of Moroccan and Arab intellectuals showed great respect for the work of Choukri. Ferial Ghazoul praised the book, as noted earlier. The distinguished Moroccan novelist and critic, Mohamed Berrada, devoted an entire chapter to Choukri's *Al-Khubz Al-Hafi*, in which he "refuted the accusation that the work is a *succès de scandale*," adding that he "consider[s] *Al-Khubz al-Hafi* an important achievement in the field of Maghrebi literature because it concretely shows a set of issues which constitute common concerns for writers and critics."[35] Alladhiqani's introduction praises Choukri's work and sees in it "a depth rarely found among contemporary Arab authors."[36] Abdellatif Akbib, a Moroccan academic and short-story writer, celebrates the "great genius of Mohamed Choukri, whose death is a loss that is as keenly felt today as it was a year ago"; Akbib adds that "Tangier is honored to have produced an artist who ranks with Chekhov, Joyce, and Hemingway."[37] Tennessee Williams describes Choukri's *Al-Khubz Al-Hafi* as a "true document of human desperation, shattering in its impact."[38] The book indeed had a tremendous impact and gained international acclaim through Paul Bowles' English translation.

Let us now move on to answer the other part of the two-sided question posed at the opening of this essay – i.e. How and, more importantly, *why* does Choukri go about treating such controversial issues, given the conservative leanings of his Moroccan society? After having addressed the *how*, let us now treat the *why*. Several factors may present themselves as good answers: a) Choukri's extraordinarily harsh life, b) his familiarity with foreign works, and c) his personal encounters with Western writers in Tangiers, particularly the Beats. Choukri did grow up in an environment of extreme poverty, starvation, and neglect. Kenneth Lisenbee, an American blogger who met Choukri while in Tangiers, states that eight of Choukri's siblings died of hunger, malnutrition, and negligence.[39] American expatriate writer Paul Bowles, who lived in Tangiers for almost half a century and translated Choukri's *Al-Khubz Al-Hafi* into English, notes that the conditions of poverty under which Choukri grew up were "excessive even for Morocco."[40] Choukri speaks in detail about his harsh life. Hunger was his constant enemy; he writes: "One afternoon I could not stop crying. I was hungry. I had sucked my fingers so much that the idea of doing it again made me sick to my stomach."[41] The pain of hunger made young Choukri opt for extreme ways to seek food: "One day when the hunger had grown too strong, I went out to Ain Ketiout to look in the garbage dump for bones and ends of dry bread."[42] Young Choukri suffered a great deal of humiliation, for his experience of eating from the garbage would haunt him throughout his life. And he was honest and brave enough to record these events in his writings.

Another hardship young Choukri had to cope with daily was his father's tyranny. Indeed, the child abuse theme surfaces in various of his works. His father treated him, his siblings, and his mother violently. Choukri recounts how one day he was starving and started crying for bread, only to receive slaps and kicks from his father, who would then shout: "Shut up! Shut up! Shut up! If you're hungry, eat your mother's heart"; Choukri goes on to add that "[he] felt [him]self lifted into the air, and he [the father] went on kicking [him] until his leg was tired."[43] We learn further that this abusive father even beat Choukri's brother Abdelqader to death. We read in *For Bread Alone* that the father seized Abdelqader's neck and twisted it around, and "blood ran out of his mouth."[44] Choukri records his reaction to this scene of filicide: "He killed him! Yes. He killed him. I saw him kill him ... He twisted his neck around, and the blood ran out of his mouth. I saw it. I saw him kill him! He killed him!"[45] This shocking murder obviously cut deeply into Choukri's psyche. He felt that he was under threat to suffer the same destiny and lived in constant fear and hatred of his father.

Choukri's father would not only beat him but would also force him to do all sorts of labor and take his wages. Choukri relates that he used to work "from six in the morning until after midnight" and that "[e]ach month [his] father went and collected the thirty pesetas [he] had earned with [his] work."[46] Having no money, Choukri developed a habit of stealing; he would steal primarily from those who used him, like the café owner.[47] Young Choukri also worked at a brick factory, "pushing a wheel-barrow full of clay or bricks back and forth for eight or nine hours a day."[48] Choukri kept moving between different manual jobs; he worked at a pottery kiln, polished the shoes of passers-by, and hawked "the daily [Spanish] paper *El Diario de África*."[49] He also helped his mother sell vegetables and fruit at an open market; his task was to shout "in a strident voice at the passers-by."[50] In the meantime, his father's violence so intensified that young Choukri finally decided to run away from home, only to end up sleeping "in the alleys along with other vagabonds."[51] In the streets of Tangiers, Choukri mingled with prostitutes, pimps, drunks, drug dealers, addicts, thieves, and the like.

It is important to mention that Choukri's parents never managed to send him to school. Only when he was twenty did he begin to think seriously about gaining literacy. Choukri tells his reader how one day he "bought a book that explained the essentials of writing and reading Arabic."[52] With the help of a Mr. Hassan, Choukri decided to go to school, a turning point in his life.[53] At the age of twenty, "Choukri – thief, small-time smuggler, male prostitute – managed to procure a place at a school in the … town of Al-Araʾesh [Larache] where he finally learned to read and write."[54] On his first day at school, Choukri "felt wretched and guilty."[55] He eventually adapted to the school environment, though not without difficulty, and became enamored with reading and writing, which "had become a sleeping and waking obsession."[56] He would shut himself away so that he could read as much as he could.[57] His passion for reading lessened his addiction to drugs and alcohol.[58] He was in the midst of an experience of "enlightenment," liberation, and rebirth. Literacy would indeed transform his entire life and grant him access to a fascinating and unusual literary career. Alladhiqani notes that Choukri excels at describing his harsh life in his works, providing thereby guidance, inspiration, and a path to "salvation" for his former friends and for all those living on the margins of society wherever they may be.[59] Needless to say, Choukri's achievement is worthy of respect.

Such an overview of Choukri's life gives insight into Choukri's leaning towards incorporate issues deemed controversial and immoral within the Moroccan framework. One could say that he felt compelled to give his reader a sense of the harsh experiences he – and others like him – had to deal with, notably during his childhood. Choukri saw (literary) writing as a precious medium to record the gloomy aspects of life around him, both major and minor. Indeed, his recording of everyday life, to a larger extent, provided a cure for his life of isolation and addiction; by writing about what he saw and experienced daily, he gave some significance and purpose to his life and offered a keen critique of the ills of Tangiers and Moroccan society at large, a society he saw was secretly – and sometimes publicly – indulging in all sorts of immoral behavior, and yet refusing to bring these issues to the public discourse. Choukri decries the state of contemporary Arab thought; he sees the state of Arabic literature, art, and literary criticism as only striving for cultural and religious conformity at the expense of "real creativity."[60] Choukri lashes out at one of his critics, who wrote that he [Choukri] was a "cursed figure of contemporary Arabic literature," a position also espoused by Muslim clerics.[61] In his work of criticism, Choukri praises such well-known Western writers as Marcel Proust, James Joyce, Virginia Woolf, and William Faulkner, for "the human being in their works imploringly feels his skin and flesh ... in an attempt to dispose of the banal traditions that dictate his life."[62] A number of remarks by Choukri show his implicit – and sometimes explicit – critique of tradition and religion. In terms of content, Choukri's works seem to have more affinities with Western literary figures of the twentieth century CE than with their Arab counterparts.

An important proposition this essay puts forward in its attempts to account for Choukri's controversial writings relates to foreign influences on our Moroccan author. When Choukri first became enamored with reading, he was introduced to a range of Western authors who left an enduring impact on him:

> I discovered Heinrich Heine before I discovered Rimbaud, Verlaine, Nerval, Baudelaire, Shelley, Keats and Byron. I knew Heine's 'I love, therefore I live' before I learned about Descartes' 'I think, therefore I am.' Then Sartre came along and planted another concept in me: 'L' enfer c' est les autres.'[63]

Jean-Jacques Rousseau's *Confessions*, in particular, influenced Choukri, who admits that Rousseau's *magnum opus* "[t]aught [him] how one can gain consolation in the appreciation of the small things that others neglect."[64] Choukri was widely read in Western literature. His familiarity with – and sometimes admiration of – Western works might explain why his works are not aligned, in a number of ways, with the mainstream Arabic literary tradition. His works are innovative, liberal, and audacious; as noted earlier, they pose a challenge to religious and social norms. With regard to their countercultural dimensions, one could say that Choukri's works have a Western feel.

The city of Tangiers was an international zone during the first half of the Twentieth Century CE, and as such housed a number of American and European writers, some of whom Choukri had the chance to know, befriend, and work with. These writers include the French Jean Genet; the British Brion Gysin; and the Americans

Paul & Jane Bowles, William Burroughs, Jack Kerouac, Allen Ginsberg, Tennessee Williams, and others. These figures feature in Choukri's biographies: *Jean Genet in Tangier* (1974),[65] *Tennessee Williams in Tangier* (1979),[66] and *Paul Bowles in Tangier* (1997).[67]

The counterculture movement of the 1960s in the US and elsewhere was partly influenced by the various writings of the Beat Generation. Johnston states that the Beats demanded "an immediate release from a culture in which the most 'freely' accessible items – bodies and ideas – seemed restricted."[68] Johnston adds that the Beat movement was a "reaction to conservatism and McCarthyism," among other things.[69] Interestingly, Choukri's works resonate with those of Jean Genet. Choukri often refers to his reading of Genet's works, especially *Le Balcon* (*The Balcony*)[70] and *Le Journal du voleur* (*The Thief's Journal*).[71] One particular passage from *Le Journal du voleur* has special value for Choukri: "My clothes were dirty and pitiful. I was hungry and cold. This was the most miserable time of my life."[72] Genet's revelations are reminiscent of Choukri's in *For Bread Alone* and *Streetwise*. Also, we learn that Choukri, the budding author, would regularly seek Genet's advice on how to improve his writing. Choukri had so much respect and admiration for Genet and his writings and indeed wanted to emulate his successful career.

Choukri was also familiar with William Burroughs' notorious *Naked Lunch*, which was conceived and written in Tangiers.[73] Choukri refers to the book on various occasions in his *In Tangier*. He reveals that Burroughs wrote it in the "Munirya Hotel" in Tangiers and that Ginsberg and Kerouac helped him in the writing process.[74] Choukri provides some curious details about Burroughs' homosexual practices and consumption of drugs and alcohol, which constantly surface in the writings of this major Beat figure:

> Only when he [Burroughs] was clinging to his lover Kiki's body was he truly euphoric. They would smoke kif and have sex. One of their erotic embraces, he claimed, lasted for sixteen hours. Burroughs was aware that Tanjawi society was going through a period of starvation, so he wasn't stingy with Kiki. In exchange for his body, he gave him almost two dollars a day ...[75]

Scenes of homosexual practices, alcohol consumption, and experimenting with different kinds of drugs abound in Burroughs' *Naked Lunch*, a vanguard, countercultural work par excellence. The publication of *Naked Lunch* was generally shocking to the American readership, because of its blatant defiance of social norms and taboos. This makes for an interesting case of comparative study with Choukri's works, notably *For Bread Alone*. Burroughs is a key figure among the Beat Generation, a social and literary movement which, according to Allen Johnston, is characterized by "alcoholism, drug addiction, mental illness, and petty thievery," which speaks to its "reaction against a seemingly aggressive and stifling social ethos."[76] Burroughs' various references to drugs are actually recollections of real life experiences. Burroughs interestingly draws on his experiences with *majoun* and *kif* while in Tangiers. To introduce Moroccan drugs to his Western audience, Burroughs writes that the "gum is called majoun, and the leaves kief. Good majoun is hard to find in Tangier," and that "Kief is identical with our marijuana, and we have here an opportunity to observe the effects of constant use on a whole population."[77] In Tangiers, Burroughs, as an American, was both an observer and a partaker in the gatherings of *majoun* eating and *kif* smoking, gatherings reminiscent of Choukri's accounts in *For Bread Alone* and *Streetwise*. Indeed, the key figures of the Beat Generation – Burroughs, Ginsberg, and Kerouac – as well as their life and works, were proximate to Choukri. In his biographies, Choukri observes the Beats observing Morocco and keenly reflects on their various works. It is not far-fetched to suggest that Choukri's proximity to the Beat writers in Tangiers and his familiarity with their works might have influenced his writing trajectory, one way or another. Choukri witnessed the unfolding of the Beat epoch in its literary, cultural, and social incarnations and was by no means hostile to the Beat literary trajectory. His liberal treatment of social taboos within Morocco resonates with the Beat style. Like the Beats, he was critical of religious/cultural conservatism and the dictates of tradition. Choukri strove to liberate the "Arab mindset" of the constraints of religion, customs, and cultural heritage, notably within the field of literature. This is a key message in his illuminating work of criticism, *Ghiwayat Al-Shahroure Al-Abyad*.

Notes

1   Mohamed Choukri, *For Bread Alone*, trans. Paul Bowles (London: Telegram, 2006).

2   Mohamed Choukri, *For Bread Alone*, trans. Paul Bowles (London: Telegram, 2006).

3   Mohamed Choukri, *Streetwise*, trans. Ed Emery (London: Telegram, 2007).

4   Mohamed Choukri, *Wujuh* (Beirut: Dar Saqi, 2006).

5   Choukri, *For Bread*, 44.

6   Ibid., 44–45.

7   Ibid., 125.

8   Ibid., 45.

9   Ibid., 98–99.

10   Ibid., 34.

11   Ibid., 66–67.

12   Mohamed Choukri, *In Tangier*, trans. Paul Bowles et al. (London: Telegram, 2008), 167–168.

13   Greg Mullins, *Colonial Affairs: Bowles, Burroughs, and Chester Write Tangier* (Madison: University of Wisconsin Press, 2002), 131.

14   Ibid., 131–132.

15   Choukri, *For Bread Alone*, 30.

16   Ibid., 121.

17   Choukri, *Streetwise*,149.

18   Mohamed Choukri, "Being and Place: An Interview with Mohamed Choukri," *Alif: Journal of Comparative Poetics* 6 (1986): 67–78, 68.

19   Ibid., 68.

20   Ferial J. Ghazoul, "When the subaltern speaks," *Al-Ahram Weekly Online* 18–24 Feb. 1999. Web. 13 March 2012.

21   Choukri, *Streetwise*, 7.

22   Ibid., 54.

23   Ibid., 56.

24   Ibid., 180.

25   Hassan Al'achaab, *Mohamed Choukri Kamaa 'Araftuhu* (Cairo: Ru'ya, 2008). 69–70.

26   Choukri, *Streetwise*, 120.

27   Nirvana Tanoukhi, "Rewriting Political Commitment for an International Canon: Paul Bowles's *For Bread Alone* as Translation of Mohamed Choukri's *Al- Khubz Al- Hafi*." *Research in African Literatures* 34.2 (2003): 127–144, 131.

28   Ariel Moriah Sheetrit, "For Water Alone: A Comparative Analysis of Tawfiq Abu Wa'il's Film 'Atash and Muhammad Shukri's Autobiographical Novels *Al-Khubz Al-Hafi* and *Al-Shuttar*." *Arab Studies Quarterly* 29.2 (2007): 17–35,19.

29   Ibid., 19.

30   Choukri, *For Bread*, 30.

31   Ibid., 30.

32   *Streetwise*, 120.

33   Muhyiddine Alladhiqani, "Al-Shahroure wa Ghiwayatuhu Al-Markaziyya," in Mohamed Choukri, *Ghiwayat Al-Shahroure Al-Abyad* (Tangier: Slaiki Brothers, 1998), 8.

34   Choukri, *Streetwise*, 150–151.

35   Ghazoul.

36   Alladhiqani, 9.

37	Abdellatif Akbib, "Bankruptcy in Mohamed Choukri's The Flower Freak," in *Writing Tangier: Currents in Comparative Romance Languages and Literatures* 169 (2009): 47–58, 48.

38	Ghazoul.

39	Kenneth Lisenbee, "Mohamed Choukri: Biography and Works," *The Authorized Paul Bowles Website*. PaulBowles.org, n.d. Web. 28 April 2011.

40	Bowles, "Introduction," 6.

41	For Bread, 9.

42	Ibid., 10.

43	Ibid., 10.

44	Ibid., 14.

45	Ibid., 14.

46	Ibid., 29.

47	Ibid., 31.

48	Ibid., 40.

49	Ibid., 41.

50	Ibid., 43.

51	Ibid., 69.

52	Ibid., 210.

53	Ibid., 210.

54	"Mohamed Choukri."

55	Choukri, *Streetwise*, 27.

56	Ibid., 41.

57	Ibid., 54.

58	Ibid., 55.

59	Ibid., 10.

60	Mohamed Choukri, *Ghiwayat Al-Shahroure Al-Abyad* (Tangier: Slaiki Brothers, 1998), 60.

61	Ibid., 87.

62	Ibid., 46.

63	Choukri, *Streetwise*, 150.

64	Ibid., 150.

65	Mohamed Choukri, *Jean Genet in Tangier*, trans. Paul Bowles (New York: Ecco Press, 1974).

66	Mohamed Choukri, *Tennessee Williams in Tangier*, trans. Paul Bowles (San Francisco: Cadmus, 1979).

67	Mohamed Choukri, *Paul Bowles in Tangier*, trans. Gretchen Head and John Garrett (Paris: Quai Voltaire, 2010).

68   Allan Johnston, "Consumption, Addiction, Vision, Energy: Political Economies and Utopian Visions in the Writings of the Beat Generation," *College Literature* 32.2 (2005): 103–126, 103.

69   Ibid., 107.

70   Jean Genet, *The Balcony*, trans. Bernard Frechtman (New York: Grove, 1966).

71   Jean Genet, *The Thief's Journal*, trans. Bernard Frechtman (New York: Grove, 1964).

72   Ibid., 24.

73   William Burroughs, *Naked Lunch* (New York: Grove, 1990).

74   Mohamed Choukri, *In Tangier*, trans. Paul Bowles et al (London: Telegram, 2010), 170.

75   Burroughs, 174.

76   Johnston, 104.

77   William S. Burroughs, "From Interzone," *Word Virus: the William S. Burroughs Reader*, ed. James Grauerholz and Ira Silverberg (New York: Grove, 1998), 121–148.

CHAPTER 9

Khatibi: A Sociologist in Literature

Sam Cherribi & Matthew Pesce

Je ne suis pas un homme de 'concept ... on a raison de me faire préciser les choses.'

ABDELKEBIR AL KHATIBI

All fantasies to which any writer will succumb, believing himself to be the holder of an infinite power over words; these can lead one to stray into a measure of 'anesthetic' aestheticism of words and things. He [Abdelkébir Khatibi] did not, however, for all that, entirely forgo what Aesthetics, as it was invested in all his work, brought to his writing, in both subtlety and density.[1]

MOHAMMED BOUDOUDOU

Abstract

This study explores the ways sociological and philosophical insights into Morocco and French speaking societies haunt and hijack the literary agenda of Abdelkebir Al Khatibi. The distinction between sociology, philosophy, and literature masks another agenda: the incompatible ways in which the three genres of writings can be bridged in composite societies like that of Morocco. Khatibi wants to bridge the unbridgeable in a society in which he is heavily invested, and yet sees the possibility of realizing his dream of being a writer as limited. The study will draw on Khatibi's writings *La Mémoire tatouée*, *La Blessure du nom propre*, *Amour bilingue*, *Un été à Stockholm*, *Chemins de Traverse: Essais de sociologie* and *Triptyque de Rabat*.

A Rich Corpus for Sociological Inquiry

Since independence, only three Moroccan sociologists have risen to international prominence: Paul Pascon, Fatema Mernissi, and Abdelkébir Khatibi. However, Khatibi's sociological work continues to be unknown in the field of social sciences outside the French speaking world. It is his oeuvre in its literary, philosophical, and stylistic dimensions that has made him famous in comparative literature, cultural studies, and humanities circles on American campuses and beyond.

Khatibi, culturally and intellectually, inhabits two worlds, Europe and the Maghreb, leading him to coin his "double critique" in order to liberate himself, the people of the Maghreb, and the Francophone countries from self-imposed, symbolic, and rigid boundaries. This process of liberation occurs through processes of socialization and acculturation. He aspires to liberate all parties from the heavy weight of ideologies linked to the formation of identities in the Maghreb since the Islamic "conquest."

His liberating approach can be seen in the same vein as the work of Pierre Bourdieu, Jacques Derrida, Roland Barthes, and Mohamed Arkoun. He sheds light on the elements of the plural identities composing the Maghreb and shows how ideology after independence depends on the formation of the nation state and other concepts related to it. The different layers of identity in the Maghreb include Arabic, Islamic, Berber, African, French, and Spanish. These elements constitute the unique stew of Maghrebi plural identities. He also examines the different influences coming from the Middle East, such as pan-Arabism and pan-Islamism as well as sub-Saharan African and European thought, through colonialism and postcolonial ideologies.

The work of Khatibi, his writings and interviews, is a corpus for sociological inquiry and investigation. For this study, this will be limited to the following titles: *La Mémoire tatouée, La Blessure du nom propre, Amour bilingue, Un été à Stockholm, Chemins de Traverse: Essais de sociologie,* and *Triptyque de Rabat*.[2] In his writing and research two themes stand out: evolution and change. His work on signs and symbols, tribal structures, the Moroccan bureaucracy, and artistic fields all focus on points of transfiguration. He also explains how Arab societies have difficulty in making a virtue of change.

Khatibi's Self-Definition: Maghreb, Europe or Both

In his own words, Khatibi reports that he was born at the intersection of three violent events: the feast of sacrifice which corresponds to ten Dhû-Hijja 1938, the beginning of the Second World War, and the experience of living in a society that was theological, feudal, and colonized by the French and Spanish. For Khatibi, these three events symbolize the dimensions of sacrifice, war, and colonization. Khatibi conceptualizes sacrifice and domination as two words that go hand in hand. His aversion to all forms of domination may come from that moment of extreme human vulnerability.

He went to Paris to study sociology at the Sorbonne with Raymond Aron and George Gurvitch in 1958. Although he hated sociology at the Sorbonne, he learned how to trade through dwellings and adventures in Paris, the cosmopolitan dimension of the city, its intellectual debates, its art, its architecture, and its margins. When he first arrived in Paris, he had already experienced it through literature, especially Baudelaire. This literature gave him the key to understanding the semiology of the city. He describes his experience as that of a professional stranger who had to mediate different cultures.

He was impressed by the work of Roger Bastide, who gave him the conceptual tools to construct an ethno-sociology of the body and its representations. The impact of Roger Bastide is felt throughout Khatibi's work. Khatibi's interest in urban spaces and architecture comes from his encounters with Henri Lefebvre. Just like the Sudanese writer Al-Tayyib Salih, Khatibi became mesmerized by the North. He loved Germany, Belgium, Scandinavia, and all the northern European countries. This fascination had more to do with northern cultures than languages.

In 1964 he returned to Morocco, where he created a new school of post-colonial sociology that transcended the orientalistic scholarship of many Moroccan educational institutions. Since 1974, Roger Bastide has inspired much of Khatibi's work. Psychoanalysis prompted him to work on the anthropology of the body, which he called "La Blessure du nom Propre."[3] These influences make of Khatibi a unique stylist of language, who uses sociology, psychology, and semiology as resources for his literary writings. Finally, he created a new genre of literature informed by sociological inquiry, which is a type of literary method for writing sociology.

Beyond these steps forward, Khatibi has a unique engagement with the societies of the Maghreb, and in particular Morocco. No other writer or sociologist understands the Moroccan psyche in all its different forms, expressions, names, signs, art, politics, and family relations as well as Khatibi. He is not only an avid reader of European literature but also a connoisseur and a lover of northern European cultures. His love for the Moroccan culture gives him a unique vantage point as a storyteller in literature with a vast knowledge of society that goes well beyond statistical evidence. This allows him to understand the logic behind certain behaviors and structures of Maghrebi societies.

In one interview Khatibi is asked, "Tell us about your Europe?". He answers with a series of questions, becoming the interviewer through a game of words. He explains how he met Europe as an heir and as a living organism. He also says, "Sometimes I use 'I' as a mask. This mask is sometimes 'I' or sometimes 'I am thinking.' If I tell you that I am at the same time Moroccan, sometimes of the Maghreb, an Arab, a European, a Muslim, a Mediterranean; if I say all this, then give you a definition of myself, is my being reducible to these attributes?" He concludes that the identity of somebody is not a closed entity "[b]ut the identity of the trace of time." It is an identity in perpetual becoming. As a researcher, Khatibi continues to deconstruct and break down binary oppositions. He denounces all kinds of humiliations and confusions to identity.[4]

Khatibi is particularly attentive to the lines that demarcate various influences on individuals and groups in Maghreb and Arab societies. This is evident in the attention he pays to the Moroccan handicraft of Safi pottery, tattoos on the faces of Berber women in the Atlas, and the symbols in henna on the hands of Moroccan brides. As an intellectual, writer and researcher, his work is as delicate as the linings of pottery from Safi.

He speaks about the complexity and subtlety of the interwoven cultures – Jewish, Islamic, and Berber – that give Morocco a special texture not only in its people but also in its landscapes, from the southern landscape of Marrakesh to the landscape surrounding the Rif region of northern Morocco. He defines the Moroccan cultural identity as a mystical community between the ones who are dead and the ones who are alive. In that sense, the Moroccan individual is very particular.[5]

Irreconcilable Divisions in the Maghreb

Khatibi exposes the dilemmas of emerging nations, like Morocco, where traditionalists and modernists who live in two opposing camps can find a modus operandi of sharing the same space of signs and symbols. He recognizes the weaknesses of post-colonial societies as a location of suffering. However, if understood, this suffering can lead to a positive turning point in the history of the Maghreb. Before 9/11, he urged Arab societies to take Islamism seriously, explaining that Islamism should be dealt with in a way that allows its members to find points of transformation that can lead to its reform and its emancipation.

He believes that Arab societies are divided into "irreconcilable" blocks. These blocks are defined by societies that accept modernity and those that refuse western hegemony and want to go back to Islam as a source of norms and values. He feels that such societies are handicapped by five factors: weakness of civil society, the tendency of hypnotic political power, the flagrant lack of savoir-faire technique, the weight of theocracy that makes it difficult to distinguish state and religion, and the weakness of the self-image that the Arab world presents. The tendency to be either pro-western or anti-western fits in with this typology.

Islamists believe that the solution lies in the past. That is why Khatibi argues the Muslim world needs a new tradition to get out of an untenable position between tradition and modernity.[6] He strongly believes that modernism and Islamism nurture one another in unhealthy reciprocity. He writes that the opposition is in every one of us, as an internal bleeding, in our apathy, in our complaisance, from our past. Islamism is a crying symptom. Our dream is to stop time, to immobilize it ... We [Muslims, Arabs and Maghrebi] suffer from our backwardness: we complain continually, but we need to work from this suffering itself.

Khatibi urges the Maghreb societies to take Islamism seriously, because it perpetuates "a profound tendency in Arab societies and their fascination with the past ... We should repeat that these societies are societies of commandment and directed servitude, voluntary or not."[7] Hence the solution is to work productively from the reality that the status quo represents.

Writing in French as Trace of Difference

When Khatibi was asked why he writes in French, his answer was that the same question was also asked of Samuel Beckett, and his response was because he liked it. He was then asked why he combined literature and sociology, to which he responded, "I am a stylist, above all, a stylist of ideas."

When Khatibi writes a text, he goes for a walk in time and space; he reads faces, and he crosses topographies. Reality for him is like carpentry. He takes only one thread, and he leaves it in his imagination taking the force of the moment. He describes this process as one in which "the one who writes wants to live at the same time in the past, the present and the future."[8] He compares writing to music, since all that is necessary is finding the right tone. He speaks of passion and love of two languages being possible without mixing them together or diminishing the value of either one. This does not break their boundaries but instead creates a harmonious parallel between words that translates emotions, perceptions, and ideas in two languages at the same time.[9]

Khatibi respects the laws that make up the structure of language. Especially in the Maghreb, he believes that many of the writers who live, speak, and write in Arabic or Berber also write in French. These individuals therefore live in two or three languages. For him, Kateb Yacine and Mohamed Dib represent this high poetic tradition.

He does not believe that Maghrebi writers' writing in French is simply a linguistic phenomenon, but instead a cultural and social one as well. It is this structural bilingualism that he calls diglossia between orality and writing. He believes that writers do not write the way they talk; in that sense there is a dissymmetry, a difference of tone, style, and rhythm.[10]

This is illustrated in a couple of different contexts. *Triptyque de Rabat* is a novel that takes the reader on a journey to discover the enigma of the city of Rabat seeped in corruption, murder and secret labyrinths. The voice narrating the story is that of a refined sociologist. Khatibi deciphers the signs and the symbols as keys to the transformations of a city with its multiple identities. In *Un été à Stockholm*, he contrasts the city of Stockholm with the city of Rabat. It is a story of fascination with a northern city. In that sense he is not like Albert Camus, who visited Amsterdam and hated its low sky.

Khatibi wants to study the dynamic nature of Moroccan culture through both its visible and masked oral and written dimensions. This study includes levels of difference, plurality and hierarchy. Khatibi believes that three large blocks of global culture in civilization are developing: the European block, the American block, and the Asian block. This reality makes him fearful of the forces of marginalization that globalization brings. He is therefore concerned about cultural marginalization.[11]

He spends more time in his academic life studying sociology than any other academic discipline. This is all the more notable, given the full mutation that has been occurring throughout Moroccan society. This is perhaps because of his interest in evolution and social change in Morocco. Themes of youth, evolution and mutations of social groups, relation of hierarchy, division of labor, distribution of wealth, and social crisis are at the heart of his work.

Since his father was a theologian, the religious question and the sacred were present early in his life. This is why he considers Islamism to be a form of ideology. He makes a link between ideology and the stressed populations that messianic religious movements create. He believes that Arab and Muslim societies are in a kind of distress because of rapid social changes that they cannot decode. It is therefore difficult to find a solution to the economic, social, and political distress of the people. The result seems to be a populism attached to religion, which has an impact on societies it affects, as do other ideological orientations such as communism.

Morocco's Unique Traits

Khatibi stresses the very peculiar character of Moroccan society. It has a very old monarchy, but there is a sense that there is a new crisis of legitimacy of the king. It also has an old civilization, which is Berber, African, Andalusian, Arab, Islamic, and European. In this sense, the country is very ethnically and religiously diverse in comparison to many of its regional peers. This ethnic and religious diversity gives rise to a host of issues that simply would not exist elsewhere.

This is illustrated by the story of a Berber woman who discussed the tattoo tradition in Morocco with Khatibi. The woman said that television had erased the tattoo tradition, which had been practiced for centuries in the country to embellish the faces and hands of women. The promotion of make-up for women on television meant that Berber women were simply no longer interested in tattoos.[12] For Khabiti, this is how new modes of being and thought are created and erase traces of cultural practices.

The Maghreb has existed as a distinct entity since the Second Century of the Hijrah of the Prophet.[13] Khatibi explains that the independence of Morocco has strengthened the monarchy. The nationalist elite has been marginalized, and a rigid mode of stratification has been created, putting an end to the aspirations of many Moroccans.[14] The state's function in turn has been to master a heterogenic society, which aggravates splits between rich and poor as well as rural and urban societies.

Khatibi refutes the idea of social mobility when it comes to power. He believes that the state developed different techniques of manipulation that he considers experimental. Such a system functions in a way that allows the state to look at a stock of elites and choose the ones it desires in every situation not because of their intellectual and individual qualities but in order to measure the level of resistance of every group with the purpose of destroying the network. In that sense, elites are privileged on account of rapid mobility. Politically, these elites, who once may have desired to change the world and make a difference, now consider it to be a great risk to make a plea for universal access to education. They may instead feel overwhelmed by the new educated classes that are now jobless.[15]

Although Khatibi died before the Arab Spring, he left an incredible theoretical toolbox that was perfected during the 50 years that followed the independence of Morocco. This toolbox will help literary critics as well as social scientists decipher the enigmas of symbols and metaphors which encompass Moroccan culture from a historical perspective. Indeed, Khatibi's work is a valuable lens for any literary or sociological endeavor into the world of signs of Morocco. Assia Belhabib's book shows clearly the complexity and ingenuity of Khatibi's work.[16]

Notes

1   Mohammed Boudoudou, On the heritage of multifarious sociological thought: (Tattooed) memories of a meeting with Abdelkébir Khatibi: The professor-researcher-writer (forthcoming).

2   Abdelkebir Khatibi, *La Mémoire tatouée* (Paris: Denoël, 1971); Abdelkebir Khatibi, *Amour bilingue* (Montpellier: Fata Morgana, 1983); Abdelkebir Khatibi, *Un été à Stockholm* (Paris: Flammarion, 1990); Abdelkebir Khatibi, *Triptyque de Rabat* (N. Blandin, 1993); Abdelkebir Khatibi, Chemins de Traverse: essais de sociologie. (Rabat: 2002).

3   Abdelkebir Khatibi, *La Blessure du nom propre* (Paris: Denoël, 1974), 7.

4   Ibid., 448.

5   Ibid., 458.

6   Ibid., 449.

7   Ibid., 450.

8   Ibid., 452.

9   Ibid., 452.

10   Ibid., 453.

11   Ibid., 457.

12   Ibid., 468.

13   Ibid., 295.

14   Ibid., 185.

15   Ibid., 188–189.

16   Assia Belhabib, *La Langue de l'hôte: Lecture de Abdelkébir Khatibi* (Casablanca: Editions Okad, 2009).

CHAPTER 10

Emigration and Quest for Identity in Laila Lalami's *Hope & Other Dangerous Pursuits*, Akbib's 'The Lost Generation,' and Fandi's *Alien ... Arab ... and Maybe Illegal in America*

Ilham Boutob

Introduction

This study explores the question of migration and its relationship to cultural identity, focusing on three Moroccan texts written in English: Laila Lalami's *Hope and Other Dangerous Pursuits*, Abdellatif Akbib's "The Lost Generation," and Mohamed Fandi's *Alien ... Arab ... and maybe Illegal in America*. Each of these books addresses issues that are raised when Moroccans attempt to leave their country, whether legally or illegally, and changes in the migrant's identity when he or she moves from the homeland to Europe or America. The protagonists of these novels provide various views of the cultural implications of migration and the tremendous frustration and wavering of both personal and cultural identities that may occur during that process.

Laila Lalami's Hope and Other Dangerous Pursuits

The main theme in Laila Lalami's novel is illegal emigration, or what is generally known in Morocco as the phenomenon of *Lahrig*: a group of young people, including Moroccans and other Africans, cross the sea to Spain in an inflatable raft with the idea that migration will improve their lives. Lalami describes the scene: "The six-meter Zodiac inflatable is meant to accommodate eight people. Thirty huddle in it now, men, women, and children, all with the anxious look of those whose destinies are in the hands of others – the captain, the coast guards, God."[1]

The writer thus points out skillfully, from the beginning, the dangers of illegal emigration by stressing that not one of the adventurers is in control of his or her destiny. Moreover, the over-crowded Zodiac raft is a precarious mode of transport, as it is liable to sink into the sea during the journey. Yet, the migrants have accepted great risks in the hope of reaching an alluring paradise, which they expect will radically alter their lives, transforming them into rich and happy people.

The opening passage of the novel sheds light on how Spain, or Europe in general, stands as a sort of paradise or Eldorado that must be reached at all costs, in the view of these desperate emigrants. The writer reveals the hopeful expectations of one of her protagonists, a young Moroccan man named Murad:

> Fourteen kilometers. Murad has pondered that number hundreds of times in the last year, trying to decide whether the risk was worth it. Some days he told himself that the distance was nothing, a brief inconvenience, that the crossing would take as little as thirty minutes if the weather was good. He spent hours thinking about what he would do once he was on the other side, imagining the job, the car, the house. Other days he could think only about the coast guards, the ice-cold water, the money he'd have to borrow, and he wondered how fourteen kilometers could separate not just two countries but two universes.[2]

If Murad manages to cross to the other side of the Mediterranean Sea, he believes it will mean that he is not just in another country but rather in a new universe, a new and superior place that will improve his poor and miserable conditions. After an adventurous "jump" of just fourteen kilometers, the poor, suffering Murad will suddenly be transformed into a happy new man with a job, a car, a house, and a lot of money. So why shouldn't he take the risk for the sake of attaining this dream, this ideal condition?

In this way Laila Lalami explores the psyche of the immigrant. Through Lalami's narration, the reader understands what motivates thousands of Moroccans and other Africans to engage in such a dangerous pursuit as illegal migration. But instead of just exposing and criticizing conditions that are responsible for this phenomenon, Lalami also blames the adventurers themselves. She does this in an indirect manner by contrasting these contemporary *harraga* (a term that refers to migrants who burn their identity cards) to the first Arabs and Moslems who, under the leadership of Tariq Ibn Ziyad, crossed the Strait of Gibraltar to conquer territory and build an Islamic civilization. Here again, the author presents these ideas through the wandering thoughts of Murad:

Murad can make out the town where they're headed. Tarifa. The mainland point of the Moorish invasion in 711. Murad used to regale tourists with anecdotes about how Tariq Ibn Ziyad had led a powerful Moor army across the Straits and, upon landing in Gibraltar, *ordered all the boats burned*. He'd told his soldiers that they could march forth and defeat the enemy or turn back and die a coward's death. The men had followed their general, toppled the Visigoths, and established an empire that ruled over Spain for more than seven hundred years. Little did they know that we'd be back, Murad thinks. Only instead of a fleet, here we are in an inflatable boat – not just Moors, but a motley mix of people from the ex-colonies, without guns or armor, without a charismatic leader.[3]

Here Lalami deliberately juxtaposes two very distant periods of history – the beginning of the eighth century CE when the Moors invaded Spain as *Fatihine* in 711 – and the beginning of the twenty-first century CE, when present-day Moors return, this time in a less glorified manner as migrant workers. Tariq and his men burned their boats when they arrived in Spain so as to fight until victory or glorious death, while the modern *harraga*[4] burn their identity cards or throw them into the sea, lest they be turned back by the Spanish authorities. It is as if they must dispense with their original identities and start new ones in Europe. This sacrifice of identity is deliberately contrasted with the eighth-century invaders who arrived in Andalusia with the strength of a conquering army and with the stated purpose of conquering territories and creating a civilization that would reflect their religious, cultural, and even economic principles; modern immigrants, instead, are often called upon to reject their cultural and religious identities in the process of migration and submit to the ruling principles of the host nation.

This sacrifice of identity is depicted vividly through the astonishing story of a female protagonist in Lalami's novel, Faten, the veiled young girl who also decides to emigrate illegally. Before the adventurous journey, Faten appears to be a devout Muslim who is so principled and pious that she manages to persuade her bourgeois college friend Noura to wear the *hijab* and become a devoted Muslim like her. But no sooner has she arrived in Europe than she not only throws off her veil, a clear symbol of her Islamic identity, but also prostitutes herself to a Spanish policeman in exchange for admission to Spain. The reasons behind this sudden and unexpected change remain ambiguous, but one of the chief causes is her fear of being deported to Morocco after setting foot on Spanish soil:

She'd managed to get to the beach, where the Spanish Guardia Civil was waiting for them. Later, in the holding cell, she saw one of the guards staring at her. She didn't need to speak Spanish to understand that he wanted to make her a deal. She remembered what her imam had said back at the underground mosque in Rabat – that extreme times sometimes demanded extreme measures. The guard had taken her to one of the private exam rooms, away from everyone else. He lifted her skirt and thrust into her with savage abandon.[5]

The grave deal Faten makes with this stranger marks the end of her innocence and the collapse of her original identity. Instead of maintaining her religious principles, she interprets the words of her imam toward her own purpose and barters her virginity for the opportunity to enter Spain without legal documents. This sexual act inaugurates a new phase in her life during which she rejects her previous values.

Abdellatif Akbib's "The Lost Generation"

Unlike Laila Lalami's characters in *Hope and Other Dangerous Pursuits*, Abdellatif Akbib's protagonist Reda, in his short story titled "The Lost Generation," has the option to emigrate to Europe legally. Even though he has an opportunity to get a job in Morocco, he insists on emigrating to France to complete his post-graduate studies. His parents have tried to convince him to stay and work in his country, but they could not persuade him to change his mind:

> But Reda was decided. His parents wielded all rhetorical devices to dissuade him, but he was of a stubborn nature ... his counter-rhetoric rested on a clear and simple premise: he knew his future could not be made in his own country; he had to look for it somewhere else, and France was where he could prosper and rise into the world. 'I have always felt out of place here,' he told his father. 'I have problems wherever I go, because people misunderstand me everywhere. I shall end up in jail some day ...'[6]

Reda's determination to leave for France and his complaint that he feels "out of place" in his homeland reveal his dissatisfaction with his identity as a Moroccan. He defends his urgent desire to escape in an attempt to find an alternative identity.

Yet when Reda claims that he will leave Morocco because of its widespread injustices, his father explains that the problem cannot be solved by escape: rather, the father explains that it is the responsibility of Moroccans, especially learned ones like Reda himself, to resist and bring about the desired changes. What is more ridiculous, according to the father, is that France itself is responsible for many of the problems from which Morocco still suffers:

> Remember, my son, that the injustice you are talking about is a virus that was sown by the very country you want to make your future in ... France did not leave Morocco out of love for Moroccans – or out of respect for human rights, for that matter. France was forced to leave the country; it had no choice. And to take revenge on nationalists, those it could not buy with money or position, the French sowed deadly viruses in the Moroccan society before leaving. The injustice you are talking about is one manifestation of that contemptible act, and your decision to go to their country is another.[7]

Here the father blames Reda for not being aware of the imperialistic "viruses" France planted in Morocco during the colonial period. It is senseless, in the father's view, to build one's future in France, because such an act implies a lack of historical understanding and a betrayal of one's cultural identity.

When the father sees that his son is so blinded by the idea of emigrating to France, he yields with one last piece of advice: "Whatever you do, don't marry a French girl,"[8] knowing that such a marriage would fully sever his son from his native Morocco and his cultural identity. The father's rhetorical questions to his son imply the complete loss of identity that would accompany such a marriage: "Would she accept to leave her own country and come to live with you here? In a third-world country? Forever? What if she doesn't? Would you sacrifice your own country, family and culture to go there for ever?"[9] The father's fears and suspicions prove to be well-founded. Although Reda promises not to marry a French woman, he fails to abide by this promise. What is worse, he neglects his parents and family as he becomes engulfed by serious problems in France: "His letters to his parents thus grew few, his phone calls fewer. Then there was no more news of him."[10]

Mohamed Fandi's Alien ... Arab ... and Maybe Illegal in America

Mohamed Fandi, the writer and the protagonist of this travel account, relates his own experience with emigration to the United States: at first as a legal migrant and later as an undocumented resident. He dedicates his book to all immigrants of the world in his opening page: "I Only Dedicate This Book To People I Don't Know ... And Particularly To Those Immigrants Who Choose To Live In The Other Side Of

Their Legitimate Frontiers."[11] This statement confirms from the beginning that the author perceives himself as an immigrant who celebrates immigration openly and identifies closely with other immigrants.

In the Preface to his book, Fandi speaks favorably about immigration and praises America for being the land of immigrants:

> America is a nation of immigrants! We are all sons and daughters of immigrants and the cultural diversity of America has served to enrich and strengthen the nation. The greatness of America is a reflection of the sacrifice, contributions, and efforts of immigrants. They have greatly enriched the history of the United States. There is reason to celebrate the richness of the cultural diversity that immigration has brought to America![12]

Here we might notice that Fandi praises and celebrates America and its immigrants: the country for its history as a site of integration for millions of immigrants from different parts of the world; the people for their role in creating a country of rich cultural diversity.

Fandi first travels to America legally through an exchange program between Morocco and the United States. When he gets there, however, he overstays his visa because he is fascinated by the country; he fears that he may never have another opportunity to return to it. He justifies his decision to stay as follows:

> It is going to be a huge decision for a Kenyan, a Mexican, a Moroccan, or even for a French immigrant to go back. It has never been easy for an alien to make up his or her mind, to leave America behind with no paper to assure the return. No one wants to risk. Nobody wants to lose the 'power' of being in the United States of America.[13]

Fandi feels that there is a privilege and a power in being an American or even being in America. He has a strong faith in the American Dream, and he even believes that all people can possibly share and live this dream. He observes, "As long as America is the first and biggest economy in the world, every human being expresses a wish to live the American dream."[14]

Fandi associates the American Dream with questions of economy and material interests; but what about the spiritual side of this dream? Fandi seems to neglect this aspect, instead focusing on the fact that America is "[t]he first and biggest economy in the world," and the land where he can have opportunities for work and unlimited access to pleasure. Rather than question the value of this materialistic approach, as did F. Scott Fitzgerald in his famous novel *The Great Gatsby*, Fandi accepts it unconditionally, claiming that the dream of materialism is uncorrupted and within reach of all people in the United States without discrimination. The reader is left to wonder when Fandi himself will be allowed to reach his share of this dream, when he remains on the margins of American society as an alien immigrant without the security of legal documents for work or residency.

During his long journey in America, Mohamed Fandi changes, especially in his religious path. He says, "I am supposed to pray at least five times a day, which I don't do anymore, shame on me."[15] He is aware of these changes and ashamed; he often considers the advice of his mother back home, who asked him not to become a different person as an immigrant, but rather to retain his original personality and his deep faith in God and his religion. Yet one of the opening chapters is entitled "The Quest For Light," which suggests that Fandi hopes to escape from what he considers "darkness" in his original country, defined, for him, as misery, injustice, and lack of opportunity for young people like him. He claims to find this light and beauty in the United States:

> I'm in the land of freedom, the land of business, the land where every day many people around the country become rich, millionaires ... What I felt? It is absolutely amazing ... The sensation to explore more freedom and that is the biggest advantage about living in America. It is actually not only freedom by itself as a result, but it also concerns the way people accomplish, fight and establish that freedom.[16]

Fandi idealizes America, for he looks on it as a kind of paradise, and he feels he must stay at any cost. As soon as he arrives in this country, he feels that he is the happiest man on earth. Though he is not himself American, but rather an immigrant without the legal documents to live freely in America, he feels proud of this country. In his view, even "Osama Bin Laden ... would be proud to be in the USA,"[17] and "more than half of my country (and each country around the world) would be ready – anytime – to visit or stay in the States."[18]

In the end, although the author is obliged to return to Morocco after living in the United States without residency or work documents for many years, he still retains that ideal image of that country as a land of freedom and an earthly paradise. This is clear from the last message he writes in his epilogue: "I needed to tell you that I was in the United States of America, that this country is the best country of the world, and that I never regretted any minute I spent there. God bless America."[19] For the reader, this unabashed enthusiasm for a country that neither nurtured Fandi nor retained him becomes a sad and ironic comment contradicting the character's perception.

The characters' quests for alternative identities in Lalami's novel, Akbib's short story, and Fandi's travel account lead to catastrophic results. Though the case of Fandi may be less complex, the examples of Faten and Reda show that emigration, whether legal or illegal, may cause the loss of one's national and cultural identity instead of helping to solve one's problems. The authors of these works, by creating characters who cannot fully realize their dreams, reveal a lost generation.

Notes

1   Laila Lalami, *Hope and Other Dangerous Pursuits* (New York: Harcourt, 2005), 1–2.

2   Ibid., 1.

3   Ibid., 2–3.

4   The term "harraga" is derived from the Arabic verb "haraqa," which means "to burn." It is actually said that some illegal emigrants burn or get rid of their papers in the hope of staying in the European countries they manage to reach.

5   Ibid., 141.

6   Abdellatif Akbib, *The Lost Generation: Collected Short Stories* (Tangier: Slaiki Brothers, 1998), 86.

7   Ibid., 87.

8   Ibid., 91.

9   Ibid., 92.

10   Ibid., 93.

11   Mohammad Fandi, *Alien … Arab … And Maybe Illegal in America* (Charleston: BookSurge, 2006).

12   Ibid.

13   Fandi, *Alien … Arab … Maybe Illegal in America*, 16–17.

14   Ibid., 14–15.

15   Ibid., 40.

16   Ibid., 13–14.

17   Ibid., 57.

18   Ibid., 14–15.

19   Ibid., 94.